Government Procedures and Operations

A Closer Look at Grant Programs

GOVERNMENT PROCEDURES AND OPERATIONS

Additional books and e-books in this series can be found on Nova's website under the Series tab.

GOVERNMENT PROCEDURES AND OPERATIONS

A CLOSER LOOK AT GRANT PROGRAMS

TABITHA REYES
EDITOR

Copyright © 2019 by Nova Science Publishers, Inc.

All rights reserved. No part of this book may be reproduced, stored in a retrieval system or transmitted in any form or by any means: electronic, electrostatic, magnetic, tape, mechanical photocopying, recording or otherwise without the written permission of the Publisher.

We have partnered with Copyright Clearance Center to make it easy for you to obtain permissions to reuse content from this publication. Simply navigate to this publication's page on Nova's website and locate the "Get Permission" button below the title description. This button is linked directly to the title's permission page on copyright.com. Alternatively, you can visit copyright.com and search by title, ISBN, or ISSN.

For further questions about using the service on copyright.com, please contact:
Copyright Clearance Center
Phone: +1-(978) 750-8400   Fax: +1-(978) 750-4470   E-mail: info@copyright.com.

NOTICE TO THE READER

The Publisher has taken reasonable care in the preparation of this book, but makes no expressed or implied warranty of any kind and assumes no responsibility for any errors or omissions. No liability is assumed for incidental or consequential damages in connection with or arising out of information contained in this book. The Publisher shall not be liable for any special, consequential, or exemplary damages resulting, in whole or in part, from the readers' use of, or reliance upon, this material. Any parts of this book based on government reports are so indicated and copyright is claimed for those parts to the extent applicable to compilations of such works.

Independent verification should be sought for any data, advice or recommendations contained in this book. In addition, no responsibility is assumed by the Publisher for any injury and/or damage to persons or property arising from any methods, products, instructions, ideas or otherwise contained in this publication.

This publication is designed to provide accurate and authoritative information with regard to the subject matter covered herein. It is sold with the clear understanding that the Publisher is not engaged in rendering legal or any other professional services. If legal or any other expert assistance is required, the services of a competent person should be sought. FROM A DECLARATION OF PARTICIPANTS JOINTLY ADOPTED BY A COMMITTEE OF THE AMERICAN BAR ASSOCIATION AND A COMMITTEE OF PUBLISHERS.

Additional color graphics may be available in the e-book version of this book.

Library of Congress Cataloging-in-Publication Data

ISBN: 978-1-53615-995-0

Published by Nova Science Publishers, Inc. † New York

CONTENTS

Preface		vii
Chapter 1	Broadband Loan and Grant Programs in the USDA's Rural Utilities Service (Updated) *Lennard G. Kruger*	1
Chapter 2	Federal Pell Grant Program of the Higher Education Act: Primer *Cassandria Dortch*	71
Chapter 3	FY2017 State Grants Under Title I-A of the Elementary and Secondary Education Act (ESEA) *Rebecca R. Skinner and Clarissa G. Cooper*	121
Chapter 4	The HUD Homeless Assistance Grants: Programs Authorized by the HEARTH Act (Updated) *Libby Perl*	129
Chapter 5	Community Services Block Grants (CSBG): Background and Funding (Updated) *Libby Perl*	189
Chapter 6	Project Safe Neighborhoods Grant Program Authorization Act of 2017 *Committee on the Judiciary*	225

Chapter 7	Maternal and Child Health Services Block Grant: Background and Funding *Victoria L. Elliott*	**241**
Index		**273**
Related Nova Publications		**283**

PREFACE

Federal grants finance essential government programs, like infrastructure, by transferring Federal dollars to State and local governments, nonprofits, and individuals. Since the earliest days of the republic, the Federal government has used grants to advance public policy. From veterans' assistance in the aftermath of the War of 1812 to land grants for railroads after the Civil War, federal grants have been part of our Nation's history for a long time. Today the Federal government awards over $700 billion in grants annually. This book looks at some of the current grant programs available from the federal government.

Chapter 1 - Given the large potential impact broadband access may have on the economic development of rural America, concern has been raised over a "digital divide" between rural and urban or suburban areas with respect to broadband deployment. While there are many examples of rural communities with state-of-the-art telecommunications facilities, recent surveys and studies have indicated that, in general, rural areas tend to lag behind urban and suburban areas in broadband deployment. According to the FCC's *First Communications Market Report*, as of 2017, 24% of Americans in rural areas lacked coverage from fixed terrestrial 25 Mbps/3 Mbps broadband, as compared to only 1.5% of Americans in urban areas. The comparatively lower population density of rural areas is likely a major reason why broadband is less deployed than in more highly populated suburban and urban areas. Particularly for wireline broadband technologies—such as cable modem and fiber—the greater the geographical distances among customers, the larger the cost to serve those customers. The Rural Utilities Service (RUS) at the U.S. Department of Agriculture (USDA) houses two ongoing assistance programs exclusively created and dedicated to financing broadband deployment: the Rural Broadband Access Loan and Loan Guarantee Program and the Community Connect Grant Program. Additionally, the Telecommunications Infrastructure Loan and Loan Guarantee Program (previously the Telephone Loan Program) funds broadband deployment in rural areas. Distance Learning and Telemedicine (DLT) grants—while not principally supporting connectivity—fund equipment and software that operate via telecommunications to rural end-users of telemedicine and distance learning applications. The Consolidated Appropriations Act, 2018 (P.L. 115-141) provided $5 million to subsidize a broadband loan level of $29.851 million, $30 million to Community Connect broadband grants, $49 million for DLT grants, and $0.863 million in loan subsidies for a total loan level of $690 million for the Telecommunications Infrastructure Loan and Loan Guarantee Program. P.L. 115- 141 also appropriated $600 million to RUS to "conduct a new broadband loan and grant pilot program." On December 14, 2018, RUS released the *Funding Opportunity Announcement* and solicitation of applications for the new pilot broadband loan and grant program, which is called the ReConnect Program. On December 20, 2018, the President signed the 2018 farm bill (P.L. 115-334, Agriculture Improvement Act of 2018). Regarding the RUS broadband programs, the act includes provisions authorizing a grant component in combination with the broadband loan program; increasing the annual authorization level from $25 million to $350 million; raising the proposed service area eligibility threshold of unserved households from 15% to 50% for broadband loans; authorizing grants, loans, and loan guarantees for middle mile infrastructure; directing improved federal agency broadband program coordination; and providing eligible applicants with technical assistance and training to prepare applications. In the 116th Congress, appropriations will determine the extent to which these programs will be funded.

Chapter 2 - The federal Pell Grant program, authorized by Title IV of the Higher Education Act of 1965, as amended (HEA; P.L. 89-329), is the single largest source of federal grant aid supporting postsecondary education students. Pell Grants, and their predecessor, Basic Education Opportunity Grants, have been awarded since 1973. The program provided approximately $29 billion in aid to approximately 7.2 million undergraduate students in FY2017. Pell Grants are need-based aid that is intended to be the foundation for all need-based federal student aid awarded to undergraduates. To be eligible for a Pell Grant, an undergraduate student must meet several requirements. One key requirement is that the student and his or her family demonstrate financial need. Financial need is determined through the calculation of an expected family contribution (EFC), which is based on applicable family financial information provided on the Free Application for Federal Student Aid (FAFSA). Although there is no absolute income threshold that determines who is eligible or ineligible for Pell Grants, an estimated 95% of Pell Grant recipients had a total family income at or below $60,000 in academic year 2015-2016. Other requirements include, but are not limited to, the student not having earned a bachelor's degree and being enrolled in an eligible program at an HEA Title IV-participating institution of higher education for the purpose of earning a certificate or degree. The maximum annual award a student may receive during an academic year is calculated in accordance with the Pell Grant award rules. The student's scheduled award is the least of (1) the total maximum Pell Grant minus the student's EFC, or (2) Cost of Attendance (COA) minus EFC. For a student who enrolls on a less-than-full-time basis, the student's maximum annual award is the scheduled award ratably reduced. For FY2019 (academic year 2019-2020), the total maximum Pell Grant is $6,195. The COA is a measure of a student's educational expenses for the academic year. Qualified students who exhaust their scheduled award and remain enrolled beyond the academic year (e.g., enroll in a summer semester) during an award year receive a *year-round* or *summer* Pell Grant. With year-round Pell Grants, qualified students may receive up to 11/2 scheduled grants in each award year. Finally, a student may receive the value of no more than 12 full-time semesters (or the equivalent) of Pell Grant awards over a lifetime. The program is funded primarily through annual discretionary appropriations, although in recent years mandatory appropriations have played an increasing role in the program. The total maximum Pell Grant is the sum of two components: the discretionary maximum award and the mandatory add-on award. The discretionary maximum award amount is funded by discretionary appropriations enacted in annual appropriations acts, and augmented by permanent and definite mandatory appropriations provided for in the HEA. For FY2019, the discretionary appropriation is $22.475 billion and the augmenting mandatory funds total $1.370 billion. The mandatory add-on award amount is funded entirely by a permanent and indefinite mandatory appropriation of such sums as necessary, as authorized in the HEA. The mandatory add-on is estimated to require $6.077 billion in FY2019. Funding provided for the Pell Grant program is exempt from sequestration. The Pell Grant program is often referred to as a *quasi-entitlement* because for the most part eligible students receive the Pell Grant award level calculated for them without regard to available appropriations. In a given year, the discretionary appropriation level may be smaller or larger than the actual cost to fund the discretionary maximum award, despite the augmenting mandatory appropriation. When the discretionary appropriation is too small, the program carries a shortfall into the subsequent fiscal year. When the discretionary appropriation is too large, the program carries a surplus into the following fiscal year. Since FY2012, the program has maintained a surplus. The surplus has variably been used to increase Pell Grant awards, expand eligibility, and either fund other programs or reduce the national deficit.

Chapter 3 - The Elementary and Secondary Education Act (ESEA), as amended by the Every Student Succeeds Act (ESSA; P.L. 114-95), is the primary source of federal aid to K-12 education. The Title I-A program is the largest grant program authorized under the ESEA. It is designed to provide supplementary educational and related services to low-achieving and other students attending elementary and secondary schools with relatively high concentrations of students from low-income families. Title I-A was funded at $15.5 billion for FY2017. Under current law, the U.S. Department of Education (ED) determines Title I-A grants to local educational agencies (LEAs) based on four separate funding formulas: Basic Grants, Concentration Grants, Targeted Grants, and Education Finance Incentive Grants (EFIG). The four Title I-A formulas have somewhat distinct allocation patterns, providing varying shares of allocated funds to different types of states. Thus, for some states, certain formulas are more favorable than others. This report provides FY2017 state grant amounts under each of the four formulas used to determine Title I-A grants. Overall, California received the largest FY2017 Title I-A grant amount ($1.8 billion, or 12.00% of total Title I-A grants). Vermont received the smallest FY2017 Title I-A grant amount ($35.3 million, or 0.23% of total Title I-A grants).

Chapter 4 - The Homeless Assistance Grants, administered by the Department of Housing and Urban Development (HUD), were first authorized by Congress in 1987 as part of the McKinney-Vento Homeless Assistance Act (P.L. 100-77). Since their creation, the grants have been composed of three or four separate programs, though for the majority of their existence, between 1992 and 2012, the grant programs were unchanged. During this time period, there were four programs authorized and funded by Congress: the Emergency Shelter Grants (ESG), the Supportive Housing Program (SHP), the Shelter Plus Care (S+C) program, and the Section 8 Moderate Rehabilitation for Single Room Occupancy Dwellings (SRO) program. Funds for the ESG program were used primarily for the short-term needs of homeless persons, such as emergency shelter, while the other three programs addressed longer-term transitional and permanent housing needs. The composition of the Homeless Assistance Grants changed when Congress enacted the Homeless Emergency Assistance and Rapid Transition to Housing (HEARTH) Act as part of the Helping Families Save Their Homes Act in the 111th Congress (P.L. 111-22). The HEARTH Act renamed the ESG program (it is now called the Emergency *Solutions* Grants) and expanded the way in which funds can be used to include homelessness prevention and rapid rehousing (quickly finding housing for families who find themselves homeless), and it consolidated SHP, S+C, and SRO into one program called the Continuum of Care (CoC) program. A third program carved out of the CoC program to assist rural communities—the Rural Housing Stability Assistance Program—was also created by P.L. 111-22. In addition, the HEARTH Act broadened HUD's definition of homelessness. The changes in P.L. 111-22 had repercussions for the way in which funds are distributed to grantees, the purposes for which grantees may use funds, and who may be served. HUD began to implement the ESG program in FY2011 and the CoC program in FY2012, and it released proposed regulations for the Rural Housing Stability (RHS) grants in March 2013 (and has not yet provided RHS grants). Funds for the ESG program, in addition to being available for homelessness prevention and rapid rehousing, can be used for emergency shelter and supportive services. CoC program funds can be used to provide permanent supportive housing, transitional housing, supportive services, and rapid rehousing. If the RHS program is implemented, rural communities will have greater flexibility in who they are able to serve (those assisted may not necessarily meet HUD's definition of "homeless individual"), and may use funds for a variety of housing and services options. HUD uses one method to distribute funds for the ESG program and another method to distribute funds for the CoC program. The ESG program distributes funds to states, counties, and metropolitan areas using the Community Development Block Grant (CDBG) program formula, while the CoC grants are distributed through a competitive process, though the CDBG formula plays a role in determining community need. In July 2016, HUD proposed to change the CoC formula so that it no longer relies on the CDBG formula distribution. Funding for the Homeless Assistance Grants has increased by almost $1 billion in the last 10 years, reaching nearly $2.4 billion in FY2017 compared to $1.4 billion in FY2007 (see Table 3). Despite funding increases, the need to renew existing grants requires the majority of funding. In FY2016, 90% of the CoC program allocation was used to renew existing grants.

Chapter 5 - Community Services Block Grants (CSBG) provide federal funds to states, territories, and tribes for distribution to local agencies to support a wide range of community-based activities to reduce poverty. These include activities to help families and individuals achieve self-sufficiency, find and retain meaningful employment, attain an adequate education, make better use of available income, obtain adequate housing, and achieve greater participation in community affairs. In addition, many local agencies receive federal funds from other sources and may administer other federal programs. Smaller related programs—Community Economic Development (CED), Rural Community Facilities (RCF), and Individual Development Accounts (IDAs)—also support antipoverty efforts. CSBG and some of these related activities trace their roots to the War on Poverty, launched more than 50 years ago in 1964. Today, they are administered at the federal level by the Department of Health and Human Services (HHS). Initial FY2018 funding for CSBG is provided by a series of continuing resolutions (CRs). As of the date of this report, the current CR funds most federal programs, including CSBG and related programs, at their FY2017 levels less an across-the-board rescission of 0.6791%, through February 8, 2018. In FY2017, CSBG and related activities were funded at a total level of $742 million through the FY2017 Consolidated Appropriations Act (P.L. 115-31). This was a reduction of nearly $30 million relative to FY2016 appropriations of $770 million, though that total was more than had been appropriated in each year from FY2012-FY2015. While the block grant was funded at the FY2016 level of $715 million, funding for CED was reduced by $10 million (from $30 million to $20 million) and funding for IDAs was eliminated for the first time since the program was created as a demonstration in 1998. Funding for RCF increased slightly to $7.5 million in FY2017, compared to $6.5 million in FY2016. Prior to enactment of the FY2018 continuing resolutions, the Administration's budget proposed to eliminate funding for CSBG, CED, and RCF, and would again have provided no funding for IDAs. Both the Senate and the House appropriations committees reported FY2018 funding bills that rejected the Administration's proposal. The House Appropriations Committee-reported bill to fund the Departments of Labor, Health and Human Services, and Education (LHHS, H.R. 3358) would provide $600 million for CSBG, $10 million for CED, $7.5 million for RCF, and no funding for IDAs. The LHHS bill approved by the Senate Appropriations Committee (S. 1771) would provide $700 million for CSBG, and maintain FY2017 funding levels for CED ($20 million) and RCF ($7.5 million). Neither the House nor the Senate committee-approved bills contain funding for IDAs. In addition, on August 16, 2017, the House passed H.R. 3354, a bill that incorporated multiple appropriations bills, as an omnibus appropriations act. However, the CR was enacted before action on H.R. 3354 was complete. Funding for CSBG and related activities in H.R. 3354 are the same as those in H.R. 3358. The Community Services Block Grant Act was last reauthorized in 1998 by P.L. 105-285. The authorization of appropriations for CSBG and most related programs expired in FY2003, but Congress has continued to make annual appropriations each year. Legislation was introduced in the 114th Congress—with bipartisan cosponsorship—to amend and reauthorize the CSBG Act through FY2023 (H.R. 1655). Similar legislation had been introduced in the 113th Congress (H.R. 3854). According to the most recent survey conducted by the National Association for State Community Services Programs, through a contract with HHS, the nationwide network of more than 1,000 CSBG grantees served 15.6 million people in 6.5 million low-income families in FY2015. States reported that the network spent $13.6 billion of federal, state, local, and private resources, including $637 million in federal CSBG funds.

Chapter 6 - This is an edited, reformatted and augmented version of House of Representatives Report to the Committee of the Whole House on the State of the Union and ordered to be printed, Publication No. 115–597, dated March 14, 2018.

Chapter 7 - The Maternal and Child Health (MCH) Services Block Grant is a federal-state partnership program that aims to improve the health of low-income pregnant women, mothers, and children. In addition, the program aims to connect low-income families with other services and programs, such as Medicaid and the State Children's Health Insurance Program (CHIP). This federal-state partnership is composed of three programs. First, formula-based block grants are provided to states and territories (collectively referred to as *states* in this report). Second, competitive grants are available through the Special Projects of Regional and National Significance (SPRANS) program. Third, competitive grants are available through the Community Integrated Service Systems (CISS) program. As a whole, these programs are administered by the Maternal and Child Health Bureau (MCHB) of the Health Resources and Services Administration (HRSA) in the Department of Health and Human Services (HHS). This block grant was authorized under Title V of the Social Security Act (SSA). Appropriations. The MCH Services Block Grant received an appropriation of $638.2 million in FY2016. Of that amount, approximately $550.8 million (86.31%) was for block grants to states, $77.1 million (12.08%) was for SPRANS, and $10.3 million (1.61%) was for CISS. Congress provided $20 million in supplemental funding to the SPRANS program to help territories respond to the Zika virus. Eligible Population. Although the MCH Services Block Grant program primarily serves low-income pregnant women, mothers, and children, individuals who are not from low-income families are also eligible to receive services. Such recipients may include nonpregnant women who are over 21 years of age. Program Services. MCH Services Block Grant funds are distributed for the purpose of funding core public health services provided by maternal and child health agencies. These core services are often divided into four categories: (1) direct health care, (2) enabling services, (3) population-based services, and (4) infrastructure building. Within these categories, the MCH Services Block Grant supports a wide array of programs, including newborn screening, health services for children with special health care needs (CSHCNs), and immunization programs. Topics Covered in This Report. This report provides background and funding information on the MCH Services Block Grant. It also includes select program and health expenditure data to provide context on issues that Congress and HRSA have sought to address through this block grant program.

In: A Closer Look at Grant Programs
Editor: Tabitha Reyes

ISBN: 978-1-53615-995-0
© 2019 Nova Science Publishers, Inc.

Chapter 1

BROADBAND LOAN AND GRANT PROGRAMS IN THE USDA'S RURAL UTILITIES SERVICE (UPDATED)[*]

Lennard G. Kruger

ABSTRACT

Given the large potential impact broadband access may have on the economic development of rural America, concern has been raised over a "digital divide" between rural and urban or suburban areas with respect to broadband deployment. While there are many examples of rural communities with state-of-the-art telecommunications facilities, recent surveys and studies have indicated that, in general, rural areas tend to lag behind urban and suburban areas in broadband deployment.

According to the FCC's *First Communications Market Report*, as of 2017, 24% of Americans in rural areas lacked coverage from fixed terrestrial 25 Mbps/3 Mbps broadband, as compared to only 1.5% of Americans in urban areas. The comparatively lower population density of rural areas is likely a major reason why broadband is less deployed than in more highly populated suburban and urban areas. Particularly for

---

[*] This is an edited, reformatted and augmented version of Congressional Research Service, Publication No. RL33816, dated December 26, 2018.

wireline broadband technologies—such as cable modem and fiber—the greater the geographical distances among customers, the larger the cost to serve those customers.

The Rural Utilities Service (RUS) at the U.S. Department of Agriculture (USDA) houses two ongoing assistance programs exclusively created and dedicated to financing broadband deployment: the Rural Broadband Access Loan and Loan Guarantee Program and the Community Connect Grant Program. Additionally, the Telecommunications Infrastructure Loan and Loan Guarantee Program (previously the Telephone Loan Program) funds broadband deployment in rural areas. Distance Learning and Telemedicine (DLT) grants—while not principally supporting connectivity—fund equipment and software that operate via telecommunications to rural end-users of telemedicine and distance learning applications.

The Consolidated Appropriations Act, 2018 (P.L. 115-141) provided $5 million to subsidize a broadband loan level of $29.851 million, $30 million to Community Connect broadband grants, $49 million for DLT grants, and $0.863 million in loan subsidies for a total loan level of $690 million for the Telecommunications Infrastructure Loan and Loan Guarantee Program. P.L. 115- 141 also appropriated $600 million to RUS to "conduct a new broadband loan and grant pilot program." On December 14, 2018, RUS released the *Funding Opportunity Announcement* and solicitation of applications for the new pilot broadband loan and grant program, which is called the ReConnect Program.

On December 20, 2018, the President signed the 2018 farm bill (P.L. 115-334, Agriculture Improvement Act of 2018). Regarding the RUS broadband programs, the act includes provisions authorizing a grant component in combination with the broadband loan program; increasing the annual authorization level from $25 million to $350 million; raising the proposed service area eligibility threshold of unserved households from 15% to 50% for broadband loans; authorizing grants, loans, and loan guarantees for middle mile infrastructure; directing improved federal agency broadband program coordination; and providing eligible applicants with technical assistance and training to prepare applications. In the 116th Congress, appropriations will determine the extent to which these programs will be funded.

BACKGROUND: BROADBAND AND RURAL AMERICA

The broadband loan and grant programs at RUS are intended to accelerate the deployment of broadband services in rural America.

"Broadband" refers to high-speed internet access and advanced telecommunications services for private homes, commercial establishments, schools, and public institutions. Currently in the United States, residential broadband is primarily provided via cable modem (from the local provider of cable television service), fiber-optic cable, mobile wireless (e.g., smartphones), or over the copper telephone line (digital subscriber line or "DSL"). Other broadband technologies include fixed wireless and satellite.

Broadband access enables a number of beneficial applications to individual users and to communities. These include ecommerce, telecommuting, voice service (voice over the internet protocol or "VOIP"), distance learning, telemedicine, public safety, and others. It is becoming generally accepted that broadband access in a community can play an important role in economic development.

Access to affordable broadband is viewed as particularly important for the economic development of rural areas because it enables individuals and businesses to participate fully in the online economy regardless of geographical location. For example, aside from enabling existing businesses to remain in their rural locations, broadband access could attract new business enterprises drawn by lower costs and a more desirable lifestyle. Essentially, broadband potentially allows businesses and individuals in rural America to live locally while competing globally in an online environment. A 2016 study from the Hudson Institute found that rural broadband providers directly and indirectly added $24.1 billion to the U.S. economy in 2015. The rural broadband industry supported 69,595 jobs in 2015, both through its own employment and the employment that its purchases of goods and services generated.[1]

Given the large potential impact broadband may have on the economic development of rural America, concern has been raised over a "digital divide" between rural and urban or suburban areas with respect to broadband deployment.

---

[1] Hanns Kuttner, Hudson Institute, *The Economic Impact of Rural Broadband*, April 2016, available at https://s3.amazonaws.com/media.hudson.org/files/publications/20160419 KuttnerTheEconomicImpactofRuralBroadband.pdf.

While there are many examples of rural communities with state-of-the-art telecommunications facilities,[2] recent surveys and studies have indicated that, in general, rural areas tend to lag behind urban and suburban areas in broadband deployment. For example

- According to the FCC's *First Communications Market Report*, "As of year-end 2017, 94% of the overall population had coverage [of fixed terrestrial broadband at speeds of 25 Mbps/3 Mbps], up from 92.3% in 2016. Nonetheless, the gap in rural and Tribal America remains notable: 24% of Americans in rural areas and 32% of Americans in Tribal lands lack coverage from fixed terrestrial 25 Mbps/3 Mbps broadband, as compared to only 1.5% of Americans in urban areas."[3]
- Also according to the FCC's *First Communications Market Report*, rural areas continue to lag behind urban areas in mobile broadband deployment. Although evaluated urban areas saw an increase of 10 Mbps/3 Mbps mobile LTE from 81.9% in 2014 to 92.6% in 2017, such deployment in evaluated rural areas remained relatively flat at about 70%."[4]
- According to January 2018 survey data from the Pew Research Center, 58% of adults in rural areas said they have a high-speed broadband connection at home, as opposed to 67% of adults in urban areas and 70% of adults in suburban areas.[5]

---

[2] See for example, National Exchange Carrier Association (NECA), *Trends: A Report on Rural Telecom Technology,* 18 pages, December 2015, available at https://www.neca.org/WorkArea/linkit.aspx?LinkIdentifier=id&ItemID= 12331&libID=12351.
[3] Draft *First Consolidated Communications Marketplace Report*, GN Docket No. 18-231, released November 21, 2018, p. 135, available at https://www.fcc.gov/document/adopting-first-consolidated-communications-marketplace-report.
[4] Draft *First Communications Market Report*, p. 138.
[5] Pew Research Center, *Internet/Broadband Fact Sheet*, February 5, 2018, available at http://www.pewinternet.org/factsheet/internet-broadband/.

- A November 2017 Census Bureau survey reported by the National Telecommunications and Information Administration (NTIA) Digital Nation Data Explorer showed 72.9% of rural residents reporting using the internet, versus 78.5% of urban residents.[6] According to NTIA, the data "indicates a fairly constant 6-9 percentage point gap between rural and urban communities' internet use over time."[7]

The comparatively lower population density of rural areas is likely the major reason why broadband is less deployed than in more highly populated suburban and urban areas. Particularly for wireline broadband technologies—such as cable modem, fiber, and DSL—the greater the geographical distances among customers, the larger the cost to serve those customers. Thus, there is often less incentive for companies to invest in broadband in rural areas than, for example, in an urban area where there is more demand (more customers with perhaps higher incomes) and less cost to wire the market area.

The terrain of rural areas can also be a hindrance, in that it is more expensive to deploy broadband technologies in a mountainous or heavily forested area. An additional added cost factor for remote areas can be the expense of "backhaul" (e.g., the "middle mile"), which refers to the installation of a dedicated line that transmits a signal to and from an internet backbone, which is typically located in or near an urban area.

Another important broadband availability issue is the extent to which there are multiple broadband providers offering competition and consumer choice. Typically, multiple providers are more prevalent in urban than in rural areas.[8]

---

[6] U.S. Department of Commerce, National Telecommunications and Information Administration, *Digital Nation Data Explorer*, June 6, 2018, available at https://www.ntia.doc.gov/data/digital-nation-dataexplorer#sel=internetUser&demo=metro&pc=prop&disp=chart.

[7] U.S. Department of Commerce, National Telecommunications and Information Administration, "The State of the Urban/Rural Digital Divide," August 10, 2016, available at https://www.ntia.doc.gov/blog/2016/state-urbanruraldigital-divide.

[8] See Table 2 in CRS In Focus IF10441, *Broadband Deployment: Status and Federal Programs*, by Lennard G. Kruger.

RURAL BROADBAND PROGRAMS AT THE RURAL UTILITIES SERVICE

Because private providers are unlikely to earn enough revenue to cover the costs of deploying and operating broadband networks in many unserved rural areas, it is unlikely that private investment alone will bring service to these areas.[9] In 2000, given the lagging deployment of broadband in rural areas, Congress and the Administration acted to initiate pilot broadband loan and grant programs within the Rural Utilities Service of the U.S. Department of Agriculture. While RUS had long maintained telecommunications loan and grant programs (Rural Telephone Loans and Loan Guarantees, Rural Telephone Bank, and more recently, the Distance Learning and Telemedicine Loans and Grants), none were exclusively dedicated to financing rural broadband deployment. Title III of the FY2001 agriculture appropriations bill (P.L. 106-387) directed USDA/RUS to conduct a "pilot program to finance broadband transmission and local dial-up Internet service in areas that meet the definition of 'rural area' used for the Distance Learning and Telemedicine Program."

Subsequently, on December 5, 2000, RUS announced the availability of $100 million in loan funding through a one-year pilot program "to finance the construction and installation of broadband telecommunications services in rural America."[10] The broadband pilot loan program was authorized under the authority of the Distance Learning and Telemedicine Program (7 U.S.C. 950aaa), and was available to "legally organized entities" not located within the boundaries of a city or town having a population in excess of 20,000.

The FY2002 agriculture appropriations bill (P.L. 107-76) designated a loan level of $80 million for broadband loans, and on January 23, 2002,

---

[9] Government Accountability Office, *Projects and Policies Related to Deploying Broadband in Unserved and Underserved Areas*, GAO-14-409, April 2014, p. 9, available at http://www.gao.gov/assets/670/662711.pdf.

[10] Rural Utilities Service, USDA, "Construction and Installation of Broadband Telecommunications Services in Rural America; Availability of Loan Funds," *Federal Register*, Vol. 65, No. 234, December 5, 2000, p. 75920.

RUS announced that the pilot program would be extended into FY2002, with $80 million in loans made available to fund many of the applications that did not receive funding during the previous year.[11]

Meanwhile, the FY2002 agriculture appropriations bill (P.L. 107-76) allocated $20 million for a pilot broadband grant program, also authorized under the Distance Learning and Telemedicine Program. On July 8, 2002, RUS announced the availability of $20 million for a pilot grant program for the provision of broadband service in rural America. The program was specifically targeted to economically challenged rural communities with no existing broadband service. Grants were made available to entities providing "community-oriented connectivity," which the RUS defined as those entities "who will connect the critical community facilities including the local schools, libraries, hospitals, police, fire and rescue services and who will operate a community center that provides free and open access to residents."[12]

The pilot program was extended into FY2003, as the Consolidated Appropriations Resolution of 2003 (P.L. 108-7) allocated $10 million for broadband grants.

Currently, RUS has four ongoing programs that have been established to incentivize and subsidize broadband infrastructure investment in unserved and underserved rural areas. These include the following:

- *Rural Broadband Access Loans*—funds the costs of construction, improvement, or acquisition of facilities and equipment needed to provide service in eligible rural areas.
- *Community Connect Grants*—funds broadband deployment into rural communities where it is not yet economically viable for private sector providers to deliver service.
- *Telecommunications Infrastructure Loans and Loan Guarantees*—funds the construction, maintenance, improvement,

---

[11] Rural Utilities Service, USDA, "Broadband Pilot Loan Program," *Federal Register*, Vol. 67, No. 15, January 23, 2002, p. 3140.
[12] Rural Utilities Service, USDA, "Broadband Pilot Grant Program," *Federal Register*, Vol. 67, No. 130, July 8, 2002, p. 45080.

and expansion of telephone service and broadband in extremely rural areas with a population of 5,000 or less.
- *Distance Learning and Telemedicine Grants*—principally funds end-user equipment to help rural communities use telecommunications to link teachers and medical service providers in one area to students and patients in another.

Table 1. Appropriations Funding for the Rural Broadband Access Loan and Loan Guarantee Program

	Direct Appropriations (subsidy level)	Loan Levels Estimated in Annual Appropriations[a]
FY2001 (pilot)	—	$100 million
FY2002 (pilot)	—	$80 million
FY2003	[b]	$80 million
FY2004	$13.1 million	$602 million
FY2005	$11.715 million	$550 million
FY2006	$10.75 million	$500 million
FY2007	$10.75 million	$500 million
FY2008	$6.45 million	$300 million
FY2009	$15.619 million	$400 million
FY2010	$28.96 million	$400 million
FY2011	$22.32 million	$400 million
FY2012	$6.0 million	$212 million
FY2013	$4 million	$42 million
FY2014	$4.5 million	$34.5 million
FY2015	$4.5 million	$24.1 million
FY2016	$4.5 million	$20.6 million
FY2017	$4.5 million	$27.0 million
FY2018	$5 million	$29.0 million

Source: Compiled by CRS from appropriations bills.

[a] Actual loan levels for a fiscal year can vary from what is estimated in annual appropriations bill.

[b] Program received $40 million composed of $20 million from FY2002 plus $20 million from FY2003 of mandatory funding from the Commodity Credit Corporation, as directed by P.L. 107-171. In the FY2004, FY2005, and FY2006 appropriations bills, mandatory funding from the CCC was canceled.

In addition, a new broadband loan and grant pilot program—the ReConnect Program—has been established and funded at $600 million by the Consolidated Appropriations Act, 2018 (P.L. 115- 141).

Table A-1 in the Appendix shows the total amount and number of awards provided by the RUS broadband programs for each state between FY2009 and FY2016.

In its April 2017 report, *Rural Broadband Deployment: Improved Consistency with Leading Practices Could Enhance Management of Loan and Grant Programs*, GAO reported that (according to RUS data) since FY2004, RUS has approved 704 broadband projects totaling almost $8.6 billion in loans and $144.8 million in grants to deploy telecommunications or broadband infrastructure networks in rural areas.[13]

Rural Broadband Access Loan and Loan Guarantee Program

Building on the pilot broadband loan program at RUS, Section 6103 of the Farm Security and Rural Investment Act of 2002 (P.L. 107-171) amended the Rural Electrification Act of 1936 to authorize a loan and loan guarantee program to provide funds for the costs of the construction, improvement, and acquisition of facilities and equipment for broadband service in eligible rural communities.[14] Section 6103 made available, from the funds of the Commodity Credit Corporation (CCC), a total of $100 million through FY2007. P.L. 107-171 also authorized any other funds appropriated for the broadband loan program. The program was subsequently reauthorized by Section 6110 of the Food, Conservation, and Energy Act of 2008 (P.L. 110-246), and by Section 6104 of the Agricultural Act of 2014 (P.L. 113-79).

Beginning in FY2004, Congress annually blocked mandatory funding from the CCC. Thus— starting in FY2004—the program was funded as part of annual appropriations in the Distance Learning and Telemedicine account within the Department of Agriculture appropriations bill. Every fiscal year, Congress approves an appropriation (loan subsidy) and a

---

[13] Government Accountability Office, *Rural Broadband Deployment: Improved Consistency with Leading Practices Could Enhance Management of Loan and Grant Program*, GAO-17-301, April 2017, p. 2, available at https://www.gao.gov/assets/690/684093.pdf.
[14] Title VI of the Rural Electrification Act of 1936 (7 U.S.C. 950bb).

specific loan level (lending authority) for the Rural Broadband Access Loan and Loan Guarantee Program. Table 1 shows—for the life of the program to date—loan subsidies and loan levels (lending authority) set by Congress in annual appropriations bills.

The Rural Broadband Access Loan and Loan Guarantee Program is codified as 7 U.S.C. 950bb. On July 30, 2015, the RUS published in the *Federal Register* the interim rule (7 C.F.R. part 1738) implementing the Rural Broadband Access Loan and Loan Guarantee Program as reauthorized by the enactment of the Agricultural Act of 2014 (P.L. 113-79),[15] and the interim rule was made final on June 9, 2016. Entities eligible to receive loans include corporations, limited liability companies, cooperative or mutual organizations, Indian tribes or tribal organizations, and state or local governments. Eligible areas for funding must be completely contained within a rural area (or composed of multiple rural areas). Additionally, at least 15% of the households in the proposed funded service areas must be unserved, no part of the proposed service area can have three or more incumbent service providers, and no part of the proposed service area can overlap with the service area of current RUS borrowers or of grantees that were funded by RUS.

Whereas RUS had previously been setting two application periods per year, the latest Notice of Solicitation of Applications (NOSA) announced that RUS is now accepting applications on a rolling basis through September 30, 2018, which will give RUS the ability to request additional information and modifications to submitted applications if necessary. RUS will evaluate the submitted applications every 90 days, and anticipates at least two evaluation periods for FY2018. The minimum loan amount is $300,000, while the maximum loan amount is $25 million. The NOSA has maintained its definition of broadband service and broadband lending speed at no less than 25 Mbps download and 3 Mbps upload for both mobile and fixed services.[16]

---

[15] Department of Agriculture, Rural Utilities Service, "Rural Broadband Access Loans and Loan Guarantees," Interim rule, 80 *Federal Register* 45397-45413, July 30, 2015, available at https://www.gpo.gov/fdsys/pkg/FR-2015-07-30/pdf/ 2015-18624.pdf.

[16] Department of Agriculture, Rural Utilities Service, "Rural Broadband Access Loan and Loan Guarantees Program," Notice of Solicitation of Applications (NOSA), 83 *Federal Register*

The 2018 farm bill, which was signed by the President on December 20, 2018 (P.L. 115-334, Agriculture Improvement Act of 2018) adds a grant component to the broadband loan program, increases the annual authorization level from $25 million to $350 million, and changes the proposed service area threshold from 15% to 50%. RUS will issue a revised regulation that implements the changes made by the 2018 farm bill. For up to one year after enactment, the Secretary shall use the previously existing rules and regulations for the broadband loan program until a final rule is issued.

For the latest application information, see http://www.rd.usda.gov/programs-services/farm-billbroadband-loans-loan-guarantees.

Community Connect Broadband Grants

The Consolidated Appropriations Act of 2004 (P.L. 108-199) appropriated $9 million "for a grant program to finance broadband transmission in rural areas eligible for Distance Learning and Telemedicine Program benefits authorized by 7 U.S.C. 950aaa." Essentially operating the same as the pilot broadband grants, the program provides grant money to applicants proposing to provide broadband on a "community-oriented connectivity" basis to currently unserved rural areas for the purpose of fostering economic growth and delivering enhanced health care, education, and public safety services. Funding for the broadband grant program is provided through annual appropriations in the Distance Learning and Telemedicine account within the Department of Agriculture appropriations bill. Table 2 shows a history of appropriations for the Community Connect Broadband Grants.

Eligible applicants for broadband grants include most state and local governments, federally recognized tribes, nonprofits, and for-profit corporations.

13225-13226, March 28, 2018, available at https://www.gpo.gov/fdsys/pkg/FR-2018-03-28/pdf/2018-06175.pdf.

Table 2. Appropriations for the Community Connect Broadband Grants

Fiscal Year	Appropriation
FY2002	$20 million
FY2003	$10 million
FY2004	$9 million
FY2005	$9 million
FY2006	$9 million
FY2007	$9 million
FY2008	$13.4 million
FY2009	$13.4 million
FY2010	$17.9 million
FY2011	$13.4 million
FY2012	$10.4 million
FY2013	$10.4 million
FY2014	$10.4 million
FY2015	$10.4 million
FY2016	$10.4 million
FY2017	$34.5 million
FY2018	$30 million

Source: Compiled by CRS from appropriations bills.

Funded projects must serve a rural area where broadband service above a specified minimum speed does not exist, deploy free broadband service for at least two years to all community facilities, and offer broadband to residential and business customers. Up to 10% of the grant may be used for the improvement, expansion, construction, or acquisition of a community center that provides online access to the public.

On May 3, 2013, RUS issued a new final rule for Community Connect grants in the *Federal Register*.[17] The final rule changes previous requirements related to matching funds, eligible communities, and application scoring criteria. The final rule also removes the previous definition of broadband service speed (200 kbps). A new threshold for broadband service speed and broadband grant speed (the speed the grantee must deliver) will be provided in an annual Notice of Funding Availability

---

[17] Department of Agriculture, Rural Utilities Service, "Community Connect Broadband Grant Program," 78 *Federal Register* 25787-25795, May 3, 2013, available at http://www.gpo.gov/fdsys/pkg/FR-2013-05-03/pdf/2013-10502.pdf.

(NOFA) in the *Federal Register*. The NOFA will also specify the deadline for applications, the total amount of funding available, and the maximum and minimum amount of funding available for each grant.

On March 15, 2018, RUS issued a Notice of Solicitation of Applications (NOSA) establishing an application window for FY2018 Community Connect grants through May 14, 2018.[18] The NOSA established a new minimum threshold for speeds constituting broadband service at 10 Mbps download and 1 Mbps upload for both fixed and mobile broadband. The minimum broadband speed that an applicant must propose to deliver is 25 Mbps download, 3 Mbps upload for both fixed and mobile service to the customer. Further information, including application materials and guidelines, is available at http://www.rd.usda.gov/programs-services/community-connect-grants.

The 2018 farm bill (P.L. 115-334) codifies the Community Connect Grant Program and authorizes the program at $50 million for each of fiscal years 2018 through 2023.

Telecommunications Infrastructure Loans and Loan Guarantees

The Telecommunications Infrastructure Loan and Loan Guarantee Program[19] provides loans and loan guarantees for the construction, maintenance, improvement, and expansion of telephone service and broadband in rural areas. The program was first authorized in 1949 to finance rural telephone service. Since 1995, RUS has required that networks funded by this program offer broadband service as well.

Loans and loan guarantees are available only to rural areas and towns with a population of 5,000 or less. Also, the program cannot fund networks that duplicate similar services in the same area.

---

[18] Department of Agriculture, Rural Utilities Service, "Announcement of Grant Application Deadlines and Funding Levels," Notice of Solicitation of Applications (NOSA), 83 *Federal Register* 11494-11499, March 15, 2018, available at https://www.gpo.gov/fdsys/pkg/FR-2018-03-15/pdf/2018-05200.pdf.

[19] For more information, see http://www.rd.usda.gov/programs-services/telecommunications-infrastructure-loans-loanguarantees.

The program is authorized to provide several different types of financing, including

- direct Treasury rate loans, which bear interest at the government's cost of money (or the current Treasury rate). Thus, the interest charged varies with the Treasury rate. As Treasury rates increase, so does the cost to the borrower for these loans.
- guaranteed loans, which are provided to borrowers of a nongovernment lender or from the Federal Financing Bank (FFB). The interest rate charged on FFB loans is the Treasury rate plus an administrative fee of one-eighth of 1%. The terms of these loans may vary significantly and allow borrowers more flexibility in meeting their financing needs.
- hardship direct loans, which bear interest at a fixed rate of 5% per year. These loans are intended only for borrowers with extremely high investment costs in terms of per subscriber service. These borrowers also have a very low number of subscribers for each mile of telecommunications line constructed. This low subscriber density inherently increases the cost to serve the most sparsely populated rural areas. Because of the high cost of the investment needed, these borrowers cannot typically afford higher interest rate loans.[20]

The annual loan level for the Telecommunications Infrastructure Loan and Loan Guarantee Program is $690 million. Currently, the 5% hardship loans are not offered—because of low interest rates, the Treasury and FFB loans can currently offer lower interest rates than the 5% offered by hardship loans.

---

[20] 2017 USDA Budget Explanatory Notes for Committee on Appropriations, p. 31-2, available at http://www.obpa.usda.gov/31rus2017notes.pdf.

Distance Learning and Telemedicine Program

The Distance Learning and Telemedicine (DLT) Program was established by the 1996 farm bill— the Federal Agriculture Improvement and Reform Act of 1996 (P.L. 104-127). Though initially providing both grants and loans, since FY2009 only DLT grants have been awarded by RUS.

DLT grants serve as initial capital assets for equipment and software that operate via telecommunications to rural end-users of telemedicine and distance learning. DLT grants do not support connectivity. Grant funds may be used for audio, video, and interactive video equipment; terminal and data terminal equipment; computer hardware, network components, and software; inside wiring and similar infrastructure; acquisition of instructional programming; broadband facilities;* and technical assistance. Eligible applicants include most entities in rural areas that provide education or health care through telecommunications, including most state and local governmental entities, federally recognized tribes, nonprofits, for-profit businesses, and consortia of eligible entities.

The 2018 farm bill (P.L. 115-334) reauthorizes the DLT program through FY2023 at $82 million per year and sets aside 20% of DLT grant funding for applications related to substance use disorder treatment services.

Broadband e-Connectivity Pilot Loan and Grant Program

Section 779 of the Consolidated Appropriations Act, 2018 (P.L. 115-141) appropriated $600 million to RUS to "conduct a new broadband loan

---

* As of FY2018, purchasing and installing broadband facilities has been added to the approved grant purposes. This purpose is limited to a maximum of 20% of the requested grant amount and must be used for providing distance learning or telemedicine services. The awardee must own the final broadband asset in order for funding to be approved. See USDA Rural Development, *Distance Learning and Telemedicine Grant Program Application Guide Fiscal Year 2018*, p. 7, available at https://www.rd.usda.gov/files/2018-DLT_App-Guide_final.pdf.

and grant pilot program." The law states that the funding is to "remain available until expended," and that

- at least 90% of the households to be served by a project receiving a loan or grant under the pilot program shall be in a rural area without sufficient access to broadband, defined for this pilot program as 10 Mbps downstream, and 1 Mbps upstream, which shall be reevaluated and redetermined, as necessary, on an annual basis by the Secretary of Agriculture;
- an entity to which a loan or grant is made under the pilot program shall not use the loan or grant to overbuild or duplicate broadband expansion efforts made by any entity that has received a broadband loan from RUS;
- in addition to other available funds, not more than 4% of the funds can be used for administrative costs to carry out the pilot program and up to 3% may be utilized for technical assistance and predevelopment planning activities to support the most rural communities; and
- RUS shall adhere to the notice, reporting, and service area assessment requirements previously established in the 2014 farm bill.

The Explanatory Statement that accompanied the FY2018 Consolidated Appropriations Act states

> The agreement reiterates that funding should be prioritized to areas currently lacking access to broadband service, and investments in broadband shall consider any technology that best serves the goals of broadband expansion. Lastly, the agreement restates the importance of coordination among federal agencies in expanding broadband deployment and adoption and expects the Department to take caution to maximize these limited resources and not overbuild or duplicate existing broadband capable infrastructure.

The Senate-passed version of H.R. 6147, which includes the FY2019 agriculture appropriations bill, includes a provision (Division C, §764) directing the Secretary of Agriculture, in administering the $600 million pilot loan and grant program, to ensure that applicants determined to be ineligible have a means of appealing or otherwise challenging that determination in a timely fashion. The legislation also directs the Secretary, in determining whether an entity may overbuild or duplicate broadband expansion efforts made by an entity that has received an RUS broadband loan, to not consider loans that were rescinded or defaulted on.

H.R. 6147, as passed by the Senate, would appropriate $425 million to the e-connectivity broadband pilot loan and grant program in FY2019. H.R. 5961, the Agriculture, Rural Development, Food and Drug Administration, and Related Agencies Appropriations Act, 2019, as approved by the House Appropriations Committee, would provide $550 million.

On July 27, 2018, RUS released a notice of inquiry and request for comments on the $600 million "Broadband e-Connectivity Pilot Program." Specifically, RUS asked for comments (due September 10, 2018) on questions including the following:

- What types of broadband technologies and services should be considered as providing "sufficient access" to broadband, defined in the law as a minimum of 10 Mbps/1 Mbps? What transmission capacity is required for rural economic development and what speed and latency is required in peak usage hours to ensure rural premises have access to coverage similar to that offered in urban areas? Should affordability of service be included in evaluating whether an area already has "sufficient access" and how should such affordability measures be benchmarked?
- How should broadband data speeds be used or verified, given the limited availability of publicly available information regarding accurate broadband speeds provided to rural households?
- What are effective methods that can measure leading indicators of potential project benefits for rural sectors such as agriculture,

manufacturing, e-commerce, transportation, health care, and education? How should RUS evaluate the viability of applications that include local utility partnership arrangements, including locally owned telecommunications companies?

On December 14, 2018, RUS released the *Funding Opportunity Announcement* (FOA) and solicitation of applications for the new pilot broadband loan and grant program, which is named the "ReConnect Program."[21] As set forth in the statute, at least 90% of the households to be served by a project receiving a loan or grant under the pilot program shall be in a rural area without sufficient access to broadband at a minimum speed of 10 Mbps/1 Mbps. RUS defines "sufficient access to broadband" as any rural area that has fixed, terrestrial broadband service delivering at least 10 Mbps downstream and 1 Mbps upstream. Mobile and satellite service will not be considered in making the determination that households in the proposed funded service area do not have sufficient access to broadband.

Approximately $560 million has been set aside for funding opportunities under the FOA, with additional budget authority available for a reserve which may be used for additional loans or grants. Award recipients must complete projects within five years. Entities eligible for awards are: states or local governments, U.S. territories, an Indian tribe, nonprofit entities, for-profit corporations, limited liability companies, and cooperative or mutual organizations.

The ReConnect Program consists of three funding categories.

100% Loan

- Up to $200 million is available.
- The maximum amount that can be requested is $50 million.
- Interest rate is set at a fixed 2%.

---

[21] U.S. Department of Agriculture, Rural Utilities Service, "Broadband Pilot Program," *Federal Register*, vol. 83, no. 240, December 14, 2018, pp. 64315-64325, available at https://www.govinfo.gov/content/pkg/FR-2018-12- 14/pdf/2018-27038.pdf.

Broadband Loan and Grant Programs ... 19

- Eligible areas are where 90% of households do not have sufficient access to broadband at 10 Mbps/1 Mbps.
- Applicants must propose to build a network capable of providing service to every premise in the proposed funded service area at a minimum speed of 25 Mbps/3 Mbps.
- Applications accepted on a rolling basis through June 28, 2019.

50% Loan/50% Grant Combination

- Up to $200 million is available.
- The maximum amount that can be requested is $25 million for the loan and $25 million for the grant. Loan and grant amounts will always be equal.
- Interest rate for the loan will be set at the Treasury rate.
- Eligible areas are where 90% of households do not have sufficient access to broadband at 10 Mbps/1 Mbps.
- Applicants must propose to build a network capable of providing service to every premise in the proposed funded service area at a minimum speed of 25 Mbps/3 Mbps
- Applications accepted on a rolling basis through May 29, 2019.

100% Grant

- Up to $200 million is available.
- The maximum amount that can be requested is $25 million.
- Applicants must provide a matching contribution equal to 25% of the cost of the overall project.
- Eligible areas are where 100% of households do not have sufficient access to broadband at 10 Mbps/1 Mbps.

- Applicants must propose to build a network capable of providing service to every premise in the proposed funded service area at a minimum speed of 25 Mbps/3 Mbps.
- Applications accepted on a rolling basis through April 29, 2019.

According to RUS, the online application portal will be open in late February. More information on the ReConnect Program is available at https://reconnect.usda.gov.

IMPACT OF UNIVERSAL SERVICE REFORM ON RUS BROADBAND LOAN PROGRAMS

RUS has three programs that provide or have provided loans for broadband infrastructure projects: the Rural Broadband Access Loan and Loan Guarantee program (also known as the Farm Bill broadband loan program), the Broadband Initiatives Program (BIP under the ARRA), and the Telecommunications Infrastructure Loan Program (established in 1949 as the Rural Telephone Loan and Loan Guarantee program).[22]

Whereas RUS broadband loans are used as up-front capital to invest in broadband infrastructure, the Federal Communications Commission's (FCC's) Universal Service Fund (USF)— specifically, the high cost fund—has functioned as an ongoing subsidy to keep the operation of telecommunications networks in high cost areas profitable for providers. Many RUS telecommunications and broadband borrowers (loan recipients) receive high cost USF subsidies. In many cases, the subsidy received from USF helps provide the revenue necessary to keep the loan viable. The Telecommunications Infrastructure Loan Program is highly dependent on high cost USF revenues, with 99% (476 out of 480 borrowers) receiving interstate high cost USF support. This is not surprising, given that the RUS

---

[22] For more information on the RUS portfolio of telecommunications and broadband programs offering loans, loan guarantees, grants, and loan/grant combinations, see CRS Report R42524, *Rural Broadband: The Roles of the Rural Utilities Service and the Universal Service Fund*, by Angele A. Gilroy and Lennard G. Kruger.

Telecommunications Infrastructure Loans are available only to the most rural and high cost areas (towns with populations less than 5,000). Regarding broadband loans, 60% of BIP (stimulus) borrowers draw from state or interstate USF support mechanisms, while 10% of Farm Bill (Rural Broadband Access Loan and Loan Guarantee Program) broadband borrowers receive interstate high cost USF support.[23]

The FCC, in an October 2011 decision, adopted an order that calls for the USF to be transformed, in stages, over a multiyear period—from a mechanism to support voice telephone service to one that supports the deployment, adoption, and use of both fixed and mobile broadband. More specifically, the high cost program is being phased out and a new fund, the Connect America Fund (CAF), which includes the targeted Mobility Fund and new Remote Areas Fund, is replacing it.[24]

During this transition, the uncertainty surrounding the FCC's proposed methodology for distributing Connect America Fund monies has led many small rural providers to postpone or cancel investment in broadband network upgrades.[25] According to RUS, "demand for RUS loans dropped to roughly 37% of the total amount of loan funds appropriated by Congress in FY2012," and "[c]urrent and prospective RUS borrowers have communicated their hesitation to increase their outstanding debt and move forward with planned construction due to the recently implemented reductions in USF support and Inter-Carrier Compensation (ICC) payments."[26]

---

[23] Jessica Zufolo, Deputy Administrator, RUS, *Overview of the RUS Telecommunications Loan and Grant Programs*, July 2011, Slide 7, http://www.narucmeetings.org/Presentations/Zufolo_7-2011.pdf.

[24] For more information, see CRS Report R42524, *Rural Broadband: The Roles of the Rural Utilities Service and the Universal Service Fund*, by Angele A. Gilroy and Lennard G. Kruger.

[25] According to a January 2013 survey conducted by NTCA—The Rural Broadband Association, 69% of member companies responding to the survey had either cancelled or postponed $492.7 million in broadband investments due to the uncertainty surrounding the transition to the FCC's Connect America Fund. See NTCA—The Rural Broadband Association, *Survey: FCC USF/ICC Impacts*, January 2013, available at http://www.ntca.org/images/stories/Documents/Advocacy/SurveyReports/FCC_USF_ICC_ImpactSurvey.pdf.

[26] Letter from RUS to the FCC, February 13, 2013, available at https://prodnet.www.neca.org/publicationsdocs/wwpdf/ 21513usda.pdf.

TASK FORCE ON AGRICULTURE AND RURAL PROSPERITY

The Interagency Task Force on Agriculture and Rural Prosperity was created on April 25, 2017 by Executive Order 13790 and was charged with identifying legislative, regulatory, and policy changes to promote agriculture, economic development, job growth, infrastructure improvements, technological innovation, energy security, and quality of life in rural America. The first recommendation of the Task Force's report to the President is to expand e-connectivity in rural and tribal areas.[27]

To help implement this recommendation, the Administration requested $500 million in a discretionary add-on to the FY2018 appropriation which would fund a combination grant/loan program at USDA/RUS to deploy broadband in rural and tribal areas. The Administration also requested $50 million for the National Telecommunications and Information Administration (NTIA) at the Department of Commerce to conduct an assessment, within 12 months, of the current state of broadband access nationwide, including identification of existing infrastructure, gaps, and opportunities for more efficient deployment. This information is intended to help RUS and other federal agencies more effectively target funding to areas where it will have the greatest impact.

The Consolidated Appropriations Act, 2018 (P.L. 115-141) appropriated $600 million to RUS to "conduct a new broadband loan and grant pilot program." The act also appropriated $7.5 million to NTIA to update the national broadband availability map in coordination with the FCC.

---

[27] U.S. Department of Agriculture, Agriculture and Rural Prosperity Task Force, Report to the President of the United States from the Task Force on Agriculture and Rural Prosperity, October 21, 2017, pp. 17-20, available at https://www.usda.gov/sites/default/files/documents/rural-prosperity-report.pdf. The Task Force recommended that the Administration establish executive leadership to expand e-connectivity across rural America, assess the state of rural e-connectivity, reduce regulatory barriers to infrastructure deployment, assess the efficacy of current programs, and incentivize private capital investment.

APPROPRIATIONS

The Rural Broadband Access Loan and Loan Guarantee Program, the Community Connect Grant Program, the Telecommunications Infrastructure Loan and Loan Guarantee program, and the Distance Learning and Telemedicine grant program are funded through the annual Agriculture, Rural Development, Food and Drug Administration, and Related Agencies Appropriations Act. The appropriations provided to the broadband loan programs are loan subsidies which support a significantly higher loan level. Table 3 shows recent and proposed appropriations for the broadband loan program, the Community Connect grant program, the DLT grant program, and Telecommunications Infrastructure loans and loan guarantees.

The Telecommunications Loan program has, for the most part, been self-sustaining and set at an annual loan level of $690 million with typically little or no annual appropriation or budget authority required to subsidize the loans.

FY2017

The Administration's FY2017 budget proposal requested zero funding for the broadband loan program and $39.492 million for the Community Connect broadband grant program. In the FY2017 budget justification, RUS stated that the budget request "shifts resources to the broadband grant program and the Distance Learning and Telemedicine grant program."[28] In 2017, RUS will focus its resources on the Broadband Opportunity Council (BOC) recommendation for a regulation rewrite of the traditional Telecommunications Loan Program to expand eligibility to allow applicants that would have been eligible for the broadband program to be eligible for this program. Currently the Telecommunications Loan program

---

[28] 2017 USDA Budget Explanatory Notes for Committee on Appropriations, p. 31-34, available at http://www.obpa.usda.gov/31rus2017notes.pdf.

(formerly the Telephone Loan program dating back to 1949) maintains an annual loan level of $690 million, and is only available to communities with populations of 5,000 or less.

Table 3. Recent and Proposed Appropriations for RUS Broadband Programs (dollars)

	FY2017 (P.L. 115-31)	FY2018 P.L. 115-141)	FY2019 (Admin. Request)	FY2019 (H.R. 5961)	FY2019 (H.R. 6147 as passed by Senate)
Broadband Loans	4.5 million (27 million loan level)	5.0 million (29.8 million loan level)	4.5 million (23.1 million loan level)	5.8 million (29.8 million loan level)	5.8 million (29.8 million loan level)
Telecom Infrastructure Loans	3 million (690 million loan level)	0.863 million (690 million loan level)	0.863 million (690 million loan level)	1.125 million (690 million loan level)	1.725 million (690 million loan level)
Community Connect Grants	34.5 million	30 million	30 million	30 million	30 million
DLT Grants	26.6 million	49 million[a]	23.6 million	32 million	30 million
Broadband Loan and Grant Pilot Program	—	600 million	—	550 million	425 million

Source: CRS, based on congressional budget documents.

[a] Includes an additional $20 million to help address the opioid epidemic in rural America.

According to RUS, funds for the broadband loan program will continue to provide loans in 2015 and 2016 for the costs of construction, improvement, and acquisition of facilities and equipment to provide broadband service to eligible rural communities. The funding in 2016 will provide for approximately three loans for the deployment of broadband infrastructure. No carryover funds will be available for 2017.

The FY2017 request of $39.492 million for the Community Connect broadband grant program is almost four times the FY2016 level. According to RUS, funding will support approximately 7 broadband grants in 2016 and 19 broadband grants in 2017.

On April 19, 2016, the House Appropriations Committee approved the FY2017 Agriculture Appropriations Act (H.R. 5054; H.Rept. 114-531). The bill provided $4.56 million to subsidize a loan level of $20 million for the broadband loan program, and $33 million for the Community Connect grant program. According to the bill report, priority for the broadband loan program is to promote broadband availability in those areas where there is not otherwise a business case for private investment in a broadband network. RUS is directed to focus on projects that bring broadband service to underserved households and areas. Additionally, the committee noted that tribal communities continue to struggle with gaining access to broadband. USDA is encouraged to provide a report that identifies the specific challenges Indian Tribal Organizations (ITOs) have in gaining access to broadband and to provide a plan for addressing these challenges, including how the Community Connect program can assist ITOs.

On May 19, 2016, the Senate Appropriations Committee approved its version of the FY2017 Agriculture Appropriations Act (S. 2956; S.Rept. 114-259). The bill provided $4.5 million to subsidize a loan level of $27.043 million for the broadband loan program, and $10.372 million for the Community Connect grant program. Regarding the broadband loan program, the committee stated

> Recognizing the positive changes the Agricultural Act of 2014 made to the Rural Broadband Access Loans and Loan Guarantees programs, the Committee continues to encourage the Department to implement a comprehensive rural broadband strategy including investment in advanced networks that will meet the needs of a 21st century economy. However, the Committee is concerned that the Department of Agriculture has not prioritized funding on cost-effectiveness on a per-household basis or on the affordability of the service being provided to consumers as factors in the awards process. The Committee believes that the best way to ensure that funds under this program are spent to promote affordable broadband availability in those unserved and underserved areas, where there is not otherwise a business case for private investment, is to prioritize awards that reach as many unserved and underserved Americans as possible for each dollar spent and to ensure that affordable

service is provided by award recipients. As such, the Committee directs the Department of Agriculture to develop criteria for the consideration of awards under this program that include the cost-effectiveness of award proposals on a per-household basis and the affordability of broadband service to potential subscribers.

Regarding the Community Connect Program's Minimum Broadband Service benchmark, the committee expressed the concern that the program is not in step with current needs and industry standards, and encouraged USDA to increase the program's Minimum Broadband Service definition, which will enable more rural communities to be eligible for Community Connect grants.

The Consolidated Appropriations Act, 2017 (P.L. 115-31) provided $4.5 million to subsidize a broadband loan level of $27.043 million, $34.5 million to Community Connect broadband grants, and $26.6 million for DLT grants. The Explanatory Statement accompanying P.L. 115-31 directed that $1.6 million of the funds for DLT grants be used to provide for upgrades to the equipment and facilities of ambulances (and other emergency transportation vehicles) and to medical facilities, such as hospitals and community health centers.

For the Telecommunications Infrastructure Loan and Loan Guarantee program, the Administration requested a loan level of $345 million in direct Treasury loans and $345 million in FFB loans. The Administration requested an appropriation (budget authority) of $3 million to subsidize the Treasury loan level, and $11 million in budget authority to subsidize modification of existing Treasury loans (thereby offering current borrowers reduced interest rates).

Both the House and Senate Appropriations Committees (H.R. 5054/H.Rept. 114-531; S. 2956/ S.Rept. 114-259) approved the Administration-requested FY2017 loan level ($345 million for Treasury loans and $345 million for FFB loans) and approved the budget authority request of $3 million to subsidize the Treasury loan level. However, neither the House nor Senate Appropriations Committees approved the Administration's request for $11 million to support loan modifications.

The Consolidated Appropriations Act, 2017 (P.L. 115-31) provided an appropriation of $3.071 million for direct treasury loans to support a total loan level of $690 million for the Telecommunications Infrastructure Loan Program.

FY2018

The Administration's FY2018 budget proposal requested the following for RUS broadband programs:

- Rural Broadband Access Loans—$4.5 million in budget authority to subsidize a broadband loan level of $27 million. According to the budget proposal, this funding level will provide for approximately 3 loans in FY2018.[29]
- Telecommunications Infrastructure Loans—$0.863 million in budget authority to subsidize a loan level of $690 million ($345 million for Treasury loans and $345 million for FFB loans). The subsidy is for Treasury loans. According to the budget proposal, this funding level will provide for approximately 40 loans in FY2018.[30]
- Community Connect and DLT grants—for FY2018, the Administration is proposing transferring Community Connect and DLT grants into a new $162 million "Rural Economic Infrastructure Program," which will also include Rural Development Community Facilities grants and Home Repair grants. Up to $80 million will be directed toward the Appalachian region. According to the Administration, the new account "combines the Rural Development grant programs into one account to provide the Administration with the flexibility to

---

[29] 2018 USDA Budget Explanatory Notes for Committee on Appropriations, Rural Utilities Service, p. 31-34, available at https://www.obpa.usda.gov/31rusexnotes2018.pdf.
[30] Ibid., p. 31-34.

place resources where significant impact can be made for economic infrastructure development."[31]

On July 12, 2017, the House Appropriations Committee approved the Agriculture, Rural Development, Food and Drug Administration, and Related Agencies Appropriations Act, 2018 (H.R. 3268; H.Rept. 115-232). The bill provided $4.521 million to subsidize a loan level of $26.991 million for the broadband loan program. Funding provided for the broadband loan program was intended to promote availability in those areas where there is not otherwise a business case for private investment in a broadband network. The committee directed RUS to focus expenditures on projects that bring broadband service to underserved households and areas.

The House bill provided $122.692 million for the new Rural Economic Infrastructure Account (24% below the Administration request), which would include both Community Connect and DLT grants, along with Community Facilities grants and Home Repair grants. The bill included language requiring at least 15% of the account resources ($18.4 million) be allocated to each program area. The committee noted that tribal communities continue to struggle with gaining access to broadband service, and encouraged the Secretary to provide a report that identifies the specific challenges Indian Tribal Organizations (ITOs) have in gaining access to broadband service and provide a plan for addressing these challenges, including how the Community Connect program can assist ITOs.

Regarding telecommunications loans, the House matched the Administration proposal, providing a loan level of $690 million ($345 million in direct Treasury loans and $345 million in FFB loans) with an appropriation of $0.863 million to subsidize direct Treasury loans.

Additionally, the House Appropriations Committee report directed USDA to continue coordinating with the FCC, NTIA, and other related federal agencies to ensure that policies tied to one federal program do not

---

[31] 2018 USDA Budget Explanatory Notes for Committee on Appropriations, Rural Development, p. 28-18, available at https://www.obpa.usda.gov/28rdexnotes2018.pdf.

undermine the objectives and functionality of another. The committee directed the department to prepare a report, in collaboration with the FCC and DOC, detailing areas of responsibility toward addressing rural broadband issues. The report shall include, but not be limited to, how the programs work complimentarily to one another; how they address broadband issues in unserved and underserved areas, including tribal lands; identify barriers to infrastructure investment in rural areas and tribal lands; data speeds which fixed, wireless, and mobile broadband users in rural areas and tribal lands experience; and cost estimates to increase speeds to 25 Mbps in unserved communities and communities currently being served by speeds less than 25 Mbps.

On July 20, 2017, the Senate Appropriations Committee approved its version of the FY2018 agriculture appropriations bill (S. 1603; S.Rept. 115-131). The bill provided $4.53 million to subsidize a loan level of $27.043 million for the broadband loan program, $30 million for the Community Connect grant program, and $26.6 million for DLT grants. Unlike the House and the Administration request, the committee did not include funding for Rural Economic Infrastructure grants. For telecommunications loans, the Senate matched the House bill and the Administration proposal, providing a loan level of $690 million ($345 million in direct Treasury loans and $345 million in FFB loans) with an appropriation of $0.863 million to subsidize direct Treasury loans.

Regarding the broadband loan program, the committee encouraged RUS to focus expenditures on projects that bring broadband service to currently unserved households, and directed RUS to report back to the committee on administrative efforts to eliminate duplicative or overbuilding of broadband technology. The committee also recommended that USDA explore a pilot grant program to demonstrate the use of multistrand fiber-optic cable that exists as part of electrical transmission infrastructure to provide state-of-the-art broadband services to currently underserved rural schools and medical centers within a mile of the existing cable.

The Consolidated Appropriations Act, 2018 (P.L. 115-141) provided $5 million to subsidize a broadband loan level of $29.851 million, $30 million to Community Connect broadband grants, and $49 million for DLT grants, which included an additional $20 million to address the opioid epidemic in rural America. P.L. 115-141 also appropriated $600 million to RUS to "conduct a new broadband loan and grant pilot program."

FY2019

The Administration's FY2019 budget proposal requested the following for RUS broadband programs:

- Rural Broadband Access Loans—$4.5 million in budget authority to subsidize a broadband loan level of $23.149 million. According to the budget proposal, this funding level will provide for approximately three loans in FY2019.[32]
- Telecommunications Infrastructure Loans and Loan Guarantees—$0.863 million in budget authority to subsidize a loan level of $690 million ($172.6 million for Treasury loans and $517.4 million for FFB loans). The subsidy is for Treasury loans. According to the budget proposal, this funding level will provide for approximately 30 loans in FY2019.[33]
- Community Connect Grants—$30 million, which will support approximately 13 broadband grants in FY2019.[34]
- Distance Learning and Telemedicine Grants—$23.6 million, which will support approximately 72 projects in FY2019.[35]

On May 16, 2018, the House Appropriations Committee approved the FY2019 Agriculture Appropriations bill (H.R. 5961; H.Rept. 115-706). The bill would provide the following:

---

[32] 2019 USDA Budget Explanatory Notes for Committee on Appropriations, Rural Utilities Service, p. 31-29, available at https://www.obpa.usda.gov/FY19explan_notes.html.
[33] Ibid., p. 31-21.
[34] Ibid., p. 31-30.
[35] Ibid., p. 31-29.

- Rural Broadband Access Loans—$5.83 million in budget authority to subsidize a broadband loan level of $29.851 million.
- Telecommunications Infrastructure Loans and Loan Guarantees—$1.125 million in budget authority to subsidize direct Treasury loans set at a level of $465 million. Along with a loan level $225 million for FFB guaranteed loans, the total loan level is $690 million.
- Community Connect Grants—$30 million.
- Distance Learning and Telemedicine Grants—$32 million.
- Broadband Loan and Grant Pilot Program—$550 million. This appropriation would continue the pilot program that was funded (at $600 million) in the FY2018 Consolidated Appropriations Act, 2018 (P.L. 115-141).

In the committee report, the committee expressed its view that "it is important for Departments to avoid efforts that could duplicate existing networks built by private investment or those built leveraging and utilizing other federal programs." As such, the committee "directs the Secretary of Agriculture to coordinate with the Federal Communications Commission (FCC) and the National Telecommunications Information Administration (NTIA) to ensure wherever possible that broadband loans and grants issued under the pilot program are being targeted to areas that are currently unserved." The committee directed USDA to use the NTIA's assessment of the current state of broadband access nationwide, and to explore using all broadband technologies, including, but not limited to, fiber, cable modem, fixed wireless, and television white space.

The committee also noted that tribal communities continue to struggle with gaining access to broadband service, and encouraged the Secretary to provide a report that identifies the specific challenges Indian Tribal Organizations (ITOs) have in gaining access to broadband service and provide a plan for addressing these challenges, including how the Community Connect program can assist ITOs.

On May 24, 2018, the Senate Appropriations Committee approved its FY2019 Agriculture Appropriations bill (S. 2976; S.Rept. 115-259). The bill would provide the following:

- Rural Broadband Access Loans—$5.83 million in budget authority to subsidize a broadband loan level of $29.851 million.
- Telecommunications Infrastructure Loans and Loan Guarantees—$1.725 million in budget authority to subsidize direct Treasury loans set at a level of $345 million. Along with a loan level of $345 million for FFB guaranteed loans, the total loan level is $690 million.
- Community Connect Grants—$30 million.
- Distance Learning and Telemedicine Grants—$30 million.
- Broadband Loan and Grant Pilot Program—$425 million.

The committee encouraged RUS to focus expenditures on projects that bring broadband service to currently unserved households, and directed RUS to report back to the committee on administrative efforts to eliminate duplicative or overbuilding of broadband technology. The committee also recommended that USDA explore a pilot grant program to demonstrate the use of multistrand fiber-optic cable that exists as part of electrical transmission infrastructure to provide state-of-the-art broadband services to currently underserved rural schools and medical centers within a mile of the existing cable; encouraged RUS to coordinate with the FCC and other relevant federal entities when making determinations of sufficient broadband access, to ensure the most accurate and up-to-date broadband coverage data are used, while being cognizant of potential problems of overbuilding; encouraged the Secretary to utilize appropriate grant program funds to locate buried, antiquated infrastructure facilities prior to construction of new utilities infrastructure financed by RUS; and urged RUS to ensure the agency's criteria and application processes provide for fair consideration of open access projects by accounting for the unique structures and opportunities such projects present in advancing broadband deployment in unserved and underserved communities.

The Senate agriculture appropriations bill was incorporated into H.R. 6147 (a "minibus" appropriations bill) and passed by the Senate on August 1, 2018.

PAST CRITICISMS OF RUS BROADBAND PROGRAMS

RUS broadband programs have been awarding funds to entities serving rural communities since FY2001. Since their inception, a number of criticisms have emerged.

Loan Approval and Application Process

Perhaps the major criticism of the broadband loan program was that not enough loans are approved, thereby making it difficult for rural communities to take full advantage of the program. As of June 22, 2009, the broadband loan program received 225 applications, requesting a total of $4.7 billion in loans. Of these, 97 applications were approved (totaling $1.8 billion), 120 were returned (totaling $2.7 billion), and 8 are pending (totaling $170 million).[36] According to RUS officials, 28% of available loan money was awarded in 2004, and only 5% of available loan money was awarded in 2005.[37]

The loan application process has been criticized as being overly complex and burdensome, requiring applicants to spend months preparing costly market research and engineering assessments. Many applications are rejected because the applicant's business plan is deemed insufficient to support a commercially viable business. The biggest reason for applications being returned has been insufficient credit support, whereby applicants do not have sufficient cash-onhand (one year's worth is required in most cases). The requirement for cash-on-hand is viewed as particularly

---

[36] Private communication, USDA, June 23, 2009.
[37] GAO, *Broadband Deployment is Extensive throughout the United States, but It Is Difficult to Assess the Extent of Deployment Gaps in Rural Areas*, p. 33.

onerous for small start-up companies, many of whom lack sufficient capital to qualify for the loan. Such companies, critics assert, may be those entities most in need of financial assistance.

In report language to the FY2006 Department of Agriculture Appropriations Act (P.L. 109-97), the Senate Appropriations Committee (S.Rept. 109-92) directed the RUS "to reduce the burdensome application process and make the program requirements more reasonable, particularly in regard to cash-on-hand requirements." The committee also directed USDA to hire more full-time employees to remedy delays in application processing times.

At a May 17, 2006, hearing held by the Senate Committee on Agriculture, Nutrition, and Forestry, the Administrator of the RUS stated that RUS is working to make the program more user friendly, while at the same time protecting taxpayer investment:

> As good stewards of the taxpayers' money, we must make loans that are likely to be repaid. One of the challenges in determining whether a proposed project has a reasonable chance of success is validating the market analysis of the proposed service territory and ensuring that sufficient resources are available to cover operating expenses throughout the construction period until such a time that cash flow from operations become sufficient. The loan application process that we have developed ensures that the applicant addresses these areas and that appropriate resources are available for maintaining a viable operation.[38]

According to RUS, the loan program was initially overwhelmed by applications (particularly during a two-week period in August 2003), and as the program matured, application review times have dropped.[39] On May 11, 2007, RUS released a Proposed Rule which sought to revise regulations for the broadband loan program. In the background material

---

[38] Testimony of Jim Andrew, Administrator, Rural Utilities Service, U.S. Department of Agriculture, "Broadband Program Administered by USDA's Rural Utilities Service," full committee hearing before the Senate Committee on Agriculture, Nutrition, and Forestry, 109th Congress, May 17, 2006.
[39] Rural Utilities Service, private communication, January 18, 2007.

accompanying the Proposed Rule, RUS stated that the average application processing time in 2006 was almost half of what it was in 2003.[40]

Eligibility Criteria

Since the inception of the broadband grant and loan programs, the criteria for applicant eligibility have been criticized both for being too broad and for being too narrow. An audit report released by USDA's Office of Inspector General (IG) found that the "programs' focus has shifted away from those rural communities that would not, without Government assistance, have access to broadband technologies."[41] Specifically the IG report found that the RUS definition of rural area has been "too broad to distinguish usefully between suburban and rural communities,"[42] with the result that, as of March 10, 2005, $103.4 million in loans and grants (nearly 12% of total funding awarded) had been awarded to 64 communities located near large cities. The report cited examples of affluent suburban subdivisions qualifying as rural areas under the program guidelines and receiving broadband loans.[43]

On the other hand, eligibility requirements have also been criticized as too narrow. For example, the limitation of assistance only to communities of 20,000 or less in population excludes small rural towns that may exceed this limit, and also excludes many municipalities seeking to deploy their own networks.[44] Similarly, per capita income requirements can preclude higher income communities with higher costs of living (e.g., rural Alaska),

---

[40] Rural Utilities Service, Department of Agriculture, "Rural Broadband Access Loans and Loan Guarantees," Proposed Rule, *Federal Register*, Vol. 72, No. 91, May 11, 2007, p. 26744.
[41] U.S. Department of Agriculture, Office of Inspector General, Southwest Region, *Audit Report: Rural Utilities Service Broadband Grant and Loan Programs*, Audit Report 09601-4-Te, September 2005, p. I, http://www.usda.gov/ oig/webdocs/09601-04-TE.pdf.
[42] Ibid., p. 6.
[43] Ibid., p. 8.
[44] Martinez, Michael, "Broadband: Loan Fund's Strict Rules Foil Small Municipalities," *National Journal's Technology Daily*, August 23, 2005.

and the limitation of grant programs only to underserved areas excludes rural communities with existing but very limited broadband access.[45]

Loans to Communities with Existing Providers

The IG report found that RUS too often has given loans to communities with existing broadband service. The IG report found that "RUS has not ensured that communities without broadband service receive first priority for loans," and that although RUS has a system in place to prioritize loans to unserved communities, the system "lacks a cutoff date and functions as a rolling selection process—priorities are decided based on the applicants who happen to be in the pool at any given moment."[46] The result is that a significant number of communities with some level of preexisting broadband service have received loans. According to the IG report, of 11 loans awarded in 2004, 66% of the associated communities served by those loans had existing service. According to RUS, 31% of communities served by all loans (during the period 2003 through early 2005) had preexisting competitive service (not including loans used to upgrade or expand existing service).[47] In some cases, according to the IG report, "loans were issued to companies in highly competitive business environments where multiple providers competed for relatively few customers."[48] At the May 1, 2007, hearing before the House Subcommittee on Specialty Crops, Rural Development, and Foreign Agriculture, then-RUS Administrator James Andrews testified that of the 69 broadband loans awarded since the program's inception, 40% of the communities approved for funding were unserved at the time of loan approval, and an additional 15% had only one broadband provider.[49]

---

[45] GAO, *Broadband Deployment is Extensive throughout the United States, but It Is Difficult to Assess the Extent of Deployment Gaps in Rural Areas*, pp. 33-34.
[46] Ibid., p. 13.
[47] Ibid., p. 14.
[48] Ibid., p. 15.
[49] Testimony of James Andrew, Administrator, Rural Utilities Service, U.S. Department of Agriculture, before the Subcommittee on Specialty Crops, Rural Development, and Foreign Agriculture, House Committee on Agriculture, May 1, 2007.

Awarding loans to entities in communities with preexisting competitive service raised criticism from competitors who already offer broadband to those communities. According to the National Cable and Telecommunications Association (NCTA), "RUS loans are being used to unfairly subsidize second and third broadband providers in communities where private risk capital already has been invested to provide broadband service."[50] Critics argued that providing loans in areas with preexisting competitive broadband service creates an uneven playing field and discourages further private investment in rural broadband.[51] In response, RUS stated in the IG report that its policies are in accordance with the statute, and that they address "the need for competition to increase the quality of services and reduce the cost of those services to the consumer."[52] RUS argued that the presence of a competitor does not necessarily mean that an area is adequately served, and additionally, that in order for some borrowers to maintain a viable business in an unserved area, it may be necessary for that company to also be serving more densely populated rural areas where some level of competition already exists.[53]

Follow-Up Audit by USDA Office of Inspector General

In 2008, as directed by the House Appropriations Committee (H.Rept. 110-258, FY2008 Agriculture appropriations bill), the IG reexamined the RUS broadband loan and loan guarantee program to determine whether RUS had taken sufficient corrective actions in response to the issues raised in the 2005 IG report. The IG concluded "the key problems identified in our 2005 report—loans being issued to suburban and exurban communities

---

[50] Letter from Kyle McSlarrow, President and CEO, National Cable & Telecommunications Association to the Honorable Mike Johanns, Secretary of the U.S. Department of Agriculture, May 16, 2006.
[51] Testimony of Tom Simmons, Vice President for Public Policy, Midcontinent Communications, before Senate Committee on Agriculture, Nutrition, and Forestry, May 17, 2006.
[52] *Audit Report: Rural Utilities Service Broadband Grant and Loan Programs*, p. 17.
[53] Rural Utilities Service, private communication, January 18, 2007.

and loans being issued where other providers already provide access—have not been resolved."[54]

Specifically, the follow-up IG report found that between 2005 and 2008, RUS broadband borrowers providing services in 148 communities were within 30 miles of cities with 200,000 inhabitants, including communities near very large urban areas such as Chicago and Las Vegas.

The IG report also found that since 2005 "RUS has continued providing loans to providers in markets where there is already competing service."[55] Of the 37 applications approved since September 2005, 34 loans were granted to applicants in areas where one or more private broadband providers already offered service. These 34 borrowers received $873 million to service 1,448 communities. The IG report found that since 2005, 77% of communities which were expected to receive service from a project financed by an approved RUS broadband loan had at least one existing broadband provider present, 59% had two or more existing providers, and 27% had three or more existing providers.[56]

In an official response to the follow-up IG report, RUS fundamentally disagreed with the IG criticisms, stating that the loans awarded between 2005 and 2008 were provided "in a way entirely consistent with the statutory requirements of the underlying legislation governing administration of the program, the regulations and guidance issued by the Department to implement the statute, and the intent of Congress."[57] Specifically, RUS argued that its May 11, 2007, Proposed Rule, and the subsequent changes to the broadband loan and loan guarantee statute made by the 2008 farm bill, both addressed concerns over loans to nonrural areas and to communities with preexisting broadband providers. However, the Final Rule based on the Proposed Rule and the 2008 farm bill had not yet been released and implemented during the 2005-2008 period examined by the IG, and RUS

---

[54] U.S. Department of Agriculture, Office of Inspector General, Southwest Region, Audit Report Rural Utilities Service Broadband Loan and Loan Guarantee Program, Report No. 09601-8-Te, March 2009, p. 9.
[55] Ibid., p. 5.
[56] Ibid., pp. 5-6.
[57] Ibid., p. 14.

was compelled by law to continue awarding broadband loans under the existing law and rules.

During 2009 and 2010, the Rural Broadband Access Loan and Loan Guarantee program was in hiatus while RUS implemented the Broadband Initiatives Program (Recovery Act grants and loans) and developed new regulations implementing the 2008 farm bill. On March 14, 2011, the new rules were released. According to then-RUS Administrator Jonathan Adelstein, "this regulation and other measures taken by the agency have addressed all the concerns raised by the OIG," and on March 24, 2011, "the OIG notified RUS that it has closed its audits of the RUS broadband loan program."[58]

2014 GAO Report

In May 2014, GAO released its report, *USDA Should Evaluate the Performance of the Rural Broadband Loan Program*.[59] In the report, GAO analyzed rural broadband loans awarded between the years 2003 and 2013. GAO found that of the 100 loans awarded (worth $2 billion), 43% were no longer active due to 25 loans rescinded and 18 defaulted (RUS rejected 149 of the 249 applications received); that RUS loans can help promote limited broadband deployment and economic development, but performance goals do not fully align with the program's purpose; and that FCC reforms of the Universal Service Fund and intercarrier compensation have created temporary uncertainty that may be hindering investment in broadband.

To address its findings, GAO made two recommendations to the Secretary of Agriculture: evaluate loans made by RUS through the broadband loan program to identify characteristics of loans that may be at risk of rescission or default; and align performance goals under the

---

[58] Testimony of Jonathan Adelstein, Administrator of RUS, before the House Subcommittee on Communications and Technology, Committee on Energy and Commerce, April 1, 2011, p. 8, http://republicans.energycommerce.house.gov/ Media/file/Hearings/Telecom/040111/ Adelstein.pdf.

[59] Government Accountability Office, *USDA Should Evaluate the Performance of the Rural Broadband Loan Program*, May 2014, 56 pp., available at http://www.gao.gov/assets/670/663578.pdf.

"enhance rural prosperity" strategic objective in the Annual Performance Report to the broadband loan program's purpose, to the extent feasible.[60]

BROADBAND LOAN REAUTHORIZATION IN THE FARM BILL

The Rural Broadband Access Loan and Loan Guarantee program is authorized by Section 601 of the Rural Electrification Act of 1936. Since the program was established in the 2002 farm bill, it has been subsequently reauthorized and modified by the 2008 and 2014 farm bills. The 2018 farm bill seeks to again reauthorize and modify the program, as well as addressing other RUS broadband programs and issues.

2008 Farm Bill

The 110th Congress considered reauthorization of the Rural Broadband Access Loan and Loan Guarantee program as part of the 2008 farm bill. The following are some key issues which were considered during the debate over reauthorization of the RUS broadband loan and loan guarantee program.

Restricting Applicant Eligibility

The RUS broadband program was criticized for excluding too many applicants due to stringent financial requirements (e.g., the requirement that an applicant have a year's worth of cash-onhand) and an application process—requiring detailed business plans and market surveys—that some viewed as overly expensive and burdensome to complete. During the reauthorization process, Congress considered whether the criteria for loan eligibility should be modified, and whether a more appropriate balance could be found between the need to make the program more accessible to

---

[60] Ibid., pp. 31-32.

unserved and often lower-income rural areas, and the need to protect taxpayers against bad loans.

Definition of "Rural Community"

The definition of which communities qualify as "rural" had been changed twice by statute since the broadband loan program was initiated. Under the pilot program, funds were authorized under the Distance Learning and Telemedicine Program, which defines "exceptionally rural areas" (under 5,000 inhabitants), "rural areas" (between 5,000 and 10,000), and "mid-rural areas" (between 10,000 and 20,000). RUS determined that communities of 20,000 or less would be eligible for broadband loans in cases where broadband services did not already exist.

In 2002, this definition was made narrower by the Farm Security and Rural Investment Act (P.L. 107-171), which designated eligible communities as any incorporated or unincorporated place with fewer than 20,000 inhabitants, and which was outside any standard metropolitan statistical area (MSA). The requirement that communities not be located within MSA's effectively prohibited suburban communities from receiving broadband loans. However, in 2004, the definition was again changed by the FY2004 Consolidated Appropriations Act (P.L. 108-199). The act broadened the definition, keeping the population limit at 20,000, but eliminating the MSA prohibition, thereby permitting rural communities near large cities to receive loans. Thus the current definition used for rural communities is the same as what was used for the broadband pilot program, except that loans can now be issued to communities with preexisting service.

The definition of what constitutes a "rural" community is always a difficult issue for congressional policymakers in determining how to target rural communities for broadband assistance. On the one hand, the narrower the definition the greater the possibility that deserving communities may be excluded. On the other hand, the broader the definition used, the greater the possibility that communities not traditionally considered "rural" or "underserved" may be eligible for financial assistance.

A related issue is the scope of coverage proposed by individual applications. While many of the loan applications propose broadband projects offering service to multiple rural communities, RUS identified a trend toward larger regional and national proposals, covering hundreds or even more than 1,000 communities.[61] The larger the scope of coverage, the greater the complexity of the loan application and the larger the possible benefits and risks to taxpayers.

Preexisting Broadband Service

Loans to areas with competitive preexisting service—that is, areas where existing companies already provide some level of broadband—sparked controversy because loan recipients are likely to compete with other companies already providing broadband service.

During reauthorization, Congress was asked to more sharply define whether and/or how loans should be given to companies serving rural areas with preexisting competitive service.[62] On the one hand, some argued that the federal government should not be subsidizing competitors for broadband service, particularly in sparsely populated rural markets which may be able only to support one provider. Furthermore, keeping communities with preexisting broadband service eligible may divert assistance from unserved areas that are most in need. On the other hand, many suburban and urban areas currently receive the benefits of competition between broadband providers—competition which can potentially drive down prices while improving service and performance. It is therefore appropriate, others argued, that rural areas also receive the benefits of competition, which in some areas may not be possible without federal financial assistance. It was also argued that it may not be economically feasible for borrowers to serve sparsely populated unserved communities unless they are permitted to also serve more lucrative areas which may already have existing providers.

---

[61] Rural Utilities Service, private communication, January 18, 2007.
[62] The statute (7 U.S.C. 950bb) allows States and local governments to be eligible for loans only if "no other eligible entity is already offering, or has committed to offer, broadband services to the eligible rural community."

Technological Neutrality

The 2002 farm bill (P.L. 107-171) directed RUS to use criteria that are "technologically neutral" in determining which projects to approve for loans. In other words, RUS is prohibited from typically valuing one broadband technology over another when assessing loan applications. As of November 10, 2008, 37% of approved and funded projects employed fiber-to-the-home technology, 17% employed DSL, 25% fixed wireless, 19% hybrid fiber-coaxial (cable), and 2% broadband over powerlines (BPL).[63] No funding has been provided for projects utilizing satellite broadband.[64]

While decisions on funded projects were required to be technologically neutral, RUS (through the Secretary of Agriculture) had the latitude to determine minimum required data transmission rates for broadband projects eligible for funding. According to the statute, "the Secretary shall, from time to time as advances in technology warrant, review and recommend modifications of rate-ofdata transmission criteria for purposes of the identification of broadband service technologies."

Some argued that the minimum speed thresholds should be raised to ensure that rural areas receive "next-generation" broadband technologies with faster data rates capable of more varied and sophisticated applications. On the other hand, significantly raising minimum data rates could exclude certain technologies—for example, typical data transmission rates for fiber and some wireless technologies exceed what is offered by "current generation" technologies such as DSL and cable. Proponents of keeping the minimum threshold at a low level argued that underserved

---

[63] USDA, Rural Utilities Service, "FCC/USDA Rural Broadband Educational Workshop," power point presentation, November 20, 2008, http://www.usda.gov/rus/telecom/broadband/workshops/FCC_USDABroadbandWorkshopNov20.pdf.

[64] According to the GAO, satellite companies state that RUS's broadband loan program requirements "are not readily compatible with their business model or technology," and that "because the agency requires collateral for loans, the program is more suited for situations where the providers, rather than individual consumers, own the equipment being purchased through the loan. Yet, when consumers purchase satellite broadband, it is common for them to purchase the equipment needed to receive the satellite signal, such as the reception dish." Satellite companies argue that in some rural areas, satellite broadband might be the most feasible and cost-effective solution. See GAO, Broadband Deployment is Extensive throughout the United States, but It Is Difficult to Assess the Extent of Deployment Gaps in Rural Areas, pp. 34-35.

rural areas are best served by any broadband technology that is economically feasible to deploy, regardless of whether it is "next" or "current" generation.

P.L. 110-246

The Food, Conservation, and Energy Act of 2008 became law on June 18, 2008 (P.L. 110-246). Section 6110, "Access to Broadband Telecommunications Services in Rural Areas," reauthorized the RUS broadband loan and loan guarantee program and addressed many of the criticisms and issues raised during the reauthorization process. The following summarizes broadband-related provisions that changed previous law.

Eligibility and Selection Criteria
- Defines rural area as any area other than (1) a city or town that has a population of greater than 20,000 and (2) an urbanized area contiguous and adjacent to a city or town with a population greater than 50,000. The Secretary may, by regulation only, consider not to be rural an area that consists of any collection of census blocks contiguous to each other with a housing density of more than 200 housing units per square mile and that is contiguous with or adjacent to an existing boundary of a rural area.
- Provides that the highest priority is to be given to applicants that offer to provide broadband service to the greatest proportion of households currently without broadband service. Eligible entities are required to submit a proposal to the Secretary that meets the requirements for a project to offer to provide service to a rural area and agree to complete build out of the broadband service within three years.
- Prohibits any eligible entity that provides telecommunications or broadband service to at least 20% of the households in the United States from receiving an amount of funds under this section for a fiscal year in excess of 15% of the funds authorized and appropriated for the broadband loan program.

- Directs the Secretary of Agriculture "from time to time as advances in technology warrant," to review and recommend modifications in rate-of-data transmission criteria for the purpose of identifying eligible broadband service technologies. At the same time, the Secretary is prohibited from establishing requirements for bandwidth or speed that have the effect of precluding the use of evolving technologies appropriate for use in rural areas.

Loans to Communities with Existing Providers
- Prohibits the Secretary from making a loan in any area where there are three or more incumbent service providers unless the loan meets all of the following requirements: (1) the loan is to an incumbent service provider that is upgrading service in that provider's existing territory; (2) the loan proposes to serve an area where not less than 25% of the households are offered service by not more than 1 provider; and (3) the applicant is not eligible for funding under another provision of the Rural Electrification Act. Incumbent service provider is defined as an entity providing broadband service to not less than 5% of the households in the service territory proposed in the application. Also prohibits the Secretary from making a loan in any area where not less than 25% of the households are offered broadband service by not more than one provider unless a prior loan has been made in the same area.

Financial Requirements
- Directs the Secretary to consider existing recurring revenues at the time of application in determining an adequate level of credit support. Requires the Secretary to ensure that the type, amount, and method of security used to secure a loan or loan guarantee is commensurate to the risk involved with the loan or loan guarantee, particularly when the loan or loan guarantee is issued to a financially healthy, strong, and stable entity. The Secretary is also required, in determining the amount and method of security, to

consider reducing the security in areas that do not have broadband service.
- Allows the Secretary to require an entity to provide a cost-share in an amount not to exceed 10% of the amount of the loan or loan guarantee.
- Retains the current law rate of interest for direct loans—which is the rate equivalent to the cost of borrowing to the Department of the Treasury for obligations of comparable maturity or 4%.
- Directs that loan or loan guarantee may have a term not to exceed 35 years if the Secretary determines that the loan security is sufficient.
- In case of substantially underserved trust areas (for example, Indian lands), where the Secretary determines a high need exists for the benefits of the program, the Secretary has the authority to provide loans with interest rates as low as 2% and may waive nonduplication restrictions, matching fund requirements, credit support requirements, or other regulations.

Loan Application Requirements
- Allows the Secretary to require an entity that proposes to have a subscriber projection of more than 20% of the broadband service market in a rural area to submit a market survey. However, the Secretary is prohibited from requiring a market survey from an entity that projects to have less than 20% of the broadband market.
- Requires public notice of each application submitted, including the identity of the applicant, the proposed area to be served, and the estimated number of households in the application without terrestrial-based broadband. Authorizes the Secretary to take steps to reduce the costs and paperwork associated with applying for a loan or loan guarantee under this section by first-time applicants, particularly those who are smaller and start-up internet providers.
- Allows the Secretary to establish a preapplication process under which a prospective applicant may seek a determination of area

eligibility. Provides that an application, or a petition for reconsideration of a decision on such an application, that was pending on the date 45 days before enactment of this act and that remains pending on the date of enactment of this act is to be considered under eligibility and feasibility criteria in effect on the original date of submission of the application.

Other Provisions
- Authorizes the Rural Broadband Access Loan and Loan Guarantee program at $25 million to be appropriated for each of fiscal years 2008 through 2012.
- Requires that the Secretary annually report to Congress on the rural broadband loan and loan guarantee program. The annual report is to include information pertaining to the loans made, communities served and proposed to be served, speed of broadband service offered, types of services offered by the applicants and recipients, length of time to approve applications submitted, and outreach efforts undertaken by USDA.
- Section 6111 provides for a National Center for Rural Telecommunications Assessment. The center is to assess the effectiveness of broadband loan programs, work with existing rural development centers to identify appropriate policy initiatives, and provide an annual report that describes the activities of the center, the results of research carried out by the center, and any additional information that the Secretary may request. An appropriation of $1 million is authorized for each of the fiscal years 2008 through 2012.
- Section 6112 directs the Chairman of the Federal Communications Commission (FCC), in coordination with the Secretary, to submit to Congress a report describing a comprehensive rural broadband strategy. Requires the report to be updated during the third year after enactment.

Implementation of P.L. 110-246

During 2009 and 2010, the Farm Bill Broadband Loan Program was on hiatus as RUS implemented the Broadband Initiatives Program (BIP) established under the American Recovery and Reinvestment Act of 2009 (P.L. 111-5). At the same time, final regulations implementing the broadband loan program as reauthorized by the 2008 farm bill were on hold and were being refined to reflect, in part, RUS experience in implementing BIP. Subsequently, on March 14, 2011, an Interim Rule and Notice was published in the *Federal Register* setting forth the rules and regulations for the broadband loan program as reauthorized by P.L. 110-246.[65] While the rule was immediately effective, RUS accepted public comment before ultimately releasing a final rule.

Meanwhile, pursuant to Section 6112 of P.L. 110-246, the FCC released on May 22, 2009, its report on rural broadband strategy, entitled *Bringing Broadband to Rural America*.[66] The report made a series of recommendations including improved coordination of rural broadband efforts among federal agencies, states, and communities; better assessment of broadband needs, including technological considerations and broadband mapping and data; and overcoming challenges to rural broadband deployment.

2014 Farm Bill

On January 27, 2014, the conference report for the Agricultural Act of 2014 was filed (H.Rept. 113-333). The conference agreement was approved by the House on January 29, approved by the Senate on February 4, and signed into law (P.L. 113-79) by the President on February 7, 2014.

P.L. 113-79 amended Section 601 of the Rural Electrification Act of 1936 (7 U.S.C. 950bb) to reauthorize the Rural Broadband Access Loan and Loan Guarantee Program through FY2018. P.L. 113-79 also included provisions to redefine project area eligibility with respect to existing

---

[65] U.S. Department of Agriculture, Rural Utilities Service, "7 CFR Part 1738, Rural Broadband Access Loans and Loan Guarantees," 76 Federal Register 13770-13796, March 14, 2011.

[66] Michael J. Copps, *Acting Chairman, Federal Communications Commission, Bringing Broadband to Rural America: Report on a Rural Broadband Strategy*, May 22, 2009, 83 pp.

broadband service, increase the program's transparency and reporting requirements, define a minimum level of broadband service, require a study on the gathering and use of address-level data, and establish a new Rural Gigabit Network Pilot Program. The conference agreement did not include a Senate bill proposal (S. 954) to create a new grant component to the existing broadband loan and loan guarantee program, nor did the conference agreement adopt the Senate bill's broadening of the definition for eligible rural areas.

Specifically, Section 6104 of P.L. 113-79 made the following changes to the Rural Broadband Access Loan and Loan Guarantee program:

- Project area eligibility—provides that an eligible area is one where not less than 15% of the households in the proposed service territory are unserved or have service levels below the minimum acceptable level of broadband service (which is set at 4 Mbps/1 Mbps).
- Priority—directs RUS to give the highest priority to applicants that offer to provide broadband service to the greatest proportion of unserved households or households that do not have residential broadband service that meets the minimum acceptable level of broadband service, as certified by the affected community, city, county, or designee; or demonstrated on the broadband map of the affected state if the map contains address-level data, or the National Broadband Map if address-level data are unavailable. RUS shall provide equal consideration to all qualified applicants, including those that have not previously received grants, loans, or loan guarantees. Also gives priority to applicants that offer to provide broadband service not predominantly for business service, but if at least 25% of customers in the proposed service territory are commercial interests.
- Evaluation period—directs RUS to establish not less than two evaluation periods for each fiscal year to compare loan and loan guarantee applications and to prioritize loans and loan guarantees to all or part of rural communities that do not have residential

broadband service that meets the minimum acceptable level of broadband service.
- Market survey requirement—provides that survey information must be certified by the affected community, city, county, or designee; and demonstrated on the broadband map of the affected state if the map contains address-level data, or the National Broadband Map if address-level data are unavailable.
- Notice requirement—directs RUS to maintain a fully searchable database on the internet that contains a list of each entity that has applied for assistance, the status of each application, and a detailed description of each application. For each entity receiving assistance, the database shall provide the name of the entity, the type of assistance being received, the purpose for which the entity is receiving the assistance, and each semiannual report submitted.
- Reporting—requires semiannual reports from loan recipients for three years after completion of the project describing in detail the use of the assistance, and the progress toward fulfilling project objectives.
- Default and deobligation—directs RUS to establish written procedures for recovering funds from loan defaults, deobligating awards that demonstrate an insufficient level of performance or fraudulent spending, awarding those funds to new or existing applicants, and minimizing overlap among programs.
- Service area assessment—directs RUS to promptly post on its website a list of the census block groups that an applicant proposes to service. RUS will provide not less than 15 days for broadband service providers to voluntarily submit information about the broadband services that the providers offer in the groups or tracts listed so that RUS may assess whether the applications submitted meet the eligibility requirements. If no broadband service provider submits this information, RUS will consider the number of providers in the group or tract to be established by reference to the most current National Broadband Map or any other data RUS may collect or obtain through reasonable efforts.

- Definition of broadband service—establishes "the minimum acceptable level of broadband service" as at least 4 Mbps downstream and 1 Mbps upstream. At least once every two years, the Secretary shall review and may adjust this speed definition and may consider establishing different minimum speeds for fixed and mobile (wireless) broadband.
- Terms and conditions—in determining the terms and conditions of assistance, the Secretary may consider whether the recipient would be serving an area that is unserved (or has service levels below the minimum acceptable level of broadband service), and if so, can establish a limited initial deferral period or comparable terms necessary to achieve the financial feasibility and long-term sustainability of the project.
- Report to Congress—adds requirements to the content of the annual report to Congress, including the number of residences and businesses receiving new broadband services; network improvements, including facility upgrades and equipment purchases; average broadband speeds and prices on a local and statewide basis; any changes in broadband adoption rates; and any specific activities that increase high-speed broadband access for educational institutions, health care providers, and public safety service providers.
- Reauthorization—reauthorizes the broadband loan and loan guarantee program through FY2018 at the current level of $25 million per year.
- Study on providing effective data for the National Broadband Map—directs USDA, in consultation with DOC and the FCC, to conduct a study of the ways data collected by RUS could most effectively be shared with the FCC to support the development and maintenance of the National Broadband Map. The study shall include a consideration of the circumstances under which address-level data could be collected by RUS and appropriately shared with the FCC.

In addition, Section 6105 authorized a new Rural Gigabit Network Pilot Program. Specifically, USDA was authorized to provide grants, loans, or loan guarantees for projects that would extend ultra-high-speed broadband service (defined as 1 gigabit per second downstream capacity) to rural areas where ultra-high-speed service is not provided in any part of the proposed service territory. The pilot program was authorized at $10 million per year for the years FY2014 through FY2018. However, no funding was appropriated for this pilot program over that period, and the Rural Gigabit Network Pilot Program was not implemented.

Implementation of P.L. 113-79

On July 30, 2015, the RUS published in the *Federal Register* the interim rule (7 C.F.R. part 1738) implementing the Rural Broadband Access Loan and Loan Guarantee Program as reauthorized by the February 7, 2014 enactment of the Agricultural Act of 2014 (P.L. 113-79).[67] Publication of the interim rule allowed the program to go forward, initially with two application periods per year. The interim rule was made final on June 9, 2016.

2018 Farm Bill

With the 2014 farm bill expiring on September 30, 2018, the 115th Congress considered reauthorization of the RUS broadband loan and loan guarantee program and other broadband-related provisions in the 2018 farm bill.

House

On April 12, 2018, H.R. 2, the Agriculture and Nutrition Act of 2018, was introduced by Representative Conaway. Subtitle B of Title VI ("Connecting Rural Americans to High Speed Broadband") would reauthorize the Rural Broadband Access Loan and Loan Guarantee Program and make a number of changes to the RUS rural broadband

---

[67] Department of Agriculture, Rural Utilities Service, "Rural Broadband Access Loans and Loan Guarantees," Interim rule, 80 *Federal Register* 45397-45413, July 30, 2015, available at https://www.gpo.gov/fdsys/pkg/FR-2015-07-30/pdf/ 2015-18624.pdf.

programs.[68] On April 18, 2018, the House Agriculture Committee approved H.R. 2 (H.Rept. 115-661) with amendments. On June 21, 2018, the House passed H.R. 2.

Senate

On June 11, 2018, the 2018 Senate farm bill, S. 3042, was introduced by Senator Roberts. The Agriculture Improvement Act of 2018 was approved on June 13, 2018 by the Committee on Agriculture, Nutrition, and Forestry and ordered to be reported with an amendment in the nature of a substitute favorably. On June 28, 2018, the Senate passed its version of H.R. 2.

Key Differences between House and Senate Bills

The following are some key differences between the House and Senate bills with respect to the rural broadband loan and loan guarantee program.

Eligible Projects

Under current law, projects eligible for rural broadband loans and loan guarantees can only (with some exceptions) serve areas in which 15% or more of households are unserved or have service levels below the minimum acceptable level of broadband service. Additionally under current law, an eligible service area can have no more than two incumbent broadband service providers. The House bill does not change the current service area eligibility threshold for rural broadband loans and loan guarantees.

On the other hand, the Senate bill would require that rural broadband loans, loan guarantees, and grants can only serve areas in which 90% or more of households are unserved or have service levels below the minimum acceptable level of broadband service. The Senate bill also provides that an eligible service area can have no more than one incumbent broadband service provider.

---

[68] See House Committee on Agriculture, "Section-by-Section, H.R. 2, the Agriculture and Nutrition Act of 2018," pp. 41-43, available at https://agriculture.house.gov/uploadedfiles/agriculture_and_nutrition_act_of_2018_section_by_section.pdf.

Grant Authority

Both the House and Senate bills add a grant component to the current farm bill broadband loan and loan guarantee program. In the House bill, grants are only available in combination with associated loans under the rural broadband, electric infrastructure, and telecommunications infrastructure loan and loan guarantee programs. Additionally, project areas must serve hard-toreach communities—specifically areas with a density of less than 12 service points per road mile and where no incumbent provider delivers fixed terrestrial broadband service at or above the minimum broadband speed. The maximum federal share of a total project cost varies by the density of the project service area, ranging from a 25% to 75% federal share.

In the Senate bill, grants are subject to the same service area eligibility criteria as broadband loans and loan guarantees (no less than 90% unserved, no more than 1 incumbent). The maximum federal share for a grant is 50%, although USDA can adjust the federal share up to 75% if the Secretary determines that the project would serve particularly remote, unserved, and low-income areas.

Definition of Minimum Broadband Service

Both the House and Senate bills set the minimum broadband service speed at 25 Mbps (download)/3 Mbps (upload), to be reviewed by the Secretary at least once every two years. Additionally, the House bill requires USDA to establish projections of minimum acceptable standards of broadband service for 5, 10, 15, 20, and 30 years into the future. Unless cost prohibitive, projects eligible for a rural broadband loan or loan guarantee must provide broadband service at the minimum level, and must be determined capable of meeting future minimum speed standards over the life of the loan or loan guarantee.

Middle Mile Projects

The House bill authorizes RUS to make rural broadband loans or loan guarantees to middle mile infrastructure projects, which are defined as any broadband infrastructure that does not connect directly to end user locations (including anchor institutions) and may include interoffice transport, backhaul, internet connectivity, data centers, or special access transport to rural areas. The Senate bill does not contain a middle mile infrastructure provision.

Reauthorization Levels

For rural broadband loans and loan guarantees, the House bill sets an authorization level of $150 million for each of fiscal years 2019 through 2023. Additionally, the House bill provides $350 million for each of fiscal years 2019 to 2023 for grants to be available in combination with associated loans and loan guarantees.

The Senate bill sets an authorization level for broadband loans, loan guarantees, and grants of $150 million for each of fiscal years 2019 through 2023.

P.L. 115-334

On December 10, 2018, the Conference Report (H.Rept. 115-1072) accompanying H.R. 2, the Agriculture Improvement Act of 2018, was filed. The Conference Report was agreed to in the House and Senate on December 11 and December 12 respectively. On December 20, 2018, the President signed the bill (P.L. 115-334).

The following summarizes the major provisions relevant to RUS broadband programs.

Section 6201. Rural Broadband Access Grant, Loan, and Loan Guarantee Program

Adds a grant component to the existing program, which is now authorized to provide grants, loans, loan guarantees, and loan/grant combinations.

- Priority—directs the Secretary to give the highest priority to applications proposing to serve rural communities that do not have any residential broadband service of at least 10 Mbps/1 Mbps. Also receiving high priority are projects that provide the maximum level of broadband service to the greatest proportion of rural households in the proposed service area. Additional priority factors include rural communities with a high percentage of low income residents, with populations under 10,000, that are experiencing outmigration, that are isolated from other population centers, or propose to provide broadband for use in various applications of precision agriculture. Projects will also receive priority if they are developed or funded by two or more stakeholders (for example, public-private partnerships).

- Grant Eligibility and Cost-Sharing—projects eligible for grants (including grant/loan combinations) must be carried out in a proposed service territory in which not less than 90% of the households are unserved. Grants shall not exceed 75% of the total project cost to an area with a density fewer than 7 people per square mile, 50% to an area with a density of 7 to 12 people per square mile, and 25% to an area with a density of 12 to 20 people per square mile. However, the Secretary has the authority to adjust the federal share of a grant up to 75% for an area of rural households without any 10 Mbps/1 Mbps broadband service, or rural communities that are under 10,000 in population, with a high percentage of low income residents, experiencing outmigration, that are isolated from other population centers, or that are proposing broadband deployment for precision agriculture applications. Additionally, the Secretary may make modifications of the density thresholds to ensure that funds are best utilized to provide broadband service in communities that are the most rural in character.
- Loan Eligibility—for broadband loans or loan guarantees, eligible proposed service areas must have not less than 50% of households unserved or below the minimum acceptable level (set at 25 Mbps/3 Mbps) of fixed broadband service, whether terrestrial or wireless. P.L. 115-334 raises the previous eligibility threshold from 15% to 50%. Left unchanged is the eligibility requirement that broadband

- Broadband Buildout Requirements—allows five years for applicants to complete the buildout of a project (up from three years). Requires the Secretary to set a current minimum acceptable standard of broadband service of 25 Mbps/3 Mbps, and to establish projections of minimum acceptable standards of broadband service of a project for 5 to 10 years, 11 to 15 years, 16 to 20 years, and more than 20 years into the future. The Secretary shall review and may adjust those minimum levels at least once every two years. Projects eligible for a rural broadband loan or loan guarantee must provide broadband service at the minimum level, and must be determined capable of meeting future minimum speed standards over the life of the loan or loan guarantee. However, if an applicant shows that it would be cost prohibitive to meet the minimum acceptable level of broadband service for the entirety of a proposed service territory due to its unique characteristics, the Secretary and the applicant may agree to utilize substitute standards for any unserved portion of the project.
- Technical Assistance and Training—the Secretary may provide to eligible applicants technical assistance and training to prepare applications, including required reports and surveys, and to improve financial management relating to the proposed project. Only applicants proposing to serve communities without residential broadband service of at least 10 Mbps/1 Mbps are eligible for technical assistance and training. Not less than 3% and not more than 5% of the annual appropriation for the broadband grant, loan, and loan guarantee program shall be used for technical assistance and training.
- Guaranteed Loan Fees—requires the Secretary to charge lenders of guaranteed loans a fee to offset subsidy costs. Fees shall be in such amounts as to bring down the cost of subsidies for guaranteed loans, but that do not act as a bar to participation in the program.

- Payment Assistance for Certain Loan and Grant Recipients—allows the Secretary to award grant funding—subject to agreed project milestones, objectives, and other considerations—that would allow a loan recipient to receive the benefit of a subsidized loan (with reduced interest rates) or a payment assistance loan.
- Authorization—sets an authorization level of $350 million for each of fiscal years 2019 through 2023 (up from $25 million per year), and delays the termination of authority to make loans and loan guarantees until September 30, 2023.

Section 6202. Expansion of Middle Mile Infrastructure into Rural Areas

Authorizes $10 million for each of fiscal years 2018 through 2023 for grants, loans, and loan guarantees towards middle mile infrastructure projects. Middle mile infrastructure connects underserved rural areas to the internet backbone; it does not connect directly to end-user locations. A project is eligible if at least 75% of the interconnection points serve eligible rural areas. A grant cannot exceed 20% of the total project cost.

Section 6203. Modifications to the Rural Gigabit Program

Renames the Rural Gigabit Network Pilot Program (which was authorized in the 2014 farm bill but never funded through appropriations) as the Innovative Broadband Advancement Program, which is authorized to provide a grant, a loan, or both to an eligible entity to demonstrate innovative broadband technologies or methods of broadband deployment that significantly decrease the cost of deployment and provide substantially faster broadband speeds than are available in a rural area. The program is authorized at $10 million for each of fiscal years 2018 through 2023.

Section 6204. Community Connect Grant Program

Codifies the existing Community Connect Grant Program and authorizes the program at $50 million for each of fiscal years 2018 through 2023. Defines an eligible service area as having broadband service capacity less than speeds of 10 Mbps download and 1 Mbps upload.

Section 6205. Outdated Broadband Systems

Requires the Secretary, beginning on October 1, 2020, to consider any portion of a service territory subject to an outstanding grant agreement as unserved for the purposes of broadband loan programs if broadband service is not provided at a minimum of 10 Mbps/1 Mbps, unless the broadband provider has begun or already constructed broadband facilities in that area which would meet the minimum acceptable broadband service standard.

Section 6206. Default and Deobligation; Deferral

Requires the Secretary to establish written procedures for all broadband programs to recover funds from loan and grant defaults, deobligate awards that demonstrate an insufficient level of performance or fraudulent spending, award those funds on a competitive basis to new or existing applicants, and minimize overlap among programs. The Secretary may establish a deferral period of not shorter than the buildout period established for the project in order to support the financial feasibility and long-term sustainability of the project.

Section 6207. Public Notice, Assessments, and Reporting Requirements

- Public Notice—requires the Secretary to make available to the public a fully searchable database on the RUS website that contains information on all broadband projects provided assistance or for which assistance is sought.
- Service Area Assessment—after giving public notice for a particular project seeking assistance, the Secretary shall provide 45 days for providers to voluntarily submit information indicating their presence in a proposed service area. If no existing provider submits such information, the Secretary may collect or obtain through reasonable efforts any other data on existing providers. In the case of applications requesting funding for unserved rural areas, the Secretary shall confirm unserved rural areas by

conferring with the FCC and NTIA, reviewing any other source relevant to service data validation, and performing site-specific testing to verify the unavailability of any retail broadband service.
- Reporting—the Secretary shall require entities receiving assistance to provide an annual report for 3 years after completion of the project that describes the use by the entity of the assistance and the progress towards fulfilling the objectives of the project. Middle mile project recipients are required to submit a semiannual report for 5 years after project completion. The recipient of assistance shall also provide complete, reliable, and precise geolocation information that indicates the location of new broadband service that is being provided. The Secretary is also required to submit an annual report to Congress that describes the extent of participation in the RUS broadband assistance programs for the preceding fiscal year.

Section 6208. Environmental Reviews

The Secretary may obligate, but not disperse, funds before the completion of otherwise required environmental, historical, or other types of reviews if the Secretary determines that a subsequent site-specific review shall be adequate and easily accomplished for the location of towers, poles, or other broadband facilities in the service area of the borrower without compromising the project or the required reviews.

Section 6209. Use of Loan Proceeds to Refinance Loans for Deployment of Broadband Service

The proceeds of any loan or loan guarantee may be used by the recipient for the purpose of refinancing an outstanding obligation on another telecommunications loan.

Section 6210. Smart Utility Authority for Broadband

Allows a recipient of grants, loans, or loan guarantees provided by the Office of Rural Development to use not more than 10% of the amount for rural broadband infrastructure projects, including both retail and nonretail activities, except for a recipient who is seeking to provide retail broadband service in any area where such service is available at the minimum broadband speeds. Additionally allows a recipient of electric grants, loans, or loan guarantees to set aside not more than 10% of the amount for retail broadband service, for use only in an area that is not being provided with the minimum acceptable level of broadband service. The funding cannot result in competitive harm to any existing grant, loan, or loan guarantee under the Rural Electrification Act of 1936.

Section 6211. Refinancing of Telephone Loans

Clarifies that the Secretary, through the RUS telephone loan program, may refinance loans of persons furnishing telephone service in rural areas, including indebtedness of recipients on another telecommunications loan made under the Rural Electrification Act. Also strikes the current law limitation that the refinancing may not constitute more than 40% of the loan.

Section 6212. Federal Broadband Coordination

- Consultation between USDA and NTIA—USDA shall consult with NTIA to assist in the verification of eligibility for USDA broadband programs. To this end, NTIA shall make available its broadband assessment and mapping capabilities.
- Consultation between USDA and FCC—USDA shall consult with the FCC before providing broadband assistance for a project to serve an area with respect to which another entity is receiving Connect America Fund or Mobility Fund support. The FCC shall consult with USDA before offering Connect America Fund or Mobility Fund support to serve an area with respect to which another entity has received RUS broadband assistance.

- Report to Congress—USDA, the FCC, and NTIA shall submit to Congress a report on how best to coordinate federally supported broadband programs and activities in order to achieve various objectives regarding long-term broadband service needs of rural residents.

Section 6213. Transition Rule

Provides that for one year after enactment, the Secretary shall use the previously existing rules and regulations for the broadband loan and Community Connect grant program until a final rule is issued.

Section 6214. Rural Broadband Integration Working Group

Establishes an interagency Rural Broadband Integration Working Group that shall consult with a wide spectrum of stakeholders to identify, assess, and determine possible actions relating to barriers and opportunities for broadband deployment in rural areas. Not later than 60 days after enactment, the Working Group shall publish a comprehensive survey of federal programs that currently support or could reasonably be modified to support broadband deployment and adoption; and all federal agency policies and rules with the direct or indirect effect of facilitating or regulating investment in, or deployment of, wired and wireless broadband networks. The Working Group will submit to the President a list of actions that federal agencies can take to support broadband deployment and adoption, including timelines to complete a list of priority actions and rulemakings.

Other Broadband-Related Provisions

- Section 6101 sets aside 20% of DLT grant funding for applications related to substance use disorder treatment services;
- Section 6102 reauthorizes the DLT program through FY2023 at $82 million per year;

- Section 6418 requires the Secretary to collect fees on loan guarantees in amounts that when combined with any appropriated funds equal the subsidy on such guarantees. The Secretary shall charge and collect from the lender fees in such amounts as to bring down the costs of subsidies for the guaranteed loan, except that the fees shall not act as a bar to participation in the program nor be inconsistent with current practices in the marketplace; and
- Section 12511 establishes the Task Force for Reviewing the Connectivity and Technology Needs of Precision Agriculture in the United States. The Task Force will develop policy recommendations to promote deployment of broadband on unserved agricultural land, with a goal of achieving reliable capabilities on 95% of agricultural land in the U.S. by 2025.

OTHER LEGISLATION IN THE 115TH CONGRESS

Aside from the 2018 farm bills and annual appropriations legislation, the following bills were introduced into the 115th Congress seeking to impact the RUS broadband programs:

- H.R. 800 (Huffman), introduced on February 1, 2017, as the New Deal Rural Broadband Act of 2017, would establish an Office of Rural Broadband within USDA; authorize a "Breaking Ground on Rural Broadband Program" to make grants, loans, or loan guarantees to eligible entities for serving rural and underserved areas ($20 billion to remain available until September 30, 2022); establish a Tribal Broadband Assistance Program ($25 million for each of fiscal years 2017 through 2022); establish a broadband grant program to accompany the Rural Broadband Loan program; modify the Telecommunications Infrastructure Loan program by raising the threshold for an eligible rural area from 5,000 to 20,000 population and by permitting RUS to give preference to loan applications that support regional telecommunications development; and direct USDA to establish and maintain an inventory of any real property that is owned, leased, or otherwise managed by the federal government on which a broadband facility could be constructed, as determined by the Under Secretary for Rural Broadband Initiatives. Referred to the Committee on Agriculture, and in addition to the Committees on Natural Resources and Energy and Commerce.

- H.R. 1084 (Kelly of Illinois), introduced on February 15, 2017, as the Today's American Dream Act, would direct GAO to submit to Congress a report on the efficiency and effectiveness of efforts by federal agencies to expand access to broadband service, including the RUS telecommunications and broadband programs. Referred to the Committee on Ways and Means, and in addition to the Committees on Education and the Workforce, Agriculture, Financial Services, Small Business, Energy and Commerce, the Judiciary, and Oversight and Government Reform.

- H.R. 4232 (Pocan), introduced on November 2, 2017, as the Broadband Connections for Rural Opportunities Program (BCROP) Act, would amend Section 601 of the Rural Electrification Act of 1936 (7 U.S.C. 950bb) to establish a broadband grant program to accompany the Rural Broadband Loan program. Also would raise the broadband loan program authorization from $25 million to $50 million. Referred to the Committees on Energy and Commerce and on Agriculture.

- H.R. 4291 (Stefanik), introduced on November 7, 2017, as the Precision Farming Act, would utilize Rural Utilities Service loans and loan guarantees under the rural broadband access program to provide broadband service for agricultural producers, and would provide universal service support for installation charges for broadband service for agricultural producers in order to improve precision farming and ranching. Referred to the Committees on Energy and Commerce and on Agriculture.

- H.R. 4308 (Lujan Grisham), introduced on November 8, 2017, as the Rural Broadband Expansion Act, would authorize the Rural Utility Service's Community Connect broadband grant program at $100 million for each of fiscal years 2019 through 2023. Referred to the Committees on Agriculture and on Energy and Commerce.
- H.R. 5172 (O'Halleran), introduced on March 6, 2018, would assist Indian tribes in maintaining, expanding, and deploying broadband systems. Referred to the Committee on Agriculture, and in addition to the Committee on Energy and Commerce.
- H.R. 5213 (Hartzler), introduced on March 8, 2018, would prohibit the Rural Utilities Service from providing assistance for the provision of broadband service with a download speed of less than 25 megabits per second or an upload speed of less than 3 megabits per second, and clarify the broadband loan and loan guarantee authority provided in Section 601 of the Rural Electrification Act of 1936. Referred to the Committee on Agriculture, and in addition to the Committee on Energy and Commerce.
- H.R. 6073 (Cramer), introduced on June 12, 2018, as the RURAL Broadband Act of 2018, would prohibit USDA from providing broadband loans or grants for projects that overbuild or otherwise duplicate broadband networks operated by another provider that have received universal service support from the FCC or previous broadband assistance from RUS. Referred to the Committee on Agriculture, and in addition to the Committee on Energy and Commerce.
- S. 1676 (Gillibrand), introduced on July 31, 2017, as the Broadband Connections for Rural Opportunities Program (BCROP) Act, would amend Section 601 of the Rural Electrification Act of 1936 (7 U.S.C. 950bb) to establish a broadband grant program to accompany the Rural Broadband Loan program. Also would raise the broadband loan program authorization from $25 million to $50 million. Referred to the Committee on Agriculture, Nutrition, and Forestry.

- S. 2654 (Smith), introduced on April 12, 2018, as the Community Connect Grant Program Act of 2018, would amend the Rural Electrification Act of 1936 to authorize the Community Connect Grant Program at an annual level of $50 million per year. Defines "eligible broadband service" as operating at or above the applicable minimum download and upload speeds established by the FCC in defining the term "advanced telecommunications capability." Referred to Committee on Agriculture, Nutrition, and Forestry.
- S. 2970 (Daines), introduced on May 24, 2018, as the RURAL Broadband Act of 2018, would prohibit USDA from providing broadband loans or grants for projects that overbuild or otherwise duplicate broadband networks operated by another provider that have received universal service support from the FCC or previous broadband assistance from RUS. Referred to the Committee on Agriculture, Nutrition, and Forestry.
- S. 3080 (Murkowski), introduced on June 18, 2018, as the Food Security, Housing, and Sanitation Improvements in Rural, Remote, and Frontier Areas Act of 2018, would amend the Rural Electrification Act of 1936 to include a satellite project or technology within the definition of broadband service. Referred to the Committee on Agriculture, Nutrition, and Forestry.
- S. 3360 (Wyden), introduced August 21, 2018, as the Broadband Internet for Small Ports Act, would establish priority for small harbors to receive RUS broadband funding. Referred to the Committee on Agriculture, Nutrition, and Forestry.

APPENDIX. RURAL DEVELOPMENT TELECOM AWARDS

Table A-1. Rural Development Telecom Awards, FY2009-FY2016 ($ millions)

	2009-2014 Amount	2009-2014 # Awards	2015 Amount	2015 # Awards	2016 Amount	2016 # Awards	TOTAL Amount	TOTAL # Awards
AL	60.4	19	1.3	3	0.45	2	62.1	24
AK	149.4	40	3.8	7	1.4	4	154.6	51
AZ	46.4	25	0	0	0.21	1	46.6	26
AR	279.8	45	25.7	3	10.3	7	315.8	55
CA	46.2	27	0.46	2	2.1	7	48.7	36
CO	85.8	29	0.26	1	0.18	1	86.2	31
FL	49.4	6	0.35	2	0	0	49.8	8
GA	112.4	20	0.90	2	1.5	6	114.8	28
HI	1.7	5	0	0	0	0	1.7	5
ID	51.3	26	0.48	1	12.7	1	64.5	28
IL	155.8	33	0.15	1	0.62	2	156.6	36
IN	128.2	14	0	0	0.55	2	128.7	16
IA	290.2	53	40.9	6	15.2	2	346.3	61
KS	373.1	47	0.14	1	26.5	3	399.7	51
KY	321.8	42	0.56	3	0.97	3	323.4	48
LA	54.8	16	0	0	1.4	3	56.3	19
ME	23.4	44	2.7	7	1.6	5	27.8	56
MD	74.4	31	0.10	1	0	0	74.5	32
MA	0.50	1	0	0	0.64	2	1.1	3
MI	126.8	24	0.98	3	0.54	2	128.3	29

Table A-1. (Continued)

	2009-2014 Amount	2009-2014 # Awards	2015 Amount	2015 # Awards	2016 Amount	2016 # Awards	TOTAL Amount	TOTAL # Awards
MN	327.4	63	30.9	4	7.8	7	366.1	74
MS	50.3	25	1.7	3	2.0	4	53.9	32
MO	214.8	56	0.67	3	0	0	215.4	59
MT	359.8	25	30.3	3	30.7	5	420.8	33
NE	153.2	34	4.2	2	0.31	2	157.7	38
NV	20.1	10	0.38	1	1.4	3	21.9	14
NH	3.9	8	0.92	2	5.5	1	10.3	11
NJ	0.32	2	0	0	0	0	0.32	2
NM	191.5	34	5.8	2	14.4	3	211.7	39
NY	64.8	42	0.48	2	0.22	1	65.5	45
NC	153.6	30	0	0	1.3	5	154.8	35
ND	376.6	39	60.3	5	55.3	2	492.3	46
OH	46.0	33	0.25	1	0.39	2	46.7	36
OK	308.6	74	22.9	4	4.5	6	336.1	84
OR	75.3	34	0.20	1	0.99	1	75.6	36
PA	4.4	18	0	0	1.0	4	5.4	22
PR	1.7	4	0	0	0	0	1.7	4
SC	205.4	21	14.0	6	1.3	4	220.7	31
SD	133.5	25	1.1	4	17.6	5	152.2	34
TN	235.9	38	0.63	2	3.5	8	240.1	48
TX	326.5	61	13.4	1	14.7	2	354.6	64
UT	22.2	15	0.33	2	0.30	1	22.8	18
VT	124.8	13	0	0	0	0	124.8	13
VA	103.8	28	3.4	2	2.4	3	109.6	33

	2009-2014		2015		2016		TOTAL	
	Amount	# Awards	Amount	# Awards	Amount	# Awards	Amount	# Awards
WA	149.4	32	0.38	1	0.46	1	150.2	34
WV	48.3	19	0	0	1.2	3	49.5	22
WI	336.9	72	9.3	7	1.1	4	347.3	83
WY	54.1	10	0	0	0	0	54.1	10
VI	0.75	1	0	0	0	0	0.75	1
Western Pacific	122.8	7	0.49	1	0	0	123.3	8
TOTAL	6,648.7	1,420	280.9	102	244.2	130	7,174.0	1,652

Source: USDA, Rural Development, *2016 Progress Report*.

Notes: Includes the four RUS loan and grant programs: Rural Broadband Loan and Loan Guarantee Program, Telecommunications Infrastructure Loan and Loan Guarantee Program, Community Connect Grant Program, and Distance Learning and Telemedicine Grant Program. Data for 2009-2014 includes the 2009-2010 Broadband Initiatives Program funds appropriated by the American Recovery and Reinvestment Act (ARRA). According to the *Rural Development 2017 Performance Report*, RUS awarded 107 telecom loans and grants in FY2017, totaling $502 million. The *2017 Performance Report* does not break down awards by state.

In: A Closer Look at Grant Programs
Editor: Tabitha Reyes

ISBN: 978-1-53615-995-0
© 2019 Nova Science Publishers, Inc.

Chapter 2

FEDERAL PELL GRANT PROGRAM OF THE HIGHER EDUCATION ACT: PRIMER*

Cassandria Dortch

The federal Pell Grant program, authorized by Title IV of the Higher Education Act of 1965, as amended (HEA; P.L. 89-329), is the single largest source of federal grant aid supporting postsecondary education students. Pell Grants, and their predecessor, Basic Education Opportunity Grants, have been awarded since 1973. The program provided approximately $29 billion in aid to approximately 7.2 million undergraduate students in FY2017. Pell Grants are need-based aid that is intended to be the foundation for all need-based federal student aid awarded to undergraduates.

To be eligible for a Pell Grant, an undergraduate student must meet several requirements. One key requirement is that the student and his or her family demonstrate financial need. Financial need is determined through the calculation of an expected family contribution (EFC), which is

---

* This is an edited, reformatted and augmented version of Congressional Research Service Publication No. R45418, dated November 28, 2018.

based on applicable family financial information provided on the Free Application for Federal Student Aid (FAFSA). Although there is no absolute income threshold that determines who is eligible or ineligible for Pell Grants, an estimated 95% of Pell Grant recipients had a total family income at or below $60,000 in academic year 2015-2016. Other requirements include, but are not limited to, the student not having earned a bachelor's degree and being enrolled in an eligible program at an HEA Title IV-participating institution of higher education for the purpose of earning a certificate or degree.

The maximum annual award a student may receive during an academic year is calculated in accordance with the Pell Grant award rules. The student's scheduled award is the least of (1) the total maximum Pell Grant minus the student's EFC, or (2) Cost of Attendance (COA) minus EFC. For a student who enrolls on a less-than-full-time basis, the student's maximum annual award is the scheduled award ratably reduced. For FY2019 (academic year 2019-2020), the total maximum Pell Grant is $6,195. The COA is a measure of a student's educational expenses for the academic year. Qualified students who exhaust their scheduled award and remain enrolled beyond the academic year (e.g., enroll in a summer semester) during an award year receive a *year-round* or *summer* Pell Grant. With year-round Pell Grants, qualified students may receive up to 11/2 scheduled grants in each award year. Finally, a student may receive the value of no more than 12 full-time semesters (or the equivalent) of Pell Grant awards over a lifetime.

The program is funded primarily through annual discretionary appropriations, although in recent years mandatory appropriations have played an increasing role in the program. The total maximum Pell Grant is the sum of two components: the discretionary maximum award and the mandatory add-on award. The discretionary maximum award amount is funded by discretionary appropriations enacted in annual appropriations acts, and augmented by permanent and definite mandatory appropriations provided for in the HEA. For FY2019, the discretionary appropriation is $22.475 billion and the augmenting mandatory funds total $1.370 billion. The mandatory add-on award amount is funded entirely by a permanent and indefinite mandatory appropriation of such sums as necessary, as authorized in the HEA. The mandatory add-on is estimated to require $6.077 billion in FY2019. Funding provided for the Pell Grant program is exempt from sequestration.

The Pell Grant program is often referred to as a *quasi-entitlement* because for the most part eligible students receive the Pell Grant award level calculated for them without regard to available appropriations. In a given year, the discretionary appropriation level may be smaller or larger than the actual cost to fund the discretionary maximum award, despite the augmenting mandatory appropriation. When the discretionary appropriation is too small, the program carries a shortfall into the subsequent fiscal year. When the discretionary appropriation is too large, the program carries a surplus into the following fiscal year. Since FY2012, the program has maintained a surplus. The surplus has variably been used to increase Pell Grant awards, expand eligibility, and either fund other programs or reduce the national deficit.

INTRODUCTION

The Federal Pell Grant program, authorized by Title IV-A-1 of the Higher Education Act of 1965, (HEA; P.L. 89-329), as amended, is the single largest source of federal grant aid supporting undergraduate students. The program provided approximately $29 billion in aid to approximately 7.2 million undergraduate students in FY2017.[1] Pell Grants are need-based aid that is intended to be the foundation for all federal need-based student aid awarded to undergraduates. In award year 2015-2016, Pell Grants represented 72% of all federal undergraduate grant aid; 53% of federal, state, and institutional undergraduate need-based grant aid;

---

[1] U.S. Department of Education, *Fiscal Year 2019 Budget*, pp. N-6–N-7.

and 28% of total grant aid for undergraduates coming from federal, state, institutional, and private sources.[2]

The discretionary statutory authority for the Pell Grant program was authorized through FY2017.[3] The discretionary authorization was extended through FY2018 under the General Education Provisions Act (GEPA), although the program has continued to receive appropriations.[4] HEA also provides permanent mandatory program appropriations.

This report provides descriptions of key elements of the Pell Grant program and information on recipient demographics, award levels, award value, program costs, and program funding.[5] The first section of the report addresses how the program works and describes the basic process for awarding Pell Grants including the application process, student eligibility requirements, award rules and calculations, and the role of the institution of higher education (IHE) in the process. This section is followed by sections on recipient characteristics and the role the program plays in relation to other student aid.[6] The report explains the complex Pell Grant funding streams and their implications. Finally, program costs and estimates are presented. In addition, the appendices provide historical Pell Grant award amounts (Appendix A), Pell Grant recipient counts (Appendix B), recent and future program funding (Appendix C), surplus and shortfall levels (Appendix D), and acronyms commonly used in the report (Appendix E).

---

[2] CRS analysis of AY2015-2016 data from the Department of Education, National Postsecondary Student Aid Study (NPSAS). This survey, which is conducted about every four or more years, was most recently conducted for award year 2015-2016.

[3] The statutory authority for the Pell Grant program was most recently reauthorized through FY2017 by the Higher Education Opportunity Act of 2008 (HEOA; P.L. 110-315).

[4] For more information on GEPA's Contingent Extension of Programs, see CRS Report R41119, *General Education Provisions Act (GEPA): Overview and Issues*.

[5] This CRS report supersedes CRS Report 422446, *Federal Pell Grant Program of the Higher Education Act: How the Program Works and Recent Legislative Changes*. The current report contains updated information.

[6] Title IV of HEA authorizes several student aid programs: Pell Grant program, Iraq and Afghanistan service grants, William D. Ford Federal Direct Loan (DL) Program, Federal Supplemental Educational Opportunity Grant (FSEOG) program, and Federal Work-Study (FWS) program. See CRS Report RL31618, *Campus-Based Student Financial Aid Programs Under the Higher Education Act*; and CRS Report R40122, *Federal Student Loans Made Under the Federal Family Education Loan Program and the William D. Ford Federal Direct Loan Program: Terms and Conditions for Borrowers*.

STUDENT ELIGIBILITY AND PROGRAM AWARD RULES

This section of the report provides an overview of the structure of the Pell Grant program and the process through which grants are made to students. It describes student eligibility, underlying concepts and award rules for determining students' grants, and the role played by postsecondary institutions in the program.

Briefly, the Pell Grant program provides grants (i.e., aid that does not have to be repaid) to financially needy undergraduates. To apply for a Pell Grant or any HEA Title IV student aid, students must complete and submit the Free Application for Federal Student Aid (FAFSA), providing requested financial and other information.[7] When the FAFSA is processed, the individual's expected family contribution (EFC) is calculated. The EFC is the amount expected to be contributed by the student and the student's family toward postsecondary education expenses for the upcoming academic year. After processing, each applicant receives a Student Aid Record (SAR). Each institution of higher education (IHE) designated by the applicant on the FAFSA receives an Institutional Student Information Record (ISIR). The SAR and ISIR contain the information submitted on the FAFSA and the individual's EFC.[8]

Institutions that receive valid SARs or valid ISIRs for eligible Pell Grant applicants are required to disburse Pell Grant funds to students who successfully enroll in approved coursework. Pell Grants are *portable aid*, that is, the grant aid follows students to the eligible postsecondary education institutions in which they enroll. In addition, the Pell Grant program is often referred to as a *quasi-entitlement* because for the most part eligible students receive the Pell Grant award level calculated for them without regard to available appropriations (for more on program funding,

---

[7] There are two ways to complete and submit a FAFSA for consideration of federal student aid. For instance, students and families may use *FAFSA on the Web,* which is an interactive online process. Alternatively, they may obtain a paper FAFSA from their financial aid office or other locations and submit it to the address listed on the form, although most applications are submitted electronically.

[8] For more information on the FAFSA processes and calculation of EFC, see CRS Report R44503, *Federal Student Aid: Need Analysis Formulas and Expected Family Contribution*.

see the "Program Funding" section).[9] The size of each student's grant is based, principally, on EFC, the total maximum Pell Grant for the award year,[10] and the student's enrollment rate, but may not exceed the student's cost of attendance.

Student Eligibility

To be eligible for a Pell Grant, a student must meet requirements that apply to HEA Title IV student aid programs in general as well as requirements specific to the Pell Grant program.[11]

Among the requirements generally applicable to the HEA Title IV student aid programs for award year (AY) 2018-2019 are the following:

- Students must be accepted for enrollment or enrolled in an eligible program at an eligible institution for the purpose of earning a certificate or degree.[12]
- Students must not be enrolled in an elementary or secondary school and must have a high school diploma (or equivalent).[13]

---

[9] Student awards have not been reduced nor recipient caps imposed since AY1990-AY1991.

[10] The Pell Grant award year begins the first day of July in a given year and ends the last day of June the following year.

[11] See Higher Education Act, as amended (hereinafter referred to as HEA), Section 484 (34 C.F.R. part 668, subpart C) for general requirements and Section 401 (34 C.F.R. part 690, subpart A) for Pell Grant specific requirements.

[12] An eligible program requires at least 16 semester hours (or the equivalent) offered during a minimum of 15 weeks. Alternatively, an eligible program may be at least 8 semester hours (or the equivalent) offered during a minimum of 10 weeks, if an associate's degree is required for admissions. One semester hour requires one hour of classroom or direct faculty instruction and at least two hours of out-of-class work each week for approximately 15 weeks. For information on HEA Title IV eligible programs and eligible institutions, see CRS Report R43159, *Institutional Eligibility for Participation in Title IV Student Financial Aid Programs*.

[13] The equivalent of a high school diploma may include a general educational development (GED) certificate; the completion of an eligible homeschool program; or the completion of one of the *ability to benefit* alternatives and either being enrolled in an eligible career pathway program or being first enrolled in an eligible postsecondary program prior to July 1, 2012. The *ability to benefit* may be demonstrated by passing an examination approved by ED to be eligible for federal student aid, or by successfully completing six credits or 225 clock hours of college work applicable to a certificate or degree offered by a postsecondary institution. A

Federal Pell Grant Program of the Higher Education Act 77

- Students must meet citizenship requirements.[14]
- Males must have registered with the selective service system when 18-25 years of age.
- Students must maintain satisfactory academic progress while enrolled. Satisfactory academic progress requires a minimum grade point average (or its equivalent) and passing a minimum percentage of attempted credits or hours.
- Students must not be in default on a Title IV student loan, or have failed to repay or make an arrangement to repay an overpayment on a Title IV grant or loan, or be subject to a judgment lien for a debt owed to the United States. Students must have repaid any Title IV funds obtained fraudulently.
- Students may be disqualified for an *unusual enrollment history*—receiving HEA Title IV aid at multiple schools in the same semester, or receiving aid and withdrawing before earning any credit.
- Students may be disqualified for a period of time for a federal or state conviction for possession or sale of drugs while receiving HEA Title IV student aid.[15]

Specific eligibility requirements for the Pell Grant program include the following:

---

career pathway program combines occupational skills training, counseling, workforce preparation, high school completion, and postsecondary credential attainment.

[14] In general, students must be U.S. citizens or permanent U.S. residents. Individuals with several other entrance statuses can qualify for aid. Individuals in the United States on a temporary basis, such as those with a student visa or an exchange visitor visa, are not eligible for federal student aid. Students with Deferred Action for Childhood Arrivals (DACA) status, conferred by the U.S. Citizenship & Immigration Services (USCIS) office in the Department of Homeland Security, are not eligible for HEA Title IV aid.

[15] Periods of ineligibility for federal student aid funds are based on whether the conviction was for the sale or possession of drugs and whether the student had previous offenses. The period of ineligibility does not apply if the conviction was reversed, set aside, removed from the student's record, or received while a juvenile (unless tried as an adult), or once the student completes a qualified drug rehabilitation program. A conviction for the sale of drugs includes convictions for conspiring to sell drugs.

- Students must not have already completed the curriculum requirements of a bachelor's or higher degree.[16]
- Students must be enrolled in non-foreign institutions.
- Students must be financially needy students as determined under the program's award rules (see below).
- Students must not be incarcerated in a federal or state penal institution.
- Students must not be subject to an involuntary civil commitment following incarceration for a sexual offense (as determined under the FBI's Uniform Crime Reporting Program).
- Students with a *significant* intellectual disability must be accepted for enrollment or enrolled in a comprehensive transition and postsecondary program.[17]

---

[16] Students with a bachelor's degree may be enrolled at least half-time in a postbaccalaureate teacher education program. Half-time enrollment is at least 6 credit hours in a standard semester. A postbaccalaureate teacher education program does not lead to a graduate degree; is offered by a school that does not also offer a bachelor's degree in education; and leads to certification or licensure necessary for employment as an elementary or secondary school teacher in the state. To be eligible for a Pell Grant, the student enrolled in the postbaccalaureate teacher education program must be pursuing an initial teacher certification or licensing credential within the state.

[17] A student with a *significant* intellectual disability has a cognitive impairment, characterized by significant limitations in intellectual and cognitive functioning and significant limitations in adaptive behavior as expressed in conceptual, social, and practical adaptive skills; and is or was eligible for a free appropriate public education under the Individuals with Disabilities Education Act. For a description of the Individuals with Disabilities Education Act, see CRS Report R41833, *The Individuals with Disabilities Education Act (IDEA), Part B: Key Statutory and Regulatory Provisions*. Comprehensive transition and postsecondary (CTP) programs are not required to lead to a recognized credential (e.g., bachelor's degree) or adhere to the same durational requirements that regular postsecondary programs must meet (e.g., a certain number of credit-bearing clock hours). Instead, CTP programs require students with intellectual disabilities to receive curriculum advising, participate at least part-time in courses or training with students who do not have intellectual disabilities, and prepare for gainful employment. A student with a *significant* intellectual disability in a CTP program does not require a high school diploma (or equivalent) and does not have to be enrolled for the purpose of obtaining a certificate or degree. A student with a *significant* intellectual disability in a CTP program must maintain satisfactory academic progress as determined by the school for the comprehensive transition and postsecondary program.

Federal Pell Grant Program of the Higher Education Act

Underlying Concepts and Award Rules

The amount of an eligible student's Pell Grant award is determined on the basis of a set of award rules. In general, these award rules are designed to ensure that the neediest students (as determined by their EFC) receive the highest Pell Grant awards in each award year.[18] As need decreases or EFC increases, Pell Grant awards decrease until they phase out completely. Students who demonstrate a level of need that falls between these two extremes are awarded Pell Grant aid on a sliding scale. Additionally, Pell Grant awards are prorated for students who attend on a lessthan-full-time, full-year basis. An important feature of the Pell Grant award rules is that the grant is determined without consideration of any other financial assistance a student may be eligible to receive or may be receiving. This reflects the intention to make the Pell Grant the foundation of federal need-based aid in a financial aid package. The Pell Grant award level is calculated without regard to other aid that may be awarded. Other HEA federal aid is added to the aid package after the Pell Grant is awarded.

Some of the underlying concepts associated with the Pell Grant program, as well as the program's award rules, are discussed below. In general, provisions are discussed as in effect for AY2018- 2019.

Award Year

The HEA Title IV award year begins the first day of July in a given year and ends the last day of June the following year. For example, award year (AY) 2018-2019 begins July 1, 2018, and ends June 30, 2019.

Academic Year

The HEA Title IV academic year is an IHE-determined instructional unit. For credit hour programs, the academic year requires a minimum of 30 weeks of instructional time. For a clock hour program, the academic year requires a minimum of 26 weeks of instructional time. A full-time, full-academic-year student is expected to complete at least 24 semester

---

[18] HEA Section 401.

hours, 36 quarter credit hours, or 900 clock hours. Each IHE establishes an academic year for each educational program. There may be more than one academic year within an award year.

Payment Period

The payment period is an academic period or period of enrollment for which Pell Grant aid is disbursed. Each academic year must have at least two payment periods. For example, an IHE on a standard semester calendar may disburse Pell Grant funds two times, once for each of two semesters: fall and spring.

Discretionary Base Maximum Award

The discretionary base maximum award is the amount specified in annual appropriations laws. For AY2018-2019, the discretionary base maximum award is $5,035. The annual appropriations laws also establish the amount of discretionary funding available to fund the discretionary base maximum award for the program for the corresponding award year. Table 1 presents the discretionary base maximum award for the last five years, and Table A-1 provides a history of discretionary base maximum award amounts since AY1973-1974.

Table 1. Pell Grant Award Amounts, AY2014-2015 through AY2018-2019

Award Year (AY)	Discretionary Base Maximum Award	Mandatory Add-On Award	Total Maximum Award
2014-2015	$4,860	$870	$5,730
2015-2016	4,860	915	5,775
2016-2017	4,860	955	5,815
2017-2018	4,860	1,060	5,920
2018-2019	5,035	1,060	6,095

Sources: U.S. Department of Education, Department of Education Budget Tables, *Congressional Action* tables for FY2015-FY2018, downloaded from https://www2.ed.gov/about/overview/budget/tables.html?src=ct.

Notes: For a history of Pell Grant award amounts since AY1973-1974, see Table A-1.

Mandatory Add-On Award

The mandatory *add-on* award is an amount established by the HEA. For AY2018-2019, the mandatory add-on award is $1,060. The HEA provides permanent and indefinite mandatory appropriations to fund the mandatory add-on award. From AY2013-2014 through AY2017-2018, statutory provisions established a formula to annually modify the mandatory add-on amount to account for inflation. For AY2017-2018 and all subsequent award years, the mandatory add-on amount remains the same in accordance with statutory provisions. Table 1 presents the mandatory add-on award for the most recent five years, and Table A-1 provides a history of mandatory add-on award amounts when provided since AY1973-1974.

Total Maximum Award

The total maximum award amount is the maximum Pell Grant amount that a student may receive in an academic year. The total maximum award is the sum of the discretionary base maximum award and the mandatory add-on award. For AY2018-2019, the total maximum award is $6,095.

Table 1 presents the total maximum award for the last five years, and Table A-1 provides a history of total maximum award amounts since AY1973-1974.

Expected Family Contribution (EFC)

The EFC is a number calculated in accordance with an HEA-defined methodology that is used to establish how much the student's family is expected to contribute to the student's educational costs. The EFC is used in conjunction with COA to determine whether a student is eligible for Title IV need-based aid (aid based on the student's and the student's family's financial need).[19] Generally, a student with an EFC greater than the maximum Pell Grant will not be eligible for a Pell Grant and a student with an EFC higher than their COA will not qualify for any federal need-

---

[19] For more information on the federal needs analysis methodology and calculation of EFC, see CRS Report R44503, *Federal Student Aid: Need Analysis Formulas and Expected Family Contribution*. See also HEA Title IV-F.

based aid. The EFC calculation methodology differs for dependent students, independent students with no dependents other than a spouse, and independent students with one or more dependents other than a spouse. Generally speaking, an independent student is an individual who is 24 years old or meets another criterion specified in the HEA.[20] A student under the age of 24 cannot qualify as independent on the basis of being financially independent of his or her parents or not being claimed on the parents' tax return. The lowest EFC is $0, and there is no maximum EFC. The EFC is determined utilizing family and financial (income and asset) information submitted by the aid applicant on the FAFSA.

Automatic (Auto) Zero EFC

Students who apply for federal student aid and meet certain qualifications automatically receive a zero EFC ($0).[21] The qualifications are based on either the family's reporting income being below a specified threshold or meeting other criteria.

Dependent students and independent students with dependents other than a spouse can qualify for an automatic zero EFC based on an AGI below a specified level and meeting other criteria. To qualify for an auto zero, the parents of the dependent student or the independent student (and spouse, as appropriate) must have an adjusted gross income (AGI) below a specific threshold and meet one of three additional criteria. The AGI threshold is $25,000 for AY2018-2019.[22]

---

[20] For HEA Title IV aid purposes, an independent student is an individual who is at least 24 years of age by December 31 of the award year; is married; is a graduate or professional student; is a veteran of the U.S. Armed Forces or is currently serving on active duty in the military; has dependents other than a spouse; has been in foster care, an orphan, or a ward of the court (anytime since the age of 13); is an emancipated minor or in legal guardianship as determined by a court; is an unaccompanied, homeless youth or self-supporting, at risk of being homeless; or is deemed independent by a financial aid officer for *other unusual circumstances*. See HEA Section 480(d).

[21] One of the benefits of qualifying for an automatic zero EFC is that it may reduce the number of questions the student must answer when completing the FAFSA. HEA Section 479(c).

[22] U.S. Department of Education, *2018-2019 Federal Student Aid Handbook*, p. AVG-40.

The additional criteria are receipt of means-tested benefits from other federal programs, eligibility to file or having filed certain federal income tax returns, and having been a dislocated worker. Independent students without dependents other than a spouse are not eligible for an automatic zero based on their financial situation.

An otherwise Pell Grant-eligible student whose parent or guardian was a member of the U.S. Armed Forces and died as a result of performing military service in Iraq or Afghanistan after September 11, 2001, receives an automatic zero EFC provided the student was under 24 years old or was enrolled at an IHE at the time of the parent or guardian's death.[23]

In cases where a student does not qualify for an automatic zero, the student may still qualify for a *calculated zero* EFC on the basis of the full EFC formula and information provided on the FAFSA.

Cost of Attendance (COA)

For Pell Grant award purposes, the cost of attendance (COA) is an IHE-determined measure of educational expenses for a student enrolled full-time for a full academic year. In general, it is the sum of (1) tuition and fees; (2) an allowance for books, supplies, transportation, and miscellaneous personal expenses; (3) an allowance for room and board; and (4) for a student with dependents, an allowance for costs expected to be incurred for dependent care.[24] Institutions may use average costs for students at their school, rather than calculating actual expenses for each student. Average COA amounts must be based on the same category of students. For example, institutions may establish separate averages by residency: in-state or out-of-state, or housing: on-campus or off-campus.

---

[23] For students who are not eligible for Pell Grants due to their EFC and who had a parent or guardian die as a result of military service in Iraq or Afghanistan after September 11, 2001, non-need-based grants called Iraq and Afghanistan Service Grants (IASG) are available. The amount of the IASG is the same as the Pell Grant the student would be eligible for if he or she had a zero EFC. IASG payments are adjusted like Pell Grants for students who are enrolled less than full time, but unlike Pell Grants, these non-need-based grants do not count as estimated financial assistance.

[24] There are exceptions and allowable additions depending on the program of study, the student's enrollment rate, whether the student has a disability, and the student's living situation. See HEA Section 472.

Scheduled Award Rule

The scheduled award is the maximum Pell Grant aid a full-time, full-academic-year student can receive. In accordance with the HEA, the scheduled award is the *least* of (1) the total maximum Pell Grant minus the student's EFC, or (2) Cost of Attendance (COA) minus EFC.[25] Most students are awarded Pell Grant aid based on the first condition of this rule (i.e., Pell Grant Award = Total Maximum Pell Grant − EFC), since the total maximum Pell Grant award available to a student in an award year is typically less than the student's COA at the attending institution. For example, a student with a zero EFC would be eligible for a scheduled Pell Grant award that is equivalent to the total maximum award, as long as the amount did not exceed the student's COA.

Annual Award Rule

The annual award is the maximum Pell Grant aid a full-academic-year student can receive at the student's enrollment rate.[26] The HEA requires ED to annually publish a schedule of annual award amounts that are proportionally reduced scheduled awards for students who are not enrolled full-time for the full academic year.[27] In practice, ED publishes four disbursement schedules: full-time; less than full-time, but at least 3/4-time; less than 3/4-time, but at least 1/2-time; and less than 1/2-time. Each schedule provides a table of annual award amounts by COA increments and EFC increments. The annual award for a student enrolled at least 1/2-time in a clock-hour or non-term credit-hour program is taken from the full-time disbursement schedule.

---

[25] The HEA prohibits the Pell Grant from exceeding the difference between the COA and the EFC. This precludes the awarding of a Pell Grant in excess of what a student might need to cover the COA after taking the EFC into account.

[26] The annual award for a student in a clock-hour or nonterm credit-hour program is always the scheduled award even if the student is attending less than full time.

[27] In recent years, ED has published the Federal Pell Grant Payment and Disbursement Schedules as a Dear Colleague Letter (DCL). For the 2018-2019 Federal Pell Grant Payment and Disbursement Schedules, see https://ifap.ed.gov/ dpcletters/GEN1804.html.

Minimum Award

The minimum Pell Grant award is the smallest annual award amount for which a student must qualify to receive a Pell Grant award. In other words, a student must qualify for at least this minimum amount to be eligible for the program. The minimum award is 10% of the total maximum award. For AY2018-2019, the minimum Pell Grant award is $610, or 10% of $6,095.[28]

Alternatively, the minimum Pell Grant award may be conceptualized as a maximum EFC. To qualify for a Pell Grant award, a student's EFC must be no more than 90% of the total maximum award. In AY2018-2019, a student with an EFC above $5,486, or 90% of $6,095 rounded to the nearest whole number, would not be eligible for a Pell Grant.

Pell Grant Award Disbursements

Pell Grant aid awards are disbursed in each payment period for which a student is eligible. Pell Grants must be paid out in installments over the academic year. In general, the annual award amount is proportionally divided among each payment period in the academic year.[29] Each academic year must have at least two payment periods. For example at an IHE on a traditional semester calendar in AY2018-2019, a full-time, full-academic-year student with a zero EFC could receive $3,047.50 in the fall semester and $3,047.50 in the spring semester. See Figure 1 for an example of Pell Grant award disbursements.

---

[28] The actual minimum award differs because ED uses midpoints for both the expected family contribution (EFC) and the cost of attendance (COA) in the annual award rule. ED's Federal Pell Grant Payment and Disbursement Schedules group COA and EFC in approximately $100 increments and calculate the award levels for each increment based on the increment midpoints. For example, the full-time, full-academic-year minimum scheduled award is based on an EFC increment of $5,401-$5,486 with a midpoint of $5,443 such that the minimum award is maximum COA − minimum EFC or $652 ($6,095 - $5,443).

[29] The proportional division takes into consideration the number of weeks of each payment period and the number of full-time credit or clock hours in each payment period in comparison to the academic year definition.

> Student A has a zero EFC and has a COA of $16,000. Student A is attending an IHE that is on a trimester calendar with three payment periods. Student A's scheduled award is $6,095 because the scheduled award is the least of
>
> 1) The total maximum Pell Grant minus the student's EFC = $6,095 – 0 = $6,095
>
> or
>
> 2) COA minus EFC = $16,000 – 0 = $16,000.
>
> If Student A plans to enroll ¾-time throughout the academic year, her annual award is $4,571.25, or ¾ × $6,095. The Pell Grant award disbursement for each payment period or trimester (fall, winter, and spring) would be one-third of the annual award or $1,523.75, or $4,571.25 ÷ 3. Student A could receive $1,523.75 in the fall, $1,523.75 in the winter, and $$1,523.5 in the spring. If Student A actually enrolls ¾-time in each quarter, the total Pell Grant award would be $4,571.25, or $1,523.75 + $1,523.75 + $1,523.75.
>
> If Student A actually enrolls ¾-time in the fall and ¾-time in the winter, she could receive $1,523.75 in the fall and $1,523.75 in the winter. Her total Pell Grant award would be $3,047.50, or $1,523.75 + $1,523.75.
>
> If Student A actually enrolls ¾-time in the fall, ½-time in the winter, and ¾-time in the spring, the winter disbursement would be based on a ½-time annual award of $3,047.50, or ½ × $6,095. Therefore, the winter disbursement would be one-third of the ½-time annual award or $1,015.83, or $3,047.50 ÷ 3. Student A could receive $1,523.75 in the fall, $1,015.83 in the winter, and $1,523.75 in the spring. The total Pell Grant award would be $4,063.33, or $1,523.75 + $1,015.83 + $1,523.75.

Source: Example created by CRS based on provisions in the HEA and information in the Department of Education, Federal Student Aid, *Federal Student Aid Handbook 2017-2018* and *2018-2019*.

Notes: Actual award amounts differ because of rounding rules and because ED uses midpoints for both the expected family contribution (EFC) and the cost of attendance (COA) in the annual award rule. The student or IHE may have to return a portion of the actual awards if the student reduces her enrollment rate during a quarter or withdraws before the end of a quarter. Alternatively, the student may receive a larger actual award if the student increases her enrollment rate.

Figure 1. Example of Pell Grant Award Disbursement.

Year-Round (Summer) Pell Grants

Since award year 2017-2018,[30] qualified students may receive up to 1½ scheduled Pell Grants, or up to 150% of the scheduled award, in each award year.[31] To qualify for the additional funds, a Pell Grant-eligible student must be enrolled at least 1/2-time in a payment period after receiving most or all of the student's scheduled award in previous payment periods of the award year. For example at an IHE on a traditional semester calendar in award year 2018-2019, a full-time, full-academic-year student

---

[30] This provision was enacted by the Consolidated Appropriations Act, 2017 (P.L. 115-31).

[31] Eligible students enrolled from July 1, 2009, to June 30, 2011, were eligible to receive so-called *year-round* Pell Grants, or up to two scheduled awards in a single award year.

Federal Pell Grant Program of the Higher Education Act 87

with a zero EFC could receive $3,047.50 in the fall semester, $3,047.50 in the spring semester, and $3,047.50 in the summer semester. Figure 2 provides an additional example.

Student B has an EFC of $500 and has a COA of $16,000. Student B is attending an IHE that is on a semester calendar. Student B's scheduled award is $5,595 because the scheduled award is the least of

1)   The total maximum Pell Grant minus the student's EFC = $6,095 − $500 = $5,595

or

2)   COA minus EFC = $16,000 − $500 = $15,500.

Student B plans to enroll ¾-time in the fall semester and full-time in the spring and the summer semesters. For the fall semester, the student's annual award is reduced in accordance with his enrollment rate to $4,196.25, or ¾ × $5,595. The fall disbursement is half of the annual award or $2,098.13, or ½ × $4,196.25. For the spring semester, the student's annual award is the scheduled award since the student is enrolled full-time. The spring disbursement is half of the annual award or $2,797.50, or ½ × $5,595. Therefore for the academic year (fall and spring), Student B has received $4,895.63, or $2,098.13 + $2,797.50, which is 87.5% of his scheduled award, or $4,895.63 ÷ $5,595.

For the summer semester, Student B's annual award is the scheduled award since the student is enrolled full-time. The summer disbursement is half of the annual award or $2,797.50, or ½ × $5,595. Therefore for the award year (fall, spring, and summer), the student would receive $7,693.13, or $2,098.13 + $2,797.50 + $2,797.50, which is 137.5% of his scheduled award, or $7,693.13 ÷ $5,595.

Source: Example created by CRS based on provisions in the HEA and information in the Department of Education, 2017 FSA Training Conference for Financial Aid Professionals, *Session 19: A Guide to Year-Round Federal Pell Grants*, dated November-December 2017.

Notes: Actual award amounts differ because of rounding rules and because ED uses midpoints for both the expected family contribution (EFC) and the cost of attendance (COA) in the annual award rule. The student or IHE may have to return a portion of the actual awards if the student reduces her enrollment rate during a quarter or withdraws before the end of a quarter. Alternatively, the student may receive a larger actual award if the student increases her enrollment rate.

Figure 2. Example of Pell Grant Award Disbursement with Year-Round (Summer) Pell Grant.

Maximum Pell Grant Lifetime Eligibility

The HEA establishes a maximum cumulative lifetime eligibility cap on Pell Grant aid.[32] Over her lifetime, a student may receive the value of no

---

[32] The HEOA amendments introduced lifetime eligibility limitations for Pell Grants. Effective for students who received their first Pell Grant on or after July 1, 2008, cumulative Pell Grant lifetime eligibility was limited to 18 full-time semesters (or the equivalent). The Consolidated Appropriations Act, 2012 (P.L. 112-74) reduced the cumulative lifetime

more than 12 full-time semesters (or the equivalent) of Pell Grant awards or six scheduled awards.[33] Pell Grant lifetime eligibility used (LEU) at a closed school from which the student did not graduate does not count toward the lifetime cap—the eligibility used is restored.[34]

Institutional Role

To be eligible for the HEA Title IV programs, including the Pell Grant program, an IHE must meet several statutory and regulatory eligibility criteria. The IHE may be a public or private nonprofit IHE, a private for-profit (sometimes referred to as proprietary) postsecondary institution, or a postsecondary vocational institution.

An eligible institution's role in administering the Pell Grant program primarily involves reviewing and verifying information submitted by students on the FAFSA, calculating awards, disbursing awards, adjusting awards to ensure students do not receive more assistance than they are eligible for, record keeping, and reporting to ED.

An eligible institution calculates a student's Pell Grant disbursement using the award rules. Generally, institutions credit a student's account with the Pell Grant disbursement payment to meet unpaid tuition, fees, room, and board; any remaining Pell Grant funds are paid directly to the student to cover other living expenses.

ED makes funds available to schools so that they can disburse Pell Grant awards. In addition, the Pell Grant program pays participating institutions an administrative cost allowance of $5 per enrolled recipient.

---

eligibility for Pell Grant aid from 18 semesters to 12 semesters starting in AY2012-2013. Any Pell Grant aid received prior to AY2012-2013 is included in a student's lifetime limit.

[33] For example, students who consistently enroll part-time in standard terms throughout their progression to a bachelor's degree could receive Pell Grant aid for 24 semesters, or 12 years. Students who consistently enroll full-time in standard terms throughout their degree progression to a bachelor's degree could receive Pell Grant aid for 12 semesters, or six years. This change does not affect the measurement of full-time enrollment for the purposes of federal student aid, which is currently 12 semester hours (or the equivalent for non-standard terms).

[34] HEA Section 437(c)(3).

DESCRIPTION OF PELL GRANT RECIPIENTS AND PARTICIPATION

This section provides descriptive statistics of Pell Grant recipients (numbers and characteristics) and the institutions that they attend. The data may inform discussion regarding the extent to which the program achieves the policy goal of improving access to higher education for financially needy individuals.

Number of Recipients

Table 2. Federal Pell Grant Recipients, AY2011-2012 to AY2015-2016

Award Year	Pell Grant Recipients	Change from Prior Year	% Change
2011-2012	9,444,000	136,000	1.46%
2012-2013	8,959,000	(486,000)	(5.14%)
2013-2014	8,663,000	(296,000)	(3.30%)
2014-2015	8,316,000	(347,000)	(4.0%)
2015-2016	7,660,000	(655,000)	(7.9%)

Source: U.S. Department of Education, AY2015-2016 Pell Grant End-of-Year Report.
Note: Recipient figures rounded to the nearest thousand. Numbers in parentheses are negative numbers. For a history of Pell Grant award amounts since AY1973-1974, see Table B-1.

The Pell Grant program reaches a significant portion of undergraduates each year. In AY2015- 2016, the latest year for which data are available, 39% of all undergraduates were estimated to have received Pell Grants.[35] Table 2 shows the number of Pell Grant recipients over the most recent five years, from AY2011-2012 to AY2015-2016, as well as the annual change and annual percentage change during this time. The number of Pell Grant recipients has declined from almost 9.5 million in AY2011-2012 to over 7.5 million in AY2015-2016. Table B-1 displays Pell Grant recipients

---

[35] CRS analysis of AY2015-2016 data from the National Postsecondary Student Aid Study (NPSAS). A CRS analysis of AY2003-2004, AY2007-2008, and AY2011-2012 NPSAS data shows that the percentage of all undergraduates estimated to have received Pell Grants in each of these academic years was 27%, 28%, and 41%, respectively.

since AY1973-1974. It is important to note that myriad factors,[36] including the labor market, can affect the number of Pell Grant recipients in any given award year.

Income of Recipients

Since Pell Grant awards are heavily dependent on EFC levels and the complex EFC formula can yield different EFCs for students with similar incomes, there is no absolute income threshold that determines who is eligible or ineligible for a Pell Grant award. Nevertheless, Pell Grant recipients are primarily low-income. In AY2016-2017, an estimated 95% of Pell Grant recipients had a total family income[37] at or below $60,000.[38] Independent Pell Grant recipients' income is generally lower than their dependent counterparts. As a point of reference, median household income for all U.S. households with or without students was $57,230 in 2015 and $59,039 in 2016.[39]

It is important to note, however, that a small percentage of Pell Grant awards go to mid- and high- income families. For the most part, these awards are smaller than the average Pell Grant award for all students and are typically provided to dependent students from families who have multiple students enrolled in postsecondary education at the same time.[40]

---

[36] Such factors include, but are not limited to, (1) amendments to the HEA that affect the federal need analysis calculation and Pell Grant award rules; (2) changes in the maximum grant level specified in annual appropriations bills; (3) trends in enrollment at postsecondary institutions; (4) demographic factors; and (5) macroeconomic and microeconomic variables.

[37] Total family income is defined here as the adjusted gross income (if a tax filer), any taxable income (if not a tax filer), and any non-taxable income.

[38] Table 70 of the *AY2016-2017 Pell Grant End-of-Year Report*.

[39] Jessica L. Semega, Kayla R. Fontenot, and Melissa A. Kollar, U.S. Census Bureau, Current Population Reports, P60- 259, *Income and Poverty in the United States: 2016*, U.S. Government Publishing Office, Washington, DC, 2017.

[40] According to Table 70 of the *AY2016-2017 Pell Grant End-of-Year Report*, approximately 5,907 Pell Grant recipients, or 0.1% of the total recipient population, had a family income of $100,000 or more. In cases where the family has more than one student enrolled in or accepted to college for the award year, the EFC is reduced to account for the number of students expected to be enrolled in the upcoming year.

Distribution of Pell Grant Recipients and Funds by Institutional Type

Table 3. Estimated Distribution of Pell Grant Recipients and Undergraduates not Receiving Pell Grants by Sector of Enrolling Institution, AY2015-2016

	Dependent Undergraduates		Independent Undergraduates	
Type and Control of Institution	% Pell Grant Recipients	% Not Receiving Pell Grant	% Pell Grant Recipients	% Not Receiving Pell Grant
Public four-year	40.5	40.2	22.0	22.9
Private nonprofit four-year	14.1	17.6	11.8	11.0
Public two-year	27.7	29.0	32.5	49.2
Private for-profit[a]	6.4	2.4	21.6	8.3
Other or more than one institution[b]	11.2	10.9	12.1	8.6
Total	100.0	100.0	100.0	100.0

Source: CRS estimates from 2015-2016 NPSAS.
Notes: Due to rounding, sum of column entries may not equal column totals.
[a] Private for-profit institutions are sometimes referred to as *proprietary* institutions.
[b] The other or more than one institution category is for students who attended an institution that is not a public four-year, private nonprofit four-year, public two-year, or private for-profit institution and for students who attended more than one eligible institution during the year.

The types of institutions in which Pell Grant recipients enroll may not reflect the overall enrollment patterns of undergraduate students who do not receive Pell Grants. For example, a larger proportion of Pell Grant recipients attend private for-profit institutions than do students not receiving Pell Grants. Table 3 shows the AY2015-2016 enrollment distribution by institutional sector of undergraduates who do not receive a Pell Grant and undergraduates who do receive Pell Grants. Each group is disaggregated for dependent and independent students. For both independent and dependent students, the share of Pell Grant recipients attending private-for profit institutions was more than double the share of undergraduate students who do not receive Pell Grants attending such institutions.

One possible explanation for this disparity is that for-profit institutions may target marketing to low-income students.[41] Most undergraduates, whether receiving Pell Grants or not, attend public four-year or public two-year institutions. For example, over half of independent Pell Grant recipients attend either public four-year (22.0%) or public two-year (32.5%) institutions.

ROLE OF THE PELL GRANT

The Pell Grant is intended to function as the foundation of federal need-based aid for financially needy undergraduates. As described earlier, other financial aid received by a student is not taken into account in determining a student's Pell Grant. This section explores the role Pell Grants and other sources of aid play in helping students meet postsecondary costs.

Purchasing Power

The total maximum Pell Grant, available to students with a zero EFC who enroll on a full-time, full-year basis, is often used as a gauge of the Pell Grant program's level of support in each year. Figure 3 compares the total maximum grant to average undergraduate tuition, fees, room, and board charges (base educational costs) at public two-year, public four-year, private two-year, and private four-year institutions between AY1973-1974 and AY2016-2017.

---

[41] "How For-Profit Colleges Sell 'Risky Education' To The Most Vulnerable," NPR, March 27, 2017; Elizabeth A. Harris, "New York City Consumer Agency Investigating Four For-Profit Colleges," *The New York Times*, April 2, 2015; and Caroline Simon, "For-Profit Colleges' Teachable Moment: 'Terrible Outcomes Are Very Profitable'," *Forbes*, March 19, 2018.

Federal Pell Grant Program of the Higher Education Act

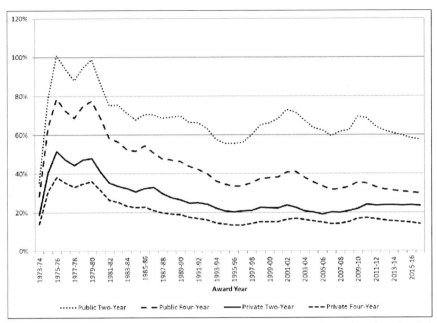

Source: CRS calculations using data from National Center for Education Statistics (NCES), *Digest of Education Statistics, 2017*, Table 330.10.

Notes: The purchasing power of the Pell Grant through AY1992-1993 was constrained by a statutory cap on the percentage of cost of attendance (COA) that a Pell Grant could cover. From AY1973-1974 to AY1984-1985, the cap was 50%; from AY1985-1986 to AY1992-1993, the cap was 60%. After that time there has been no absolute limit on the percentage of COA that can be covered.

Figure 3. Percentage of Tuition, Fees, Room, and Board Covered by the Total Maximum Pell Grant, by Institutional Sector: AY1973-1974 to AY2016-2017.

It is evident that the maximum was at its peak relative to these average charges during the 1970s. Since the 1990s, the extent to which the total maximum Pell Grant covers average base educational costs has been variable; however, despite some increases, the total maximum Pell Grant has lost ground relative to average base educational costs at public four-year institutions. In AY2016-2017, the total maximum grant ($5,815) covered approximately 58% of the average base educational costs at public two-year institutions, 30% at public four-year institutions, 23% at private two-year institutions, and 14% at private four-year institutions.[42]

It is also important to note that in all sectors of higher education, published tuition, fees, and room and board have consistently risen more rapidly than average prices in the economy for a number of years. An analysis of the purchasing power of the Pell Grant maximum award, therefore, could also include an examination of why published prices at institutions of higher education have risen at such a rapid rate and what is the role of federal student aid, including Pell Grants, in contributing to rising published prices.[43]

Receipt of Pell Grants and Other Aid

The Pell Grant is intended to be the foundation of federal need-based student aid from Title IV of the HEA.[44] In AY2015-2016, an estimated 16% of Pell Grant recipients relied on a Pell Grant as their only source of aid from all sources, and 34% of Pell Grant recipients did not receive other HEA Title IV aid funds.[45]

Most Pell Grant recipients (84%) participate in other student aid programs. For those Pell Grant recipients with a zero EFC, Table 4 shows estimates of the average percentage of cost of attendance (COA) covered by their Pell Grant award, their loans from all sources, and their total aid package in AY2015-2016, by total family income.

---

[42] Under Section 472 of the HEA, other allowances for the cost of attendance for the purpose of awarding Pell Grant aid are provided, such as costs associated with transportation and dependent care expenses. These costs are not considered in this section of the report in order to maintain a comparable trend across institutional sectors. If these costs are included, the average amount of coverage by the Pell Grant maximum would be less for all types of institutions.

[43] For more information on college prices and potential explanations for escalating college prices, see CRS Report R43692, *Overview of the Relationship between Federal Student Aid and Increases in College Prices*.

[44] Federal need-based student aid from the HEA is defined here as Pell Grants, Federal Supplemental Educational Opportunity Grants (FSEOG), Federal Work-Study earnings, and Direct Subsidized Loans.

[45] CRS estimates from 2015-2016 NPSAS.

Table 4. Pell Grant Aid, Student Loans, and Total Aid from All Sources as Average Percentages of Cost of Attendance for Undergraduate Students Who Have a Zero EFC and Received a Pell Grant, by Total Family Income (2014) (AY2015-2016)

	Pell Grant Aid as a Percentage of COA	All Loans[a] as a Percentage of COA	Total Aid[b] as a Percentage of COA
All Zero EFC Pell Grant Recipients	27.1%	20.3%	62.9%
Total Family Income (Dependent)[c]			
Less than $20,000	29.7%	15.0%	63.8%
$20,000 to $29,999	29.6%	15.9%	66.6%
$30,000 to $49,999	27.7%	14.7%	67.3%
$50,000 or more	NR	NR	NR
Total Family Income (Independent)[d]			
Less than $20,000	25.6%	23.6%	61.7%
$20,000 to $29,999	25.9%	24.6%	62.2%
$30,000 to $49,999	25.8%	22.1%	61.8%
$50,000 or more	25.5%	24.8%	62.2%

Source: CRS estimates from 2015-2016 NPSAS.

Notes: NR means reporting standards were not met. COA means cost of attendance.

[a] All loans column includes federal loans to students, state loans, institutional loans, Direct PLUS loans to parents, and other private commercial or alternative loans. Data include loan amounts for Pell Grant recipients who did not borrow as well as those who did borrow.

[b] Total aid includes all federal, state, institutional, and private financial aid received by the student in the form of grants, loans, work-study assistance, or other types of aid.

[c] Includes income of dependent student and parents.

[d] Includes income of independent student and spouse when applicable.

This table allows for examination of the extent to which Pell Grants and other aid helped Pell Grant recipients with a zero EFC meet their COA.[46] Table 4 shows, for example, that among all Pell Grant recipients, Pell Grant aid covered, on average, 27.1% of the COA and all loan sources covered, on average, an additional 20.3% of the COA for these recipients. For Pell Grant recipients, total aid from all sources supplies less than two-thirds (62.9%) of the COA, on average.

---

[46] The cost of attendance is the sum of tuition and fees and non-tuition expenses for students who attended only one institution. The cost is adjusted to accommodate private alternative loans that may exceed total aid (federal, state, institutional, and private financial aid received by the student in the form of grants, loans, work-study assistance, or other types of aid).

PROGRAM FUNDING

This section of the report reviews the latest Pell Grant program funding trends and reviews Pell Grant funding sources and procedures. As a *quasi entitlement* that makes grant payments to eligible students who apply for aid and enroll in eligible programs notwithstanding the appropriation level available in any one year, the program may operate with a surplus or shortfall of discretionary funding. Funding provided for the Pell Grant program is exempt from sequestration, pursuant to provisions included in Section 255(h) of the Balanced Budget and Emergency Deficit Control Act of 1985 (BBEDCA, Title II of P.L. 99-177, as amended). Given the somewhat unique funding characteristics of this program, this section of the report explores funding concepts, funding levels, and insight into how shortfalls and surpluses of discretionary funding in the program have been addressed.

The Pell Grant program since approximately FY2008 has been funded through three funding streams. A discretionary appropriation is the primary source of funds for the discretionary award amounts. There are two mandatory funding streams. The smaller mandatory funding stream augments the discretionary appropriations to fund the discretionary award level. Therefore, a portion of the discretionary award level is funded through mandatory appropriations. A larger mandatory appropriation funds the mandatory add-on award amounts. Recent and historical discretionary maximum award levels and mandatory add-on award levels are shown in Table 1 and Appendix A, respectively. Appendix C presents the three distinct funding streams and enacting legislation since FY2008.

Role of Discretionary Funding

Annual discretionary appropriation bills provide the largest portion of funding for the Pell Grant program, and this funding typically remains available for use for two fiscal years. An annual appropriation is usually available for obligation on October 1 of the fiscal year for which the appropriation is made and remains available for obligation through September 30 of the following fiscal year.[47] Thus, while FY2018 funds are provided with the purpose of supporting awards made from July 1, 2018, to June 30, 2019, these funds are available for obligation from October 1, 2017, to September 30, 2019, and may support multiple award years. This multiyear availability allows the discretionary appropriation to operate at a surplus or shortfall in any given year. As mentioned earlier, annual discretionary appropriation bills also establish the base discretionary maximum grant for each applicable award year.

Role of Mandatory Funding

Specified Mandatory Appropriations to Augment Discretionary Funding

The SAFRA Act (enacted as part of the Health Care and Education Reconciliation Act of 2010; P.L. 111-152), the FY2011 Continuing Appropriations Act (P.L. 112-10), the Budget Control Act of FY2011 (P.L. 112-25), and most recently the FY2012 Consolidated Appropriations Act (P.L. 112-74) amended the HEA to provide specified mandatory appropriations for the Pell Grant program to augment current and future discretionary appropriations. That is, these funds, while mandatory from a budgetary perspective, can be used to pay for costs in the program for which annual discretionary appropriations are typically provided. The concept of providing advance mandatory funding to augment or supplant discretionary funding in the program is relatively new. Prior to FY2007, mandatory funding had been infrequently provided for the Pell Grant program, but usually to supplement discretionary funding to pay for accumulated funding shortfalls.[48]

---

[47] The annual appropriation for the Pell Grant program is available immediately upon enactment at any point on or after October 1. In the event the annual appropriation is not enacted at the beginning of the fiscal year, a continuing resolution typically provides prorated funding for the program until an appropriation measure is enacted.

[48] For example, mandatory funding in the amount of $4.3 billion was provided in P.L. 109-149 to pay exclusively for the accumulated funding shortfall through AY2005-2006.

Permanent, Indefinite Mandatory Appropriations for the Add-On Award

The SAFRA Act also established permanent, indefinite mandatory appropriations for the program to provide for the mandatory add-on award amount in FY2010 and beyond.[49] Although the mandatory appropriations that fund add-on award amounts are available permanently for *such sums as necessary*, the amount provided for each year will be determined based on actual costs associated with the applicable add-on amount.

Summary of Recent and Projected Funding

Table 5 provides a summary of recent and projected Pell Grant program funding from FY2012 through FY2021.[50] A distinction is made between discretionary appropriations, mandatory appropriations provided to augment discretionary appropriations, and mandatory appropriations provided to fund add-on award amounts. Table 5 also displays the mandatory appropriations that have been provided through FY2021.

From a budgetary perspective, these recent mandatory appropriations have been offset largely by enacted provisions that were estimated to have resulted in savings from the federal student loan programs, which are classified as mandatory programs. Additionally, some of the mandatory appropriations provided for the program in the FY2011 Continuing Appropriations Act and FY2012 Consolidated Appropriations Act were offset by enacted provisions that resulted in mandatory savings in other aspects of the Pell Grant program.[51]

---

[49] Prior to the SAFRA Act, the College Cost Reduction and Access Act of 2007 (CCRAA) provided annual specified mandatory appropriation levels from FY2008 to FY2017 to fund annual add-on award amounts. The SAFRA Act eliminated the specified mandatory appropriation levels for FY2010 and all subsequent years and replaced these levels with indefinite mandatory appropriations, while revising the add-on award amounts.

[50] Table D-1 in this report provides a more comprehensive history of the discretionary funding levels in the program since FY1973.

[51] Since the enactment of the SAFRA Act, legislative changes that affect the eligibility and award rules of the Pell Grant program are measured separately on the budget ledger between discretionary and mandatory funding. That is, a distinction is made between savings or additional costs associated with funding the discretionary base maximum

Federal Pell Grant Program of the Higher Education Act 99

Table 5. Pell Grant Funding (FY2012 to FY2021) (dollars in millions)

Fiscal Year[a]	Funds Supporting Discretionary Award Amounts		Funds Supporting Mandatory Add-On Award Amounts		Total Funding
	Discretionary Appropriation	Mandatory Appropriation	Subtotal	Mandatory Appropriation	
2012	22,824	13,795	36,619	4,950[b]	41,569
2013	22,778	7,587	30,365	4,854[c]	35,219
2014	22,778	588	23,366	4,835[d]	28,201
2015	22,475	0	22,475	5,153e	27,628
2016	22,475	0	22,475	4,840[f]	27,316
2017	22,475g	1,320h	23,796	5,680i	29,476
2018	22,475	1,334j	23,809	5,977k	29,682
2019	22,475[g]	1,370[l]	23,845	SSAN	TBD
2020	TBD	1,430	TBD	SSAN	TBD
2021	TBD	1,145[m]	TBD	SSAN	TBD

Source: CRS analysis of the HEA, as amended, President's budget FY2016-FY2019, and respective appropriations measures.

Notes: Totals may not add due to rounding;

TBD = to be determined;

SSAN = Such sums as necessary. In effect, this means the amount of mandatory appropriations that will be necessary to fully fund the add-on award amount specified in the HEA for a given year. In other words, mandatory funding has been available to support the add-on amount beginning in FY2010 onward permanently, but the amount required in each year is indefinite and cannot be reported until the add-on amount is determined and all funds are disbursed to eligible students.

For the specific amounts provided by enacting legislation since FY2008, see Table C-1.

[a] The fiscal year in this table represents the first year the funds appropriated in each column are available for use. Most funds are available for two fiscal years.

[b] This is the amount of mandatory appropriations required to increase the discretionary base maximum grant by $690 in AY2012-2013, as estimated in the President's FY2016 budget.

[c] This is the amount of mandatory appropriations required to increase the discretionary base maximum grant by $785 in AY2013-2014, as estimated in the President's FY2016 budget.

[d] This is the amount of mandatory appropriations required to increase the discretionary base maximum grant by $870 in AY2014-2015, as estimated in the President's FY2019 budget.

[e] This is the amount of mandatory appropriations required to increase the discretionary base maximum grant by $915 in AY2015-2016, as estimated in the President's FY2019 budget.

[f] This is the amount of mandatory appropriations required to increase the discretionary base maximum grant by $965 in AY2016-2017, as estimated in the President's FY2019 budget.

[g] This amount reflects the annual discretionary appropriation level and excludes any rescission of the Pell Grant program cumulative surplus.

---

award and the mandatory add-on award when changes to the program are enacted. For example, eliminating eligibility for a student to receive two scheduled Pell Grant awards in one award year resulted in savings associated with both the discretionary base maximum award and the mandatory add-on award. In general, savings associated with the mandatory award was redirected back to the program as specified mandatory appropriations for future use in specified years.

h. This amount reflects a $254 million rescission enacted by the Consolidated Appropriations Act, 2017 (P.L. 115-31).
i. This is the amount of mandatory appropriations required to increase the discretionary base maximum grant by $1,060 in AY2017-2018, as estimated in the President's FY2019 budget.
j. This amount reflects a $48 million rescission enacted by the Consolidated Appropriations Act, 2018 (P.L. 115-141).
k. This is the amount of mandatory appropriations required to increase the discretionary base maximum grant by $1,060 in AY2018-2019, as estimated in the President's FY2019 budget.
l. This amount reflects a $39 million rescission enacted by the Department of Defense and Labor, Health and Human Services, and Education Appropriations Act, 2019 and Continuing Appropriations Act, 2019 (P.L. 115-245).
m. Additional annual mandatory appropriations in the amount of $1,145,000,000 are also provided for each succeeding year beyond FY2021.

Mandatory appropriations that will be necessary to fully fund the add-on award amount are available permanently, but the specific amount required in each year cannot be reported until the add-on amount is determined and all funds are disbursed to eligible students.

ED does, however, estimate the amount of mandatory appropriations provided required to fund add-on award amounts for the current and subsequent fiscal years.

Discretionary Funding Shortfalls and Surpluses

The Pell Grant program is often referred to as a *quasi-entitlement* and has for the most part been operated as an appropriated entitlement. An *appropriated entitlement* is a program that receives mandatory funding in the annual appropriations acts, but the level of spending is not controlled through the annual appropriations process.[52] Instead, the level of mandatory spending for appropriated entitlements, like other entitlements, is based on the benefit and eligibility criteria established in law, and the amount provided in appropriations acts is based on meeting this projected level. The Pell Grant program is not an entitlement because the program is primarily funded through discretionary appropriations.

---

[52] For more information about appropriated entitlements, see CRS Report RS20129, *Entitlements and Appropriated Entitlements in the Federal Budget Process*.

In addition in the past, statutory benefit and eligibility criteria were adjusted so that spending would not exceed appropriations. Finally, annual Pell Grant discretionary appropriations are determined on the basis of estimates of program costs and other policy considerations.

To the extent that the annual appropriation may be higher or lower than actual program costs, the program may operate at a surplus or shortfall. The surplus or shortfall may accumulate over more than one year. The HEA requires that the Secretary of Education, when she has determined that the appropriated funds are insufficient to satisfy all Pell Grant entitlements,[53] notify each chamber of Congress of the funding shortfall, identifying how much more funding is needed to meet those entitlements. The Secretary can respond to a shortfall in Pell Grant funding by allocating funds from the most recently enacted appropriation to pay for obligations incurred in previous award years.[54] For example, although the FY2019 appropriation is expected to fund award year 2019- 2020 program costs, the appropriation may fund award year 2018-2019 costs since obligations for these costs occur in FY2019. This permits ED to use funds from multiple fiscal years' appropriations to meet one award year's cost.

The misalignment between estimated program costs (appropriations) and actual expenditures is often related to economic and statutory changes. When the general economy weakens, postsecondary enrollment often increases and thus Pell Grant participation and cost increases.

Table 6 provides a 10-year history of funding of estimated shortfall or surplus levels, funding for the discretionary award amounts, and estimated expenditures (Appendix D provides data from FY1973 to FY2018).

---

[53] The authorizing statue speaks of *entitlements* when it describes the award determined for a student based on the published award schedule.

[54] This response to the shortfall is only feasible if ED determines enough funds are available from the most recently enacted appropriation to meet obligations from multiple award years. A series of legal opinions at ED and other agencies in the 1990s provides the basis for the authority to use funds in an annual appropriation for multiple award years. In general, absent specific language in an annual appropriations measure limiting funds to a specific award year or purpose, the Secretary may use such funds for any award year during the period of availability specified in an appropriations measure.

Table 6. Annual and Cumulative Discretionary Funding Shortfalls in the Pell Grant Program, FY2009-FY2018 (dollars in millions)

Fiscal Year	Award Year	Annual Funding for Discretionary Award Amounts[a]	Estimated Total Expenditures[b]	Annual Surplus or (Shortfall)	Cumulative Surplus or (Shortfall)
2009	2009-2010	32,928c	26,844	6,084	3,427
2010	2010-2011	17,495	30,491	(12,996)	(9,569)
2011	2011-2012	36,456d	28,796	7,660	(1,909)
2012	2012-2013	36,619e	27,512	9,107	7,198
2013	2013-2014	30,365f	26,481	3,884	11,082
2014	2014-2015	23,366g	25,320	(1,954)	9,128
2015	2015-2016	22,475	23,361	(886)	8,242
2016	2016-2017	22,475	21,788	687	8,929
2017	2017-2018	22,485h	23,377	(892)	8,037
2018	2018-2019	23,809i	24,436	(627)	7,410

Sources: Congressional Budget Office, Pell Grant Program—CBO'S April 2018 Baseline.

Notes: Numbers in parentheses are negative numbers. For a history of surpluses and shortfalls in the Pell Grant program since AY1973-1974, see Table D-1.

a. This number includes annual discretionary appropriations and may include additional mandatory and discretionary funding.
b. All estimates of expenditures are subject to change.
c. Includes approximately $15.6 billion in supplemental discretionary appropriations provided in the American Recovery and Reinvestment Act (ARRA; P.L. 111-5).
d. Includes $13.5 billion in mandatory appropriations that were provided in the SAFRA Act for general use in the program through FY2012 and $22,956 million in discretionary appropriations provided in the FY2011 Continuing Appropriations Act.
e. The funding sources are the FY2011 Continuing Appropriations Act that provided $3,183 million in mandatory appropriations for general use in the program for FY2012; the Budget Control Act of 2011 (P.L. 112-25) that provided $10 billion in mandatory appropriations for general use in the program for FY2012; and the FY2012 Consolidated Appropriations Act (P.L. 112-74) that provided $22,824 million in discretionary appropriations for FY2012 and $612 million in mandatory appropriations for general use in the program for FY2012.
f. The funding sources are the Budget Control Act of 2011 (P.L. 112-25) that provided $7 billion in mandatory appropriations for general use in the program for FY2013; and the FY2012 Consolidated Appropriations Act (P.L. 112-74) that provided $587 million in mandatory appropriations for general use in the program for FY2013.
g. The funding sources are the FY2012 Consolidated Appropriations Act (P.L. 112-74) that provided $588 million in mandatory appropriations for general use in the program for FY2014; and the Consolidated Appropriations Act, 2014 (P.L. 113-76) that provided $22,778 million in discretionary appropriations for FY2014.
h. The funding sources are the FY2011 Continuing Appropriations Act that provided $1.060 million in mandatory appropriations; the FY2012 Consolidated Appropriations Act (P.L. 112-74) that provided $514 million in mandatory appropriations; and the Consolidated

Federal Pell Grant Program of the Higher Education Act 103

Appropriations Act, 2017 (P.L. 115-31) that provided $22.475 million in discretionary appropriations, rescinded $1.310 million of the surplus, and reduced the cumulative mandatory appropriation of $1.574 million from the FY2011 Continuing Appropriations Act and the FY2012 Consolidated Appropriations Act to $1.320 million.

i. The funding sources are the FY2011 Continuing Appropriations Act that provided $1.125 million in mandatory appropriations; the FY2012 Consolidated Appropriations Act (P.L. 112-74) that provided $257 million in mandatory appropriations; and the Consolidated Appropriations Act, 2018 (P.L. 115-141) that provided $22.475 million in discretionary appropriations and reduced the cumulative mandatory appropriation of $1.382 million from the FY2011 Continuing Appropriations Act and the FY2012 Consolidated Appropriations Act to $1.334 million.

Although discretionary award amounts are funded by discretionary and mandatory appropriations, the surplus or shortfall is accounted for using only discretionary funding. The annual funding shortfall or surplus differs from the cumulative shortfall or surplus, which may accumulate over multiple award years.[55] It is also important to note that Congress may have provided a reduced appropriation level in a given year when a funding surplus was available for use from the previous year. Conversely, Congress may have provided additional appropriations in a given year to pay for an estimated funding shortfall from the previous year.

Policy Implications and Measures to Address Funding Shortfalls

For the most part, funding shortfalls in the Pell Grant program have been recognized as common occurrences. Persistent or high funding shortfalls, as in FY2010, may be viewed as fiscally irresponsible. In essence when there is a shortfall, the program is in debt, and eventually the debt must be paid. The higher the debt level, the more difficult it is to resolve.

Generally speaking, with input from the Administration and other stakeholders, Congress adopts legislation that controls spending across the

---

[55] In general, the annual surplus or shortfall is a measure of the difference between one year's appropriation, which is typically provided for a particular award year, and the estimated expenditures for that particular award year. The cumulative surplus is a measure that, in addition to including the annual surplus or shortfall, takes into account the prior year's surplus or shortfall amount.

federal government and for specific programs.[56] Through the budget resolution process, a 302(b) allocation is established for each of the 12 appropriations bills. These allocations, referred to as 302(b) subdivisions, establish the maximum discretionary amount that can be spent through each bill. Therefore generally but with exceptions, individual program-level discretionary appropriations within the annual Departments of Labor, Health and Human Services, and Education, and Related Agencies appropriations bill must be balanced within its established 302(b) allocation. In other words, increased discretionary appropriations for one program may coincide with decreased discretionary appropriations for one or more other programs. Resolving a Pell Grant program shortfall may lead to a difficult decision about which program(s) to reduce discretionary funding.

Over the years, federal policymakers and Congress have taken a variety of measures to address the vexing issues associated with funding shortfalls in the Pell Grant program. The measures have included modified budget scoring, reductions in students' awards, recipient caps, reductions in program costs, and supplemental appropriations.

Reductions in Students' Awards and Recipient Caps Before 1992

From the inception of the program in 1972 until the enactment of the Higher Education Amendments of 1992 (P.L. 102-325), the Secretary of Education had statutory authority under the HEA to reduce awards to respond to a shortfall in appropriated funds.[57] Reductions were made in awards in eight years using this authority (the last in AY1990-AY1991).

---

[56] For more information on the budget and appropriations process, see CRS Report R40472, *The Budget Resolution and Spending Legislation*.

[57] Some form of authority to reduce awards was available to the Secretary between the inception of the program in 1972 and the 1992 amendments. Immediately prior to its repeal in 1992, the HEA provision permitted reduction in awards only within certain limits. No award could be reduced for students whose expected family contribution (EFC) was $200 or less (i.e., the awards for the neediest students would be protected). A schedule of reductions for other awards had to use a *single linear reduction formula* that applied uniformly. No award could be made to a student whose initial award was reduced to less than $100 under the reduction formula. The original language creating the Basic Educational Opportunity Grants (BEOG), the predecessor to Pell Grants, in the Education Amendments of 1972 allowed for payments on a pro rata reduced basis and specified a minimum grant of $50 whenever the program was less than fully funded.

After this HEA authority was repealed, appropriations legislation for FY1994-FY2001 continued to provide the Secretary with reduction authority, but that authority was not used.[58] FY2002 and subsequent appropriations legislation have not included such language.

CBO Scoring Rule

Congress took steps in FY2006 to limit the possibility of large accumulated funding shortfalls in the future. H.Con.Res. 95 (109th Congress) established a permanent rule that applies to the scoring[59] of the Pell Grant program by the Congressional Budget Office (CBO). The rule provides that if the appropriation of new discretionary budget authority[60] enacted for the program is insufficient to cover the full estimated costs in the upcoming year—including any funding surplus or shortfall from prior years—the budget authority counted against the bill for the program will be equal to the adjusted full cost (i.e., total need). The full estimated costs must be based on the maximum discretionary award amount and any changes to the eligibility criteria. For most discretionary programs, CBO equates the budget authority to the level provided in each appropriation bill.

As a result of the scoring rule, Congress cannot fund new programs or increase the funding of existing programs subject to discretionary appropriations while providing less funding than required for the Pell Grant program. The scoring rule, however, cannot fully account for the challenges of estimating the cost of the program. Discretionary program costs are estimated in advance of the award year they are intended to support, and based on the chosen discretionary base maximum award level and estimated program participation. The scoring rule does constrain the accumulation of

---

[58] The appropriations legislation during this time period required the Secretary to reduce awards using fixed or variable percentages, or using a fixed dollar reduction, if, prior to issuing the payment schedules, he or she determined that appropriated funds could not fully fund the appropriated maximum grant. A schedule of reduced grants would then be published.

[59] CBO *keeps score* for Congress by monitoring the results of congressional action on individual authorization, appropriation, and revenue bills against budget authority and outlay targets that are specified in the concurrent resolutions.

[60] Budget authority is defined as the broad responsibility conferred by Congress that empowers government agencies to spend federal funds.

the funding shortfall by requiring Congress to annually reconcile previous years' appropriation levels with updated estimates of previous years' program obligations.

Reductions in Program Costs

Given the CBO scoring rule, there are several levers that have been used to reduce or prevent an increase in Pell Grant program costs and thus reduce or eliminate a shortfall.

- The discretionary maximum award level has been reduced or not increased.
- Statutory provisions that establish Pell Grant award rules have been modified to reduce the amount of funds that some students may receive. For example, *year-round* Pell Grants were eliminated beginning in AY2011-2012.
- Statutory provisions that establish Pell Grant eligibility have been modified to reduce the number of recipients. For example, the qualifying minimum award amount was increased beginning in AY2012-2013.
- Statutory provisions that establish the calculation of EFC have been modified to reduce the numbers of students eligible for Pell Grants and other HEA Title IV need-based financial aid. For example, the income threshold for an automatic zero EFC was increased beginning in AY2012-2013 in order to reduce the number of students receiving an automatic zero EFC.
- Statutory provision that establish student eligibility for any HEA Title IV aid programs have been amended to reduce eligibility. For example, the ability of new students without a high school diploma (or equivalent) to qualify for HEA Title IV aid was temporarily eliminated from July 1, 2012, through June 30, 2014.

Supplementary Appropriations

In addition to reducing program costs or in lieu of reducing program costs to reduce or eliminate a funding shortfall, legislation has provided supplementary appropriations to address the CBO scoring rule.

- Supplementary mandatory appropriations have been provided for general use in the program, often by generating savings in the Direct Loan program that is funded by mandatory budget authority.
- Supplementary discretionary appropriations have been provided during periods of expansionary fiscal policy such as through the American Recovery and Reinvestment Act (ARRA; P.L. 111-5).

In addition to supplementary appropriations, the regular discretionary appropriations amount may be increased.

Policy Implications and Measures to Address Funding Surpluses

The policy implications of a funding surplus are very different from those of a shortfall. An increasing or high cumulative surplus may be viewed as presenting a potential opportunity. The surplus may be viewed as representing a pot of available funding. The surplus may be invested back into the Pell Grant program or it may be used to pursue other policy priorities.

There are several approaches for investing the surplus into the program.

- Appropriations levels and statutory provisions may be maintained under the assumption that Pell Grant program costs would eventually use the surplus. For example as the U.S. population grows, postsecondary enrollment and Pell Grant participation may grow.

- Award levels for Pell Grant recipients may be increased in order to increase the size of a Pell Grant. For example, the discretionary base maximum award was increased from $4,860 in FY2009-FY2017 to $5,035 in FY2018.
- Student eligibility for Pell Grants may be expanded. For example, increasing the discretionary base maximum award from $4,860 in FY2009-FY2017 to $5,035 in FY2018 also increases the number of students who are eligible.
- Statutory provisions that establish Pell Grant award rules may be modified to increase the amount of funds that some students may receive. For example, *year-round* Pell Grants were reauthorized beginning in AY2017-2018.
- Statutory provisions that establish the calculation of EFC may be modified to increase the numbers of students eligible for Pell Grants and other HEA Title IV need-based financial aid.
- Statutory provision that establish student eligibility for any HEA Title IV aid programs may be amended to increase eligibility.

Alternatively, the surplus may be used to fund or increase funding for other programs or to reduce a budget deficit. All or a portion of the surplus may be rescinded in an appropriations act. For example, the Consolidated Appropriations Act, 2017 (P.L. 115-31) included a rescission of $1.3 billion from the Pell Grant program surplus. The rescission offsets the cost of appropriations in the act.

ESTIMATED PROGRAM COSTS FOR RECENT AND FUTURE YEARS

Grant payments are made to eligible students who apply for aid and enroll in eligible programs notwithstanding the prescribed appropriation levels in any one year in such a way that some liken the program to a *quasi entitlement*. Costs for the Pell Grant program are award year-specific and

Federal Pell Grant Program of the Higher Education Act 109

are primarily affected by the number of eligible students who apply for aid and enroll in eligible programs, the total maximum award amount, and award rules. The number of eligible students may be affected by economic conditions and legislative changes to the federal need analysis methodology and award rules. As discussed earlier, the total maximum award amount is determined by both the annual appropriations act and the HEA. Other factors that contribute to changes in program costs include the cost of higher education.

The Congressional Budget Office reports and estimates program costs at least annually. Table 7 provides a summary of current and future estimated Pell Grant program costs from AY2012-2013 through AY2021-2022, as of April 2018. Costs associated with the discretionary base maximum award and costs associated with the mandatory add-on award are specified. Table 7 shows that the total program cost has declined from AY2012-2013 to AY2016-2017 and is estimated to increase thereafter.

Table 7. Estimated Pell Grant Program Costs, AY2012-2013 to AY2021-2022 (dollars in billions)

Award Year (AY)	Cost Associated with Discretionary Award Levels	Cost Associated with Mandatory Award Levels	Total Program Cost
AY2012-2013	27.5	5.0	32.5
AY2013-2014	26.5	5.1	31.6
AY2014-2015	25.3	5.5	30.8
AY2015-2016	23.4	5.7	29.0
AY2016-2017	21.8	5.4	27.2
AY2017-2018	23.4	5.9	29.2
AY2018-2019	24.4	6.1	30.6
AY2019-2020	24.6	6.2	30.8
AY2020-2021	25.0	6.3	31.3
AY2021-2022	25.5	6.4	31.9

Source: Congressional Budget Office (CBO), Discretionary Baseline, Cumulative Surplus/Shortfall, and Funding Gap of the Federal Pell Grant Program—Baseline dated March 2012, May 2013, April 2014, March 2015, March 2016, June 2017, and April 2018.

Notes: Estimates of program costs are not adjusted for inflation and are subject to change.

From AY2012-2013 to AY2015-2016, the number of Pell Grant recipients decreased annually (Table 2) although the total maximum award amount increased annually since AY2013-2014 (Table A-1). Declining undergraduate enrollment in degree-granting postsecondary institutions from 28.2 million in AY2011-2012 to 26.3 million in AY2015-2016 is reflected in a reduction of Pell Grant recipients.[61] The decrease in the number of Pell Grant recipients from AY2012-2013 to AY2015-2016, which is particularly evident in the decrease in costs related to the discretionary award level, outweighs the increase in the total maximum award, which is demonstrated in increased costs associated with mandatory award levels.

Program costs after AY2016-2017 are estimated to increase (Table 7). The increase would primarily be a result of an estimated increase in the number of Pell Grant recipients and the awarding of year-round Pell Grants. The CBO baseline does not account for any potential a change in the total maximum Pell Grant award after the AY2018-2019 discretionary maximum award increase included in the Consolidated Appropriations Act, 2018 (P.L. 115-141).

APPENDIX A. HISTORICAL PELL GRANT AWARD AMOUNTS

Table A-1. Pell Grant Award Amounts, AY1973-1974 and Subsequent Years

Award Year (AY)	Authorized Maximum Award[a]	Discretionary Base Maximum Award	Mandatory Add-On Award	Total Maximum Award	Effective Minimum Award[b]
1973-1974	$1,400	$452	N/A	$452	$50
1974-1975	1,400	1,050	N/A	1,050	50
1975-1976	1,400	1,400	N/A	1,400	200
1976-1977	1,400	1,400	N/A	1,400	200
1977-1978	1,800	1,400	N/A	1,400	200
1978-1979	1,800	1,600	N/A	1,600	50

---

[61] National Center for Education Statistics (NCES), *Digest of Education Statistics 2017*, Table 308.20.

Federal Pell Grant Program of the Higher Education Act   111

1979-1980	1,800	1,800	N/A	1,800	200
1980-1981	1,800	1,750	N/A	1,750	150
1981-1982	1,900	1,670	N/A	1,670	120
1982-1983	2,100	1,800	N/A	1,800	50
1983-1984	2,300	1,800	N/A	1,800	200
1984-1985	2,500	1,900	N/A	1,900	200
1985-1986	2,600	2,100	N/A	2,100	200
1986-1987	2,600	2,100	N/A	2,100	100
1987-1988	2,300	2,100	N/A	2,100	200
1988-1989	2,500	2,200	N/A	2,200	200
1989-1990	2,700	2,300	N/A	2,300	200
1990-1991	2,900	2,300	N/A	2,300	100
1991-1992	3,100	2,400	N/A	2,400	200
1992-1993	3,100	2,400	N/A	2,400	200
1993-1994	3,700	2,300	N/A	2,300	400
1994-1995	3,900	2,300	N/A	2,300	400
1995-1996	4,100	2,340	N/A	2,340	400
1996-1997	4,300	2,470	N/A	2,470	400
1997-1998	4,500	2,700	N/A	2,700	400
1998-1999	4,500	3,000	N/A	3,000	400
1999-2000	4,500	3,125	N/A	3,125	400
2000-2001	4,800	3,300	N/A	3,300	400
2001-2002	5,100	3,750	N/A	3,750	400
2002-2003	5,400	4,000	N/A	4,000	400
2003-2004	5,800	4,050	N/A	4,050	400
2004-2005	5,800	4,050	N/A	4,050	400
2005-2006	5,800[c]	4,050	N/A	4,050	400
2006-2007	5,800[c]	4,050	N/A	4,050	400
2007-2008	5,800[c]	4,310	N/A	4,310	400
2008-2009	5,800[c]	4,241	$490	4,731	523[d]
2009-2010	6,000	4,860	490	5,350	609[d]
2010-2011	None Specified	4,860	690	5,550	555
2011-2012	None Specified	4,860	690	5,550	555
2012-2013	None Specified	4,860	690	5,550	577e
2013-2014	None Specified	4,860	758	5,645	582[e]
2014-2015	None Specified	4,860	870	5,730	587[e]
2015-2016	None Specified	4,860	915	5,775	581e
2016-2017	None Specified	4,860	955	5,815	591e
2017-2018	None Specified	4,860	1,060	5,920	593e
2018-2019	None Specified	5,035	1,060f	6,095	611e
2019-2020	None Specified	5,135	1,060f	6,195	TBD

Source: HEA; appropriations acts, FY2010-FY2016; U.S. Department of Education, Department of Education Budget Tables, Congressional Action FY2013-FY2016; and U.S. Department of Education, *Federal Pell Grant Payment and Disbursement Schedules*, 2009-2010 to 2014-2015.

Notes: TBD = to be determined; N/A = not applicable.

Table A-1. (Continued)

a. The authorized maximum award was the annual maximum Pell Grant specified for each award year in the HEA. The authorization is intended to provide guidance regarding the appropriate amount of funds to carry out the policy objectives of a program. The SAFRA Act eliminated the authorized maximum award levels from the HEA.

b. The effective minimum award is the minimum amount of Pell Grant aid available to a student in any given year as determined by law. The effective minimum award for AY2010-2011 and all future years is equal to 10% of the total maximum award amount. Since the FY2012 Consolidated Appropriations Act eliminated the bump award beginning on July 1, 2012, the qualifying minimum award and effective minimum award are now the same.

c. Prior to the reauthorization of the HEA by the HEOA in 2008, Congress passed measures to extend the HEA allowing for the continuation of the Pell Grant program. The last authorized maximum award specified in law prior to the HEOA was $5,800 for AY2003-2004; therefore, the authorized maximum award is listed as $5,800 from AY2004-2005 through AY2008-2009 in this table.

d. This amount is the minimum amount of aid awarded to a student attending on a less-than-half-time basis.

e. Although the statutory effective minimum is 10% of the total maximum, the actual minimum award differs because ED uses midpoints for both the EFC and COA. ED's Federal Pell Grant Payment and Disbursement Schedules group COA and EFC in approximately $100 increments and calculate the award levels for each increment based on the increment midpoints. For example, the full-time, full-academic-year minimum scheduled award is based on an EFC increment of $5,401-$5,486 with a midpoint of $5,443 such that the minimum award is maximum COA – minimum EFC or $652 ($6,095 - $5,443).

f. Under current statutory provisions, the mandatory add-on award will remain at $1,060 permanently.

APPENDIX B. FEDERAL PELL GRANT RECIPIENTS, AY1973-1974 TO AY2015-2016

Table B-1. Federal Pell Grant Recipients, AY1973-1974 to AY2015-2016

Award Year	Pell Grant Recipients	Annual Change	% Change
1973-1974	176,000	N/A	N/A
1974-1975	567,000	391,000	222.2%
1975-1976	1,217,000	650,000	114.6%
1976-1977	1,944,000	727,000	59.7%

Federal Pell Grant Program of the Higher Education Act

Award Year	Pell Grant Recipients	Annual Change	% Change
1977-1978	2,011,000	67,000	3.4%
1978-1979	1,893,000	(118,000)	(5.9%)
1979-1980	2,538,000	645,000	34.1%
1980-1981	2,708,000	170,000	6.7%
1981-1982	2,709,000	1,000	0.0%
1982-1983	2,523,000	(186,000)	(6.9%)
1983-1984	2,759,000	236,000	9.4%
1984-1985	2,747,000	(12,000)	(0.4%)
1985-1986	2,813,000	66,000	2.4%
1986-1987	2,660,000	(153,000)	(5.4%)
1987-1988	2,882,000	222,000	8.3%
1988-1989	3,198,000	316,000	11.0%
1989-1990	3,322,000	124,000	3.9%
1990-1991	3,405,000	83,000	2.5%
1991-1992	3,786,000	381,000	11.2%
1992-1993	4,002,000	216,000	5.7%
1993-1994	3,756,000	(246,000)	(6.1%)
1994-1995	3,675,000	(81,000)	(2.2%)
1995-1996	3,612,000	(63,000)	(1.7%)
1996-1997	3,666,000	54,000	1.5%
1997-1998	3,733,000	67,000	1.8%
1998-1999	3,855,000	122,000	3.27%
1999-2000	3,764,000	(91,000)	(2.36%)
2000-2001	3,899,000	135,000	3.59%
2001-2002	4,341,000	442,000	11.34%
2002-2003	4,779,000	438,000	10.09%
2003-2004	5,140,000	361,000	7.55%
2004-2005	5,308,000	168,000	3.27%
2005-2006	5,168,000	(140,000)	(2.64%)
2006-2007	5,165,000	(3,000)	(0.06%)
2007-2008	5,543,000	378,000	7.32%
2008-2009	6,157,000	614,000	11.08%
2009-2010	8,094,000	1,937,000	31.46%
2010-2011	9,308,000	1,214,000	15.00%
2011-2012	9,444,000	136,000	1.46%
2012-2013	8,959,000	(486,000)	(5.14%)
2013-2014	8,663,000	(296,000)	(3.30%)
2014-2015	8,316,000	(347,000)	(4.01%)
2015-2016	7,660,000	(655,000)	(7.88%)

Source: U.S. Department of Education, *AY2015-16 Pell Grant End-of-Year Report.*

Note: Recipient figures rounded to the nearest thousand. Numbers in parentheses are negative numbers.

Appendix C. Program Funding: FY2008-FY2021

Table C-1. Pell Grant Annual Funding: FY2008-FY2021 (dollars in millions)

Fiscal Year[a] Legislation	FY2008	FY2009	FY2010	FY2011	FY2012	FY2013	FY2014	FY2015	FY2016	FY2017	FY2018	FY2019	FY2020	FY2021
Discretionary Appropriations														
Annual Appropriations	14,215	17,288	17,495	22,956	22,824	22,778	22,778	22,475	22,475	22,475	22,475	22,475	TBD	TBD
ARRA	—	15,640	—	—	—	—	—	—	—	—	—	—	—	—
Consolidated Appropriations Act, 2017	—	—	—	—	—	—	—	—	—	(1,310)	—	—	—	—
Department of Defense and Labor, Health and Human Services, and Education Appropriations Act, 2019 and Continuing Appropriations Act, 2019	—	—	—	—	—	—	—	—	—	—	—	(600)	—	—
Total Discretionary	14,215	32,928	17,495	22,956	22,824	22,778	22,778	22,475	22,475	21,165	22,475	21,875	TBD	TBD
Mandatory Appropriations Provided to Augment Discretionary Appropriations														
SAFRA Act	—	—	—	13,500	—	—	—	—	—	—	—	—	—	—
FY2011 Continuing Appropriations Act	—	—	—	—	3,183	0	0	0	0	1,060	1,125	1,125	1,140	1,145b
Budget Control Act of 2011	—	—	—	—	10,000	7,000	—	—	—	—	—	—	—	—

Fiscal Year[a]	FY2008	FY2009	FY2010	FY2011	FY2012	FY2013	FY2014	FY2015	FY2016	FY2017	FY2018	FY2019	FY2020	FY2021
FY2012 Consolidated Appropriations Act	—	—	—	612	587	588	0	0	0	514	257	284	290	0
Consolidated Appropriations Act, 2017	—	—	—	—	—	—	—	—	—	(254)	—	—	—	—
Consolidated Appropriations Act, 2018	—	—	—	—	—	—	—	—	—	—	(48)	—	—	—
Department of Defense and Labor, Health and Human Services, and Education Appropriations Act, 2019 and Continuing Appropriations Act, 2019	—	—	—	—	—	—	—	—	—	—	—	(39)	—	—
Total Mandatory to Augment Discretionary	—	—	—	13,500	13,795	7,587	588	0	0	1,574	1,382	1,370	1,430	1,145c
Mandatory Appropriations Provided to Fund Add-On Award Amounts														
CCRAA	2,041c	2,090	3,030	3,090	5,050	105	4,305	4,400	4,600	4,900	—	—	—	—
ARRA	—	643	831	—	—	—	—	—	—	—	—	—	—	—
FY2009 Technical Amendments to the HEA	—	—	—	—	153	—	—	152	—	—	—	—	—	—
SAFRA Act[d]	—	—	(3,861)	(3,090)	(5,050)	(258)	(4,305)	(4,452)	(4,600)	(4,900)	—	—	—	—
SAFRA Act[d]	—	—	5,300e	5,560f	4,950g	4,854h	4,835i	5,153j	4,840k	5,680l	5,977m	6,103n	SSAN	SSAN
Total Mandatory for Add On Awards	2,041	2,733	5,300	5,560	4,950	4,854	4,835	5,153	4,840	5,680	5,977	6,103	SSAN	SSAN

Fiscal Year[a]	FY2008	FY2009	FY2010	FY2011	FY2012	FY2013	FY2014	FY2015	FY2016	FY2017	FY2018	FY2019	FY2020	FY2021
Total Pell Grant Funding Excluding Surplus (Discretionary and Mandatory)														
Total Funding	16,256	35,661	22,795	42,016	41,569	35,219	28,202	27,628	27,316	29,476	29,834	29,348	TBD	TBD

Source: CRS analysis of the HEA and respective legislation.

Notes: TBD = to be determined; "—" means that no appropriations were provided beyond the initial year(s) specified. Numbers in parentheses are negative numbers.

SSAN = Such sums as necessary. In effect, this means the amount of mandatory appropriations that will be necessary to fully fund the add-on award amount specified in the HEA for a given year. In other words, mandatory funding has been available to support the add-on amount beginning in FY2010 onward indefinitely, but the specific amount required in each year cannot be reported until the add-on amount is determined and all funds are disbursed to eligible students

a. The fiscal year in this table represents the first year the funds appropriated in each column are available for use. Most funds are available for two fiscal years.
b. Additional annual mandatory appropriations in the amount of $1,145,000,000 are also provided for each succeeding year beyond FY2021 per the FY2011 Continuing Appropriations Act.
c. Includes $11 million for the elimination of the tuition sensitivity rule in AY2007-2008.
d. The SAFRA Act rescinded advance appropriation provided in the CCRAA, ARRA, and FY2009 Technical Amendments to the HEA. The SAFRA Act provided indefinite and permanent mandatory appropriations for the mandatory add-on award. The positive amounts shown are the actual amounts required for the mandatory add-on award.
e. This is the amount of mandatory appropriations required for a $690 mandatory add-on award in AY2010-2011, as reported in the President's FY2015 budget.
f. This is the amount of mandatory appropriations required for a $690 mandatory add-on award in AY2011-2012, as reported in the President's FY2016 budget.
g. This is the amount of mandatory appropriations required for a $690 mandatory add-on award in AY2012-2013, as reported in the President's FY2017 budget.
h. This is the amount of mandatory appropriations required for a $785 mandatory add-on award in AY2013-2014, as reported in the President's FY2018 budget.
i. This is the amount of mandatory appropriations required for an $870 mandatory add-on award in AY2014-2015, as reported in the President's FY2019 budget.
j. This is the amount of mandatory appropriations required for a $915 mandatory add-on award in AY2015-2016, as reported in the President's FY2019 budget.
k. This is the amount of mandatory appropriations required for a $965 mandatory add-on award in AY2016-2017, as reported in the President's FY2019 budget.
l. This is the amount of mandatory appropriations required for a $1,060 mandatory add-on award in AY2017-2018, as reported in the President's FY2019 budget.
m. This is the amount of mandatory appropriations required for a $1,060 mandatory add-on award in AY2018-2019, as reported in the President's FY2019 budget.
n. This is the amount of mandatory appropriations required for a $1,060 mandatory add-on award in AY2019-2020, as reported in the President's FY2019 budget

APPENDIX D. ANNUAL AND CUMULATIVE DISCRETIONARY FUNDING SHORTFALLS AND SURPLUSES IN THE PELL GRANT PROGRAM, FY1973-FY2018

Table D-1. Annual and Cumulative Discretionary Funding Shortfalls and Surpluses in the Pell Grant Program, FY1973-FY2018 (dollars in millions)

Fiscal Year	Award Year	Funds Available for the Discretionary Award Level	Estimated Total Expenditures[a]	Annual Surplus or (Shortfall)[b]	Cumulative Surplus or (Shortfall)
1973	1973-1974	$122	$48	$74	N/A
1974	1974-1975	475	358	117	N/A
1975	1975-1976	840	926	(86)	N/A
1976	1976-1977	1,326	1,475	(149)	N/A
1977	1977-1978	1,904	1,524	380	N/A
1978	1978-1979	2,160	1,541	619	N/A
1979	1979-1980	2,431	2,357	74	N/A
1980	1980-1981	2,157	2,387	(230)	N/A
1981	1981-1982	2,604	2,300	304	N/A
1982	1982-1983	2,419	2,421	(2)	N/A
1983	1983-1984	2,419	2,797	(378)	N/A
1984	1984-1985	2,800	3,053	(253)	N/A
1985	1985-1986	3,862	3,597	265	N/A
1986	1986-1987	3,580	3,460	120	N/A
1987	1987-1988	4,187	3,754	433	N/A
1988	1988-1989	4,260	4,476	(216)	N/A
1989	1989-1990	4,484	4,770	(75)	($75)
1990	1990-1991	4,804	4,904	(231)	(306)
1991	1991-1992	5,376	5,772	(396)	(702)
1992	1992-1993	5,503	6,156	18	(684)
1993	1993-1994	6,462	5,621	460	(224)
1994	1994-1995	6,637	5,504	808	584
1995	1995-1996	6,147	5,466	716	1,300
1996	1996-1997	4,914	5,784	(870)	429
1997	1997-1998	5,919	6,315	(396)	33
1998	1998-1999	7,345	7,236	109	142

Table D-1. (Continued)

Fiscal Year	Award Year	Funds Available for the Discretionary Award Level	Estimated Total Expenditures[a]	Annual Surplus or (Shortfall)[b]	Cumulative Surplus or (Shortfall)
1999	1999-2000	7,704	7,233	471	613
2000	2000-2001	7,640	7,996	(356)	256
2001	2001-2002	8,756	9,985	(1,229)	(908)
2002	2002-2003	11,314[c]	11,653	(339)	(1,247)
2003	2003-2004	11,365	12,713	(1,348)	(2,595)
2004	2004-2005	12,007	13,152	(1,145)	(3,740)
2005	2005-2006	12,365	12,695	(330)	(4,070)
2006	2006-2007	17,345[d]	12,825	4,520	220
2007	2007-2008	13,661	14,699	(1,038)	(818)
2008	2008-2009	14,215	16,054	(1,839)	(2,657)
2009	2009-2010	32,928[e]	26,844	6,084	3,427
2010	2010-2011	17,495	30,491	(12,996)	(9,569)
2011	2011-2012	36,456f	28,796	7,660	(1,909)
2012	2012-2013	36,619[g]	27,512	9,107	7,198
2013	2013-2014	30,365[h]	26,481	3,884	11,082
2014	2014-2015	23,366[i]	25,320	(1,954)	9,128
2015	2015-2016	22,475	23,361	(886)	8,242
2016	2016-2017	22,475	21,788	687	8,929
2017	2017-2018	22,485[j]	23,377	(892)	8,037
2018	2018-2019	23,809[k]	24,436	(627)	7,410

Sources: (1) U.S. Department of Education (ED), *AY2010-11 Federal Pell Grant Program End-of-Year Report;* (2) unpublished data provided by ED; (3) data provided by CBO in May 2013, April 2014, and March 2015; and (4) respective appropriations measures.

Notes: TBD = to be determined. N/A = not available. Numbers in parentheses are negative numbers. Data on the cumulative shortfall or surplus prior to AY1989-1990 could not be verified and therefore are not provided. Prior to 1980, the program was called the Basic Educational Opportunity Grant (BEOG) Program.

[a.] The estimated total expenditure totals for AY1973-1974 through AY1988-1989 are taken from the U.S. Department of Education, *AY2009-10 Federal Pell Grant Program End-of-Year Report* and do not include administrative cost allowance payments to institutions. The expenditure totals for AY1989-1990 to AY2005-2006 are taken from unpublished data provided by ED and reflect administrative cost allowance payments to institutions. Estimates of all data after AY2005-2006 are provided by CBO and also include administrative cost allowance payments to institutions. All estimates of expenditures are subject to change. In years in which mandatory appropriations were available to fund the discretionary award levels, expenditures include discretionary and mandatory appropriations.

[b.] The annual shortfall or surplus amount reflects account transfers and other adjustments and may not equal the difference between the annual appropriation and estimated total expenditures in each year.

[c.] Includes $1 billion in supplemental discretionary funding to pay for the FY2001 cumulative shortfall.

[d.] Includes $4.3 billion in mandatory funding provided in FY2006 to exclusively supplement the discretionary funding necessary to retire the cumulative funding shortfall through AY2005-2006, as originally estimated in the President's FY2006 budget. The mandatory funds that exceeded the actual cumulative funding shortfall were returned to the U.S. Department of the Treasury. The discretionary appropriation for FY2006 was $13,045 million.

e. Includes approximately $15.7 billion in supplemental discretionary appropriations provided in the American Recovery and Reinvestment Act (ARRA).

f. Includes $13.5 billion in mandatory appropriations that were provided in the SAFRA Act for general use in the program through FY2012 and $22,956 million in discretionary appropriations provided in the FY2011 Continuing Appropriations Act.

g. This number includes mandatory and discretionary funding from the following sources: The FY2011 Continuing Appropriations Act provided $3,183 million in mandatory appropriations for general use in the program for FY2012. The Budget Control Act of 2011 (P.L. 112-25) provided $10 billion in mandatory appropriations for general use in the program for FY2012. Finally, the FY2012 Consolidated Appropriations Act (P.L. 112-74) provided $22,824 million in discretionary appropriations for FY2012 and $612 million in mandatory appropriations for general use in the program for FY2012.

h. This number includes mandatory and discretionary funding from the following sources: The Budget Control Act of 2011 (P.L. 112-25) provided $7 billion in mandatory appropriations for general use in the program for FY2013. Additionally, the FY2012 Consolidated Appropriations Act (P.L. 112-74) provided $587 million in mandatory appropriations for general use in the program for FY2013.

i. This number includes mandatory and discretionary funding from the following sources: The FY2012 Consolidated Appropriations Act (P.L. 112-74) provided $588 million in mandatory appropriations for general use in the program for FY2014. The Consolidated Appropriations Act, 2014 (P.L. 113-76) provided $22,778 million in discretionary appropriations for FY2014.

j. This number includes mandatory and discretionary funding from the following sources: The FY2011 Continuing Appropriations Act provided $1.060 million in mandatory appropriations; the FY2012 Consolidated Appropriations Act (P.L. 112-74) provided $514 million in mandatory appropriations; and the Consolidated Appropriations Act, 2017 (P.L. 115-31) provided $22.475 million in discretionary appropriations, rescinded $1.310 million of the surplus, and reduced the cumulative mandatory appropriation of $1.574 million from the FY2011 Continuing Appropriations Act and the FY2012 Consolidated Appropriations Act to $1.320 million.

k. This number includes mandatory and discretionary funding from the following sources: The FY2011 Continuing Appropriations Act provided $1.125 million in mandatory appropriations; the FY2012 Consolidated Appropriations Act (P.L. 112-74) provided $257 million in mandatory appropriations; and the Consolidated Appropriations Act, 2018 (P.L. 115-141) provided $22.475 million in discretionary appropriations and reduced the cumulative mandatory appropriation of $1.382 million from the FY2011 Continuing Appropriations Act and the FY2012 Consolidated Appropriations Act to $1.334 million.

APPENDIX E. GLOSSARY/ACRONYMS

ARRA	American Recovery and Reinvestment Act (P.L. 111-5)
CBO	Congressional Budget Office
CCRAA	College Cost Reduction and Access Act of 2007 (P.L. 110-84)

COA	Cost of Attendance
Direct Loan	William D. Ford Direct Loan program
ED	U.S. Department of Education
EFC	Expected Family Contribution
FAFSA	Free Application for Federal Student Aid
HEA	Higher Education Act of 1965 (P.L. 89-329), as amended
HEOA	Higher Education Opportunity Act of 2008 (P.L. 110-315)
IHE	Institution of Higher Education
ISIR	Institutional Student Information Record
NPSAS	U.S. Department of Education, National Postsecondary Student Aid Study
Private for-profit	Sometimes referred to as proprietary
SAFRA Act	Title II-A of the Health Care and Education Reconciliation Act of 2010 (P.L. 111-152)

In: A Closer Look at Grant Programs
Editor: Tabitha Reyes

ISBN: 978-1-53615-995-0
© 2019 Nova Science Publishers, Inc.

Chapter 3

FY2017 STATE GRANTS UNDER TITLE I-A OF THE ELEMENTARY AND SECONDARY EDUCATION ACT (ESEA)[*]

Rebecca R. Skinner and Clarissa G. Cooper

ABSTRACT

The Elementary and Secondary Education Act (ESEA), as amended by the Every Student Succeeds Act (ESSA; P.L. 114-95), is the primary source of federal aid to K-12 education. The Title I-A program is the largest grant program authorized under the ESEA. It is designed to provide supplementary educational and related services to low-achieving and other students attending elementary and secondary schools with relatively high concentrations of students from low-income families. Title I-A was funded at $15.5 billion for FY2017.

Under current law, the U.S. Department of Education (ED) determines Title I-A grants to local educational agencies (LEAs) based on four separate funding formulas: Basic Grants, Concentration Grants, Targeted Grants, and Education Finance Incentive Grants (EFIG). The

---

[*] This is an edited, reformatted and augmented version of Congressional Research Service Publication No. R44873, updated November 19, 2018.

four Title I-A formulas have somewhat distinct allocation patterns, providing varying shares of allocated funds to different types of states. Thus, for some states, certain formulas are more favorable than others.

This report provides FY2017 state grant amounts under each of the four formulas used to determine Title I-A grants. Overall, California received the largest FY2017 Title I-A grant amount ($1.8 billion, or 12.00% of total Title I-A grants). Vermont received the smallest FY2017 Title I-A grant amount ($35.3 million, or 0.23% of total Title I-A grants).

INTRODUCTION

The Elementary and Secondary Education Act (ESEA) is the primary source of federal aid to elementary and secondary education. Title I-A is the largest program in the ESEA, funded at $15.5 billion for FY2017. The program is designed to provide supplementary educational and related services to low-achieving and other students attending elementary and secondary schools with relatively high concentrations of students from low-income families. The U.S. Department of Education (ED) determines Title I-A grants to local educational agencies (LEAs) based on four separate funding formulas: Basic Grants, Concentration Grants, Targeted Grants, and Education Finance Incentive Grants (EFIG).

The ESEA was comprehensively reauthorized by the Every Student Succeeds Act (ESSA; P.L. 114-95) on December 10, 2015.[1] The ESSA made few changes to the Title I-A formulas. These changes took effect in FY2017.[2]

This report provides FY2017 state grant amounts under each of the four formulas used to determine Title I-A grants.[3]

---

[1] For more information on the ESSA, see CRS Report R44297, Reauthorization of the Elementary and Secondary Education Act: Highlights of the Every Student Succeeds Act.
[2] While the ESSA included provisions for changes to the Title I-A formula grant allocation process to take effect on July 1, 2016, the Consolidated Appropriations Act of 2016 (P.L. 114-113) changed the effective date of these provisions to July 1, 2017.
[3] This version of this report updates an earlier version, replacing estimated grant amounts with actual grant amounts. For more information about FY2016 Title I-A grants to states, see CRS Report R44486, FY2016 State Grants Under Title I-A of the Elementary and Secondary Education Act (ESEA). For more information about FY2015 Title I-A grants to states, see CRS Report R44097, FY2015 State Grants Under Title I-A of the Elementary and Secondary Education Act (ESEA).

Under Title I-A, funds are allocated to LEAs via state educational agencies (SEAs) using the four Title I-A formulas. Annual appropriations bills specify portions of each year's Title I-A appropriation to be allocated to LEAs and states under each of the formulas. In FY2017, about 42% of Title I-A appropriations were allocated through the Basic Grants formula, 9% through the Concentration Grants formula, and 25% each through the Targeted Grants and EFIG formulas. Once funds reach LEAs, the amounts allocated under the four formulas are combined and used jointly.

For each formula, a maximum grant is calculated by multiplying a *formula child count*, consisting primarily of estimated numbers of school-age children in poor families, by an *expenditure factor* based on state average per-pupil expenditures for public elementary and secondary education. In some formulas, additional factors are multiplied by the formula child count and expenditure factor. These maximum grants are then reduced to equal the level of available appropriations for each formula, taking into account a variety of state and LEA minimum grant provisions. In general, LEAs must have a minimum number of formula children and/or a minimum formula child rate to be eligible to receive a grant under a specific Title I-A formula. Some LEAs may qualify for a grant under only one formula, while other LEAs may be eligible to receive grants under multiple formulas.

Under three of the formulas—Basic, Concentration, and Targeted Grants—funds are initially calculated at the LEA level. State grants are the total of allocations for all LEAs in the state, adjusted for state minimum grant provisions. Under EFIG, grants are first calculated for each state overall and then are subsequently suballocated to LEAs within the state using a different formula.

FY2017 grants included in this report were calculated by ED. The percentage share of funds allocated under each of the Title I-A formulas was calculated for each state by dividing the total grant received by the total amount allocated under each respective formula.

FY2017 Title I-A Grants

Table 1 provides each state's grant amount[4] and percentage share of funds allocated under each of the Title I-A formulas for FY2017.[5] Total Title I-A grants, calculated by summing the state level grant for each of the four formulas, are also shown in *Table 1*.

Overall, California received the largest total Title I-A grant amount ($1.8 billion) and, as a result, the largest percentage share (12.00%) of Title I-A grants. Vermont received the smallest total Title I-A grant amount ($35.3 million) and, as a result, the smallest percentage share (0.23%) of Title IA grants.

In general, grant amounts for states vary among formulas due to the different allocation amounts for the formulas. For example, the Basic Grant formula receives a greater share of overall Title IA appropriations than the Concentration Grant formula, so states generally receive higher grant amounts under the Basic Grant formula than under the Concentration Grant formula.

Among states, Title I-A grant amounts and the percentage shares of funds vary due to the different characteristics of each state. For example, Texas has a much larger population of children included in the formula calculations than North Carolina and, therefore, receives a higher grant amount and larger share of Title I-A funds.

---

[4] For the purposes of the Title I-A program, Puerto Rico is considered a state.

[5] The Bureau of Indian Education (BIE) and the Outlying Areas receive 0.7% and 0.4%, respectively, of overall Title IA appropriations, less a reservation of funds for the U.S. Census Bureau. Of the funds allocated to the Outlying Areas, $1 million is taken off the top for a grant to Palau and the remaining funds are allocated to each of the Outlying Areas based on poverty levels. If appropriations for Title I-A for FY2017 or a subsequent fiscal year are insufficient to provide a total amount of funds to make grants to states that is at least as much as the total amount of funds available to make grants to states in FY2016, the reservation of funds for the BIE and Outlying Areas will be implemented as required by law prior to the enactment of the ESSA. In FY2017, this appropriations threshold was met, and the BIE received $108.1 million, American Samoa $18.9 million, Guam $20.5 million, the Northern Mariana Islands $11.5 million, and the Virgin Islands $9.9 million.

Within a state, the percentage share of funds allocated may vary by formula, as certain formulas are more favorable to certain types of states (e.g., EFIG is generally more favorable to states with comparatively equal levels of spending per pupil among their LEAs). If a state's share of a given Title I-A formula exceeds its share of overall Title I-A funds, this is generally an indication that this particular formula is more favorable to the state than formulas for which the state's share of funds is below its overall share of Title I-A funds.

For example, Florida and New York received a substantially higher percentage share of Targeted Grants than of overall Title I-A funds, indicating that the Targeted Grant formula is more favorable to them than other Title I-A formulas may be. At the same time, both states received a smaller percentage share of Basic Grants than of overall Title I-A funds, indicating that the Basic Grant formula is less favorable to them than other Title I-A formulas may be.[6]

In the four states (North Dakota, South Dakota, Vermont, and Wyoming) that receive a minimum grant under all four formulas, the shares received under the Targeted Grant and EFIG formulas are greater than under the Basic Grant or Concentration Grant formulas, due to higher state minimums under these formulas. If a state received the minimum grant under a given Title I-A formula, the grant amount is denoted with an asterisk (*) in *Table 1*.

---

[6] Both Florida and New York received their largest grant amounts under the Basic Grants formula, but this is due to the larger appropriation provided for Basic Grants. An examination of the percentage share each state receives under each of the four formulas provides an indication of which formulas are most beneficial to a particular state. In general, a state would receive a larger overall Title I-A grant if a greater percentage of the Title I-A appropriation was provided to the formula(s) under which the state benefits the most.

Table 1. FY2017 Title I-A State Grants and Percentage Share of Funds, by Funding Formula (Dollars in thousands)

State	Basic Grants Grant Amount	Basic Grants Percentage Share of Total Allocation	Concentration Grants Grant Amount	Concentration Grants Percentage Share of Total Allocation	Targeted Grants Grant Amount	Targeted Grants Percentage Share of Total Allocation	EFIG Grant Amount	EFIG Percentage Share of Total Allocation	Total Title I-A Grants Grant Amount	Total Title I-A Grants Percentage Share of Total Allocation
Total, United States	$6,383,403	100.00%	$1,347,316	100.00%	$3,777,040	100.00%	$3,777,040	100.00%	$15,284,799	100.00%
Alabama	103,331	1.62%	23,571	1.75%	59,166	1.57%	64,672	1.71%	250,740	1.64%
Alaska	17,106*	0.27%	2,745	0.20%	11,514*	0.30%	11,488*	0.30%	42,853	0.28%
Arizona	145,520	2.28%	31,663	2.35%	88,056	2.33%	84,221	2.23%	349,461	2.29%
Arkansas	68,933	1.08%	15,679	1.16%	36,250	0.96%	42,277	1.12%	163,139	1.07%
California	767,150	12.02%	165,625	12.29%	476,730	12.62%	424,350	11.23%	1,833,855	12.00%
Colorado	66,541	1.04%	11,859	0.88%	35,597	0.94%	38,237	1.01%	152,235	1.00%
Connecticut	58,941	0.92%	9,211	0.68%	26,586	0.70%	34,986	0.93%	129,724	0.85%
Delaware	19,750	0.31%	4,698	0.35%	13,220*	0.35%	13,220*	0.35%	50,887	0.33%
District of Columbia	17,744*	0.28%	4,118	0.31%	12,877	0.34%	12,659*	0.34%	47,398	0.31%
Florida	327,854	5.14%	77,313	5.74%	243,813	6.46%	207,998	5.51%	856,978	5.61%
Georgia	219,086	3.43%	50,503	3.75%	137,192	3.63%	133,145	3.53%	539,926	3.53%
Hawaii	20,926	0.33%	4,828	0.36%	13,465	0.36%	14,522	0.38%	53,740	0.35%
Idaho	25,886	0.41%	5,579	0.41%	13,220*	0.35%	13,886	0.37%	58,571	0.38%
Illinois	293,028	4.59%	57,926	4.30%	171,879	4.55%	155,592	4.12%	678,426	4.44%
Indiana	115,569	1.81%	23,859	1.77%	57,362	1.52%	68,779	1.82%	265,568	1.74%
Iowa	44,617	0.70%	7,378	0.55%	18,130	0.48%	27,235	0.72%	97,360	0.64%

	Basic Grants		Concentration Grants		Targeted Grants		EFIG		Total Title I-A Grants	
State	Grant Amount	Percentage Share of Total Allocation	Grant Amount	Percentage Share of Total Allocation	Grant Amount	Percentage Share of Total Allocation	Grant Amount	Percentage Share of Total Allocation	Grant Amount	Percentage Share of Total Allocation
Kansas	48,567	0.76%	9,103	0.68%	22,806	0.60%	27,267	0.72%	107,743	0.70%
Kentucky	95,480	1.50%	21,972	1.63%	54,232	1.44%	59,704	1.58%	231,388	1.51%
Louisiana	129,167	2.02%	30,972	2.30%	77,990	2.06%	78,262	2.07%	316,392	2.07%
Maine	22,998	0.36%	4,563	0.34%	13,220*	0.35%	13,220*	0.35%	54,000	0.35%
Maryland	93,423	1.46%	18,369	1.36%	60,461	1.60%	58,529	1.55%	230,782	1.51%
Massachusetts	109,661	1.72%	19,092	1.42%	52,904	1.40%	62,712	1.66%	244,368	1.60%
Michigan	213,226	3.34%	44,147	3.28%	118,457	3.14%	129,612	3.43%	505,442	3.31%
Minnesota	75,753	1.19%	10,670	0.79%	33,996	0.90%	43,238	1.14%	163,656	1.07%
Mississippi	81,652	1.28%	19,123	1.42%	48,542	1.29%	50,848	1.35%	200,166	1.31%
Missouri	110,493	1.73%	23,066	1.71%	54,706	1.45%	63,386	1.68%	251,651	1.65%
Montana	17,744*	0.28%	3,693	0.27%	13,220*	0.35%	13,220*	0.35%	47,877	0.31%
Nebraska	32,938	0.52%	6,188	0.46%	16,610	0.44%	19,453	0.52%	75,189	0.49%
Nevada	49,206	0.77%	11,468	0.85%	40,040	1.06%	29,769	0.79%	130,483	0.85%
New Hampshire	17,465*	0.27%	2,657	0.20%	11,347*	0.30%	11,728*	0.31%	43,198	0.28%
New Jersey	163,123	2.56%	27,713	2.06%	77,970	2.06%	95,984	2.54%	364,789	2.39%
New Mexico	48,217	0.76%	11,264	0.84%	29,561	0.78%	30,622	0.81%	119,665	0.78%
New York	484,962	7.60%	102,964	7.64%	341,911	9.05%	278,163	7.36%	1,208,000	7.90%
North Carolina	184,190	2.89%	43,018	3.19%	110,654	2.93%	113,105	2.99%	450,967	2.95%
North Dakota	14,735*	0.23%	2,042*	0.15%	10,101*	0.27%	10,108*	0.27%	36,986	0.24%
Ohio	241,679	3.79%	49,199	3.65%	125,588	3.33%	140,083	3.71%	556,549	3.64%
Oklahoma	72,528	1.14%	15,477	1.15%	37,590	1.00%	43,515	1.15%	169,110	1.11%
Oregon	66,426	1.04%	14,272	1.06%	32,204	0.85%	39,484	1.05%	152,387	1.00%

Table 1. (Continued)

State	Basic Grants Grant Amount	Basic Grants Percentage Share of Total Allocation	Concentration Grants Grant Amount	Concentration Grants Percentage Share of Total Allocation	Targeted Grants Grant Amount	Targeted Grants Percentage Share of Total Allocation	EFIG Grant Amount	EFIG Percentage Share of Total Allocation	Total Title I-A Grants Grant Amount	Total Title I-A Grants Percentage Share of Total Allocation
Pennsylvania	269,685	4.22%	51,500	3.82%	149,640	3.96%	150,614	3.99%	621,439	4.07%
Puerto Rico	166,420	2.61%	42,256	3.14%	94,463	2.50%	105,121	2.78%	408,260	2.67%
Rhode Island	22,526	0.35%	4,135	0.31%	13,220*	0.35%	13,370	0.35%	53,251	0.35%
South Carolina	100,838	1.58%	23,501	1.74%	57,836	1.53%	61,138	1.62%	243,314	1.59%
South Dakota	17,744*	0.28%	3,179*	0.24%	12,992*	0.34%	13,020*	0.34%	46,934	0.31%
Tennessee	126,222	1.98%	29,058	2.16%	75,751	2.01%	75,730	2.01%	306,762	2.01%
Texas	577,591	9.05%	128,319	9.52%	363,688	9.63%	352,211	9.33%	1,421,810	9.30%
Utah	38,226	0.60%	6,456	0.48%	20,096	0.53%	22,375	0.59%	87,154	0.57%
Vermont	13,904*	0.22%	2,265*	0.17%	9,574*	0.25%	9,587*	0.25%	35,330	0.23%
Virginia	115,804	1.81%	21,836	1.62%	59,395	1.57%	62,152	1.65%	259,186	1.70%
Washington	102,484	1.61%	19,839	1.47%	46,831	1.24%	59,408	1.57%	228,563	1.50%
West Virginia	40,950	0.64%	9,318	0.69%	19,805	0.52%	26,511	0.70%	96,585	0.63%
Wisconsin	91,227	1.43%	16,173	1.20%	44,813	1.19%	56,776	1.50%	208,988	1.37%
Wyoming	14,167*	0.22%	1,892*	0.14%	9,769*	0.26%	9,748*	0.26%	35,576	0.23%

Source: Table prepared by CRS based on unpublished data provided by the U.S. Department of Education (ED), Budget Service. Title I-A grant amounts were calculated by ED. Percentage shares of FY2017 allocation amounts were calculated by CRS.

Notes: Details may not add to totals due to rounding. Percentages calculated based on unrounded numbers. Amounts shown in the table only reflect Title I-A funds provided to states. These amounts are determined after funds have been reserved from the total Title I-A appropriation for the Census Bureau, Bureau of Indian Education, and Outlying Areas.

An asterisk (*) denotes minimum grants.

*: State received a minimum grant.

In: A Closer Look at Grant Programs
Editor: Tabitha Reyes

ISBN: 978-1-53615-995-0
© 2019 Nova Science Publishers, Inc.

Chapter 4

THE HUD HOMELESS ASSISTANCE GRANTS: PROGRAMS AUTHORIZED BY THE HEARTH ACT (UPDATED)[*]

Libby Perl

ABSTRACT

The Homeless Assistance Grants, administered by the Department of Housing and Urban Development (HUD), were first authorized by Congress in 1987 as part of the McKinney-Vento Homeless Assistance Act (P.L. 100-77). Since their creation, the grants have been composed of three or four separate programs, though for the majority of their existence, between 1992 and 2012, the grant programs were unchanged. During this time period, there were four programs authorized and funded by Congress: the Emergency Shelter Grants (ESG), the Supportive Housing Program (SHP), the Shelter Plus Care (S+C) program, and the Section 8 Moderate Rehabilitation for Single Room Occupancy Dwellings (SRO) program. Funds for the ESG program were used primarily for the short-term needs of homeless persons, such as

---

[*] This is an edited, reformatted and augmented version of Congressional Research Service, Publication No. RL33764, dated August 30, 2017.

emergency shelter, while the other three programs addressed longer-term transitional and permanent housing needs.

The composition of the Homeless Assistance Grants changed when Congress enacted the Homeless Emergency Assistance and Rapid Transition to Housing (HEARTH) Act as part of the Helping Families Save Their Homes Act in the 111th Congress (P.L. 111-22). The HEARTH Act renamed the ESG program (it is now called the Emergency *Solutions* Grants) and expanded the way in which funds can be used to include homelessness prevention and rapid rehousing (quickly finding housing for families who find themselves homeless), and it consolidated SHP, S+C, and SRO into one program called the Continuum of Care (CoC) program. A third program carved out of the CoC program to assist rural communities—the Rural Housing Stability Assistance Program—was also created by P.L. 111-22. In addition, the HEARTH Act broadened HUD's definition of homelessness. The changes in P.L. 111-22 had repercussions for the way in which funds are distributed to grantees, the purposes for which grantees may use funds, and who may be served.

HUD began to implement the ESG program in FY2011 and the CoC program in FY2012, and it released proposed regulations for the Rural Housing Stability (RHS) grants in March 2013 (and has not yet provided RHS grants). Funds for the ESG program, in addition to being available for homelessness prevention and rapid rehousing, can be used for emergency shelter and supportive services. CoC program funds can be used to provide permanent supportive housing, transitional housing, supportive services, and rapid rehousing. If the RHS program is implemented, rural communities will have greater flexibility in who they are able to serve (those assisted may not necessarily meet HUD's definition of "homeless individual"), and may use funds for a variety of housing and services options.

HUD uses one method to distribute funds for the ESG program and another method to distribute funds for the CoC program. The ESG program distributes funds to states, counties, and metropolitan areas using the Community Development Block Grant (CDBG) program formula, while the CoC grants are distributed through a competitive process, though the CDBG formula plays a role in determining community need. In July 2016, HUD proposed to change the CoC formula so that it no longer relies on the CDBG formula distribution.

Funding for the Homeless Assistance Grants has increased by almost $1 billion in the last 10 years, reaching nearly $2.4 billion in FY2017 compared to $1.4 billion in FY2007 (see Table 3). Despite funding increases, the need to renew existing grants requires the majority of funding. In FY2016, 90% of the CoC program allocation was used to renew existing grants.

AN INTRODUCTION TO THE HOMELESS ASSISTANCE GRANTS

Homelessness in America has always existed, but it did not come to the public's attention as a national issue until the 1970s and 1980s, when the characteristics of the homeless population and their living arrangements began to change. Throughout the early and middle part of the 20th century, homelessness was typified by "skid rows"—areas with hotels and single-room occupancy dwellings where transient single men lived.[1] Skid rows were usually removed from the more populated areas of cities, and it was uncommon for individuals to actually live on the streets.[2] Beginning in the 1970s, however, the homeless population began to grow and become more visible to the general public. According to studies from the time, homeless persons were no longer almost exclusively single men, but included women with children; their median age was younger; they were more racially diverse (in previous decades the observed homeless population was largely white); they were less likely to be employed (and therefore had lower incomes); they were mentally ill in higher proportions than previously; and individuals who were abusing or had abused drugs began to become more prevalent in the population.[3]

A number of reasons have been offered for the growth in the number of homeless persons and their increasing visibility. Many cities demolished skid rows to make way for urban development, leaving some residents without affordable housing options.[4] Other possible factors contributing to homelessness include the decreased availability of affordable housing generally, the reduced need for seasonal unskilled labor, the reduced likelihood that relatives will accommodate homeless family members, the decreased value of public benefits, and changed admissions standards at

---

[1] Peter H. Rossi, *Down and Out in America: The Origins of Homelessness* (Chicago: The University of Chicago Press, 1989), pp. 20-21, 27-28.
[2] Ibid., p. 34.
[3] Ibid., pp. 39-44.
[4] Ibid., p. 33.

mental hospitals.[5] The increased visibility of homeless people was due, in part, to the decriminalization of actions such as public drunkenness, loitering, and vagrancy.[6]

In the 1980s, Congress first responded to the growing prevalence of homelessness with several separate grant programs designed to address the food and shelter needs of homeless individuals.[7] Then, in 1987, Congress enacted the Stewart B. McKinney Homeless Assistance Act (McKinney Act), which created a number of new programs to comprehensively address the needs of homeless people, including food, shelter, health care, and education (P.L. 100-77). The act was later renamed the McKinney-Vento Homeless Assistance Act (McKinney-Vento) in P.L. 106-400 after its other prominent sponsor, Bruce F. Vento.[8]

Among the programs authorized in the McKinney-Vento Act were four grants to provide housing and related assistance to homeless persons: the Emergency Shelter Grants (ESG) program, the Supportive Housing Demonstration program, the Supplemental Assistance for Facilities to Assist the Homeless (SAFAH) program, and the Section 8 Moderate Rehabilitation Assistance for Single Room Occupancy Dwellings (SRO) program. These four programs, administered by the U.S. Department of Housing and Urban Development (HUD), were created to provide temporary and permanent housing to homeless persons, along with supportive services. Over the years, Congress changed the makeup of the Homeless Assistance Grants, but for 20 years, from 1992 to 2012, the same four grant programs composed the Homeless Assistance Grants. These

---

[5] Ibid., pp. 181-194, 41. See, also, Martha Burt, *Over the Edge: The Growth of Homelessness in the 1980s* (New York: Russell Sage Foundation, 1992), pp. 31-126.

[6] *Down and Out in America*, p. 34; *Over the Edge*, p. 123.

[7] These programs included the Emergency Food and Shelter Program (P.L. 98-8), the Emergency Shelter Grants Program (P.L. 99-591), and the Transitional Housing Demonstration Program (P.L. 99-591). In 1987, all three were incorporated into the Stewart B. McKinney Homeless Assistance Act (P.L. 100-77), although the Transitional Housing Demonstration Program was renamed the Supportive Housing Demonstration Program.

[8] For information about other programs created by the McKinney Act, see CRS Report RL30442, *Homelessness: Targeted Federal Programs*, coordinated by Libby Perl.

were the ESG program, the Supportive Housing Program (SHP), the Shelter Plus Care (S+C) program, and the SRO program.[9]

On May 20, 2009, for the first time since 1992, the Homeless Assistance Grants were reauthorized as part of the Helping Families Save Their Homes Act (P.L. 111-22). The law is often referred to as the "HEARTH Act" after its title in P.L. 111-22 (the Homeless Emergency Assistance and Rapid Transition to Housing Act). The HEARTH Act changed the makeup of the four existing grants—the SHP, S+C, and SRO programs were combined into one grant called the "Continuum of Care" (CoC) program; the ESG program was renamed the "Emergency Solutions Grants"; and rural communities were to have the option of competing for funds under a new Rural Housing Stability Assistance Program (RHS). The way in which the funds are distributed, the purposes for which grantees may use funds, and the people who may be served have also changed. The HEARTH Act authorized the Continuum of Care Program, together with the Emergency Solutions Grants Program, at $2.2 billion in FY2010 and such sums as necessary for FY2011.

Report Organization

In FY2011, HUD first awarded funds under the new ESG program, and FY2012 was the first year that funds were awarded pursuant to the CoC program. New regulations regarding the definition of homelessness became effective on January 5, 2012, and HUD released proposed regulations for the RHS program on March 27, 2013 (with comments due by May 28, 2013). This report has multiple sections describing the implementation of the HEARTH Act provisions. It describes

- the HEARTH Act changes to the definition of homelessness in the section "The Definition of Homelessness";

---

[9] Both the SHP and the SRO program were part of the original McKinney Act in 1987, and the S+C program was added in 1990 as part of the Stewart B. McKinney Homeless Assistance Amendments Act of 1990 (P.L. 101-645).

- the way in which ESG operated prior to HEARTH Act implementation as well as the changes made beginning in FY2011 in the section "The Emergency Solutions Grants Program (ESG)";
- components of the competitive Homeless Assistance Grants prior to enactment of the HEARTH Act, and how they have been absorbed in the CoC program in the section "Transition to the Continuum of Care Program";
- how funds are distributed pursuant to the CoC program in the section "Distribution of Continuum of Care Program Funds"; and
- the housing and services that are authorized to be provided through the RHS program and how communities are to receive funds in the section "Rural Housing Stability Assistance Program."

THE DEFINITION OF HOMELESSNESS

The way in which homelessness is defined is an important part of how the Homeless Assistance Grants operate, as it determines who communities may assist with the grants they receive. The definition had been the subject of debate for a number of years, with some finding that the definition governing the HUD homeless programs was too restrictive when compared to definitions used in other federal programs that assist those experiencing homelessness.

Until enactment of the HEARTH Act, "homeless individual" was defined in Section 103(a) of the McKinney-Vento Act as

> (1) an individual who lacks a fixed, regular, and adequate nighttime residence; and (2) an individual who has a primary nighttime residence that is—(A) a supervised publicly or privately operated shelter designed to provide temporary living accommodations (including welfare hotels, congregate shelters, and transitional housing for the mentally ill); (B) an institution that provides a temporary residence for individuals intended to be institutionalized; or (C) a public or private place not designed for, or ordinarily used as, a regular sleeping accommodation for human beings.

This definition was sometimes described as requiring one to be literally homeless in order to meet its requirements[10]—either living in emergency accommodations or having no place to stay.

The HEARTH Act expanded the definition of "homeless individual,"[11] and on December 5, 2011, HUD issued final regulations clarifying aspects of the HEARTH Act definition of homelessness.[12] The regulation took effect on January 4, 2012. The HEARTH Act retained the original language of the definition with some minor changes, but also added provisions that move away from the requirement for literal homelessness and toward housing instability as a form of homelessness. Each subsection below explains separate ways in which the HEARTH Act changed the definition of homelessness.

The Original McKinney-Vento Act Language

The HEARTH Act made minor changes to the existing language in the McKinney-Vento Act. The law continues to provide that a person is homeless if they lack "a fixed, regular, and adequate nighttime residence," and if their nighttime residence is a place not meant for human habitation, if they live in a shelter, or if they are a person leaving an institution who had been homeless prior to being institutionalized. The HEARTH Act added that those living in hotels or motels paid for by a government entity or charitable organization are considered homeless, and it included all those persons living in transitional housing, not just those residing in transitional housing for the mentally ill as in prior law. The amended law also added locations that are not considered suitable places for people to sleep, including cars, parks, abandoned buildings, bus or train stations, airports, and campgrounds.

---

[10] See, for example, the Department of Housing and Urban Development, *The Third Annual Homeless Assessment Report to Congress*, July 2008, p. 2, footnote 5, http://www.hudhre.info/documents/ 3rdHomelessAssessmentReport.pdf.
[11] 42 U.S.C. §11302.
[12] U.S. Department of Housing and Urban Development, "Homeless Emergency Assistance and Rapid Transition to Housing: Defining "Homeless"," 76 *Federal Register* 75994-76019, December 5, 2011.

When HUD issued its final regulation in December 2011, it clarified that a person exiting an institution cannot have been residing there for more than 90 days and still be considered homeless.[13] In addition, where the law states that a person "who resided in a shelter or place not meant for human habitation" prior to institutionalization, the "shelter" means emergency shelter, and does not include transitional housing.[14]

Imminent Loss of Housing

P.L. 111-22 added to the current definition those individuals and families who meet all of the following criteria:

- They will "imminently lose their housing," whether it be their own housing, housing they are sharing with others, or a hotel or motel not paid for by a government or charitable entity. Imminent loss of housing is evidenced by an eviction requiring an individual or family to leave their housing within 14 days; a lack of resources that would allow an individual or family to remain in a hotel or motel for more than 14 days; or credible evidence that an individual or family would not be able to stay with another homeowner or renter for more than 14 days.
- They have no subsequent residence identified.
- They lack the resources or support networks needed to obtain other permanent housing.

HUD practice prior to passage of the HEARTH Act was to consider individuals and families who would imminently lose housing within seven days to be homeless.

---

[13] Ibid., p. 76000.
[14] Ibid.

Other Federal Definitions

P.L. 111-22 added to the definition of "homeless individual" unaccompanied youth and homeless families with children who are defined as homeless under other federal statutes. The law did not define the term youth, so in its final regulations HUD defined a youth as someone under the age of 25.[15] In addition, the HEARTH Act did not specify which other federal statutes would be included in defining homeless families with children and unaccompanied youth. In its regulations, HUD listed seven other federal programs as those under which youth or families with children can be defined as homeless: the Runaway and Homeless Youth program; Head Start; the Violence Against Women Act; the Healthcare for the Homeless program; the Supplemental Nutrition Assistance Program (SNAP); the Women, Infants, and Children nutrition program; and the McKinney-Vento Education for Children and Youth program.[16]

Five of these seven programs (all but Runaway and Homeless Youth and Health Care for the Homeless programs) either share the Education for Homeless Children and Youths definition, or use a very similar definition.

- The Department of Education defines homeless children and youth in part by reference to the Section 103 definition of homeless individuals as those lacking a fixed, regular, and adequate nighttime residence.[17] In addition, however, the ED program defines children and youth who are eligible for services to include those who are (1) sharing housing with other persons due to loss of housing or economic hardship; (2) living in hotels or motels, trailer parks, or campgrounds due to lack of alternative arrangements; (3) awaiting foster care placement; (4) living in substandard housing; and (5) children of migrant workers.[18]

---

[15] Ibid., p. 75996.
[16] Ibid.
[17] 42 U.S.C. §11434a.
[18] Migratory children are defined at 20 U.S.C. §6399.

- The Runaway and Homeless Youth program defines a homeless youth as either ages 16 to 22 (for transitional housing) or ages 18 and younger (for short-term shelter) and for whom it is not possible to live in a safe environment with a relative or for whom there is no other safe alternative living arrangement.[19]
- Under the Health Care for the Homeless program, a homeless individual is one who "lacks housing," and the definition includes those living in a private or publicly operated temporary living facility or in transitional housing.[20]

Youth and families who are defined as homeless under another federal program must meet each of the following criteria:

- They have experienced a long-term period without living independently in permanent housing. In its final regulation, HUD defined "long-term period" to mean at least 60 days.
- They have experienced instability as evidenced by frequent moves during this long-term period, defined by HUD to mean at least two moves during the 60 days prior to applying for assistance.[21]
- The youth or families with children can be expected to continue in unstable housing due to factors such as chronic disabilities, chronic physical health or mental health conditions, substance addiction, histories of domestic violence or childhood abuse, the presence of a child or youth with a disability, or multiple barriers to employment. Under the final regulation, barriers to employment may include the lack of a high school degree, illiteracy, lack of English proficiency, a history of incarceration, or a history of unstable employment.[22]

---

[19] 42 U.S.C. §5732a(3).
[20] 42 U.S.C. §254b(h)(5)(A).
[21] 76 *Federal Register* 76017.
[22] Ibid.

Communities are limited to using not more than 10% of Continuum of Care program funds to serve individuals and families defined as homeless under other federal statutes unless the community has a rate of homelessness less than one-tenth of 1% of the total population.[23]

Domestic Violence

Another change to the definition of homeless individual was added as subsection 103(b) to McKinney-Vento. The law now considers to be homeless anyone who is fleeing a situation of "domestic violence, dating violence, sexual assault, stalking, or other dangerous or life-threatening conditions in the individual's or family's current housing situation, including where the health and safety of children are jeopardized."[24] The law also provides that an individual must lack the resources or support network to find another housing situation. The final regulation issued by HUD in December 2011 specified that the conditions either must have occurred at the primary nighttime residence or made the individual or family afraid to return to their residence.[25]

Documenting Homeless Status

For the first time, the regulations governing the Homeless Assistance Grants specify how housing and service providers should verify the homeless status of the individuals and families that they serve. (Previously, guidance had been provided in program handbooks.) The final regulations issued in December 2011 create different requirements depending both on the part of the statutory definition under which individuals or families find themselves homeless as well as the type of service provided. In general, it is preferred that service providers have third party documentation that an

---

[23] 42 U.S.C. §11382(j).
[24] 42 U.S.C. §11302(b).
[25] 76 *Federal Register* 76014.

individual or family is homeless (such as an eviction order or verification from a family member with whom a homeless individual or family had lived). However, under some circumstances, it may also be acceptable to confirm homelessness based on intake worker observation or certification from the person or head of household who is homeless.[26] Where someone is seeking assistance at an emergency shelter, through a street outreach program, or from a victim service provider, failure to separately verify homeless status should not prevent an individual or family from receiving immediate assistance.

Definition of Chronically Homeless Person

P.L. 111-22 also expanded the definition of "chronically homeless person," which had been defined in regulation.[27] Under the regulation, the term had been defined as an *unaccompanied individual* who has been homeless continuously for one year or on four or more occasions in the last three years, and who has a disability.[28] A regulation released by HUD on December 4, 2015 (and effective January 4, 2016) clarifies that four or more occasions of homelessness in the last three years must total at least 12 months, with at least seven nights separating each occasion.[29]

The HEARTH Act added to the definition of chronically homeless those homeless *families* with an adult head of household (or youth where no adult is present) who has a disability. The definition of disability specifically includes post traumatic stress disorder and traumatic brain injury. Note, however, that to be considered chronically homeless, an

---

[26] Ibid., p. 76017.
[27] 24 C.F.R. §91.5.
[28] In proposed regulations, HUD has elaborated on the chronic homelessness definition to specify that the periods of homelessness over a three-year period add up to at least a year. See U.S. Department of Housing and Urban Development, "Homeless Emergency Assistance and Rapid Transition to Housing: Rural Housing Stability Assistance Program and Revisions to the Definition of "Chronically Homeless"; Proposed Rule," 78 *Federal Register* 18729, March 27, 2013.
[29] U.S. Department of Housing and Urban Development, "Homeless Emergency Assistance and Rapid Transition to Housing: Defining "Chronically Homeless"," 80 *Federal Register* 75791, December 4, 2015.

individual or family has to be living in a place not meant for human habitation, a safe haven, or an emergency shelter; the HEARTH Act's changes to the definition of "homeless individual" do not apply to chronic homelessness. In addition, a person released from an institution will be considered chronically homeless as long as, prior to entering the institution, they otherwise met the definition of chronically homeless person, and had been institutionalized for fewer than 90 days. HUD began using the new definition in its administration of the Homeless Assistance Grants as part of the FY2010 competition.[30]

THE EMERGENCY SOLUTIONS GRANTS PROGRAM (ESG)

The Emergency Solutions Grants, until enactment of the HEARTH Act known as the Emergency Shelter Grants, was the first of the Homeless Assistance Grants to be authorized. It was established one year prior to enactment of McKinney-Vento as part of the Continuing Appropriations Act for FY1987 (P.L. 99-591).[31] Funds are distributed to grantee states and local communities to assist those experiencing homelessness (see the next section for information on how funds are distributed). From its creation through FY2010, the funds distributed through the ESG program were provided primarily for the emergency shelter and service needs of homeless persons. However, when the ESG program was reauthorized as part of the HEARTH Act (P.L. 111-22), it not only changed its name, but the focus of the program was broadened to include an expanded role for homelessness prevention and rapid rehousing (assistance to quickly find permanent housing for individuals or families who find themselves homeless). On December 5, 2011, HUD issued interim regulations for the

---

[30] See U.S. Department of Housing and Urban Development, *FY2010 Notice of Funding Availability (NOFA) for the Continuum of Care Homeless Assistance Program*, September 14, 2010, p. 6, http://archives.hud.gov/funding/2010/ cocsec.pdf.

[31] The ESG program was initially part of H.R. 5313, which was incorporated into H.Rept. 99-1005, the Conference Report to accompany H.J.Res. 738, which became P.L. 99-591.

ESG program, and they became effective on January 4, 2012.[32] Funding for the program's new purposes was made available as part of a second round of funding in FY2011.[33] In FY2012 and thereafter, all funds awarded could be used for the ESG program activities as authorized by the HEARTH Act.

Eligible Activities Prior to Enactment of the HEARTH Act

Prior to enactment of the HEARTH Act, ESG funds could be used for four main purposes: (1) the renovation, major rehabilitation, or conversion of buildings into emergency shelters; (2) services such as employment counseling, health care, and education; (3) homelessness prevention activities such as assistance with rent or utility payments; and (4) operational and administrative expenses.[34] States and communities that received ESG funds were limited to using not more than 30% of the total ESG funds they received for services, not more than 30% for homelessness prevention activities, not more than 10% for staff costs, and not more than 5% for administrative costs.

Additional Eligible Activities after Enactment of the HEARTH Act

As amended by the HEARTH Act, ESG allows grantees to use a greater share of funds for homelessness prevention and rapid rehousing. Specifically, funds may be used for short- or medium-term rental assistance (tenant- or project-based) and housing relocation and

---

[32] U.S. Department of Housing and Urban Development, "Homeless Emergency Assistance and Rapid Transition to Housing: Emergency Solutions Grants Program and Consolidated Plan Conforming Amendments," 76 *Federal Register* 75954-75994, December 5, 2011.

[33] For a list of grantees and the amount received by each in both the first and second rounds of funding, see http://hudhre.info/documents/FY2011ESGAllocation2_11.15.2011.pdf.

[34] 42 U.S.C. §11374(a)(1)-(4).

stabilization services for individuals and families who are homeless or at risk of homelessness.

At Risk of Homelessness

The law defines the term "at risk of homelessness" to include an individual or family with income at or below 30% of area median income and who has insufficient resources to attain housing stability. An individual or family must also meet one of the following conditions:[35]

- have moved for economic reasons at least twice during the last 60 days;
- are living with someone else due to economic hardship;
- have been notified in writing that their current housing will be terminated within 21 days;
- are living in a hotel or motel not paid for by a government or charitable entity;
- are living in overcrowded housing (more than 2 persons in an efficiency unit or more than 1.5 people per room otherwise);
- are leaving an institution such as a health or mental health care facility, foster care, or correctional facility; or
- are living in a housing situation that is unstable in some other way.

In addition, families with children and youth defined as homeless under other federal statutes are considered "at risk" of homelessness. As with the definition of homelessness generally, the other federal programs under which children and youth may be considered homeless are the Runaway and Homeless Youth program; Head Start; the Violence Against Women Act; the Healthcare for the Homeless program; the Supplemental Nutrition Assistance Program (SNAP); the Women, Infants, and Children nutrition program; and the McKinney Vento Education for Homeless Children and Youth program.[36] Under the updated ESG program in the

---

[35] While defined in law at 42 U.S.C. §11360, the ESG regulations provide additional detail about what it means to be at risk of homelessness. See 76 *Federal Register* 75974.
[36] 76 *Federal Register* 75974.

HEARTH Act, the amount of funds that grant recipients can use for emergency shelter and related supportive services are limited to the greater of 60% of their ESG allocation or the amount they had used prior to enactment of the HEARTH Act for emergency shelter and related services.

Funding for the ESG Program

Until enactment of P.L. 111-22, the allocation of funds for ESG had not exceeded $160 million in all the years of the program's existence. The HEARTH Act provided that 20% of funds made available by Congress for the Homeless Assistance Grants would go to the newly named program (traditionally, HUD had reserved somewhere between 10% and 15% of funds for the ESG program). However, in appropriations laws since enactment of the HEARTH Act, Congress has not required HUD to allocate 20% of funds to ESG, and has instead specified a dollar amount for ESG, which has ranged from $215 million to $286 million.[37] The percentage of funds that recipients can use for administrative costs also changed pursuant to the HEARTH Act. Prior to its enactment, recipients could use up to 5% of their grants for administrative costs. This was raised to 7.5% by the HEARTH Act.[38]

Distribution of ESG Funds

ESG funds are distributed to both local communities (called "entitlement areas" and defined as metropolitan cities and urban counties)[39]

---

[37] For example, the FY2011 appropriations law specified that at least $225 million be set aside for ESG; the FY2012 appropriations law, not less than $250 million; the FY2013 appropriations law, not less than $200 million; and the FY2014 through FY2016 laws, not less than $250 million. HUD provided $250 million for ESG in FY2011 (13% of total Homeless Assistance Grant funding), $286 million in FY2012 (15%), $215 million in FY2013 (11%), $250 million in FY2014 (12%), $266 million in FY2015 (12%), and $270 million in FY2016 (12%).

[38] 42 U.S.C. §11378.

[39] See 42 U.S.C. 11373(a), which refers to the statute governing the Community Development Block Grant program at 42 U.S.C. §§5302(a)(4)-(6). A metropolitan city is the central city within a metropolitan statistical area, or a city of 50,000 or more within a metropolitan

and states (called "non-entitlement areas") for distribution in communities that do not receive funds directly, through the Community Development Block Grant (CDBG) program formula.[40] Puerto Rico is considered a state and its cities are entitlement areas under the CDBG formula, and the District of Columbia is also an entitlement area. The four territories of Guam, the Commonwealth of the Northern Mariana Islands, the U.S. Virgin Islands, and American Samoa also receive ESG funds. The interim regulations governing ESG changed the allocations to these four territories, however. Previously, regulations provided that the four territories receive 0.2% of total funds, but the interim regulations provide that the territories receive "up to 0.2 percent, but not less than 0.1 percent" of the ESG allocation.[41] Funds are then distributed among the four territories based on population.[42] Tribes do not receive funds through ESG; instead, funds for homeless assistance are distributed through the Indian Community Development Block Grant.[43]

The CDBG program formula is meant to distribute funds based on a community's need for development; the ESG program has used the CDBG formula to target funds for homeless assistance since its inception, and the HEARTH Act did not alter this part of the law. The formula awards funds to metropolitan cities and urban counties (70% of funds) and to the states for use in areas that do not receive funds directly (30% of funds).[44]

As a condition for receiving ESG funds, states and communities must present HUD with a consolidated plan explaining how they will address community development needs within their jurisdictions.

---

statistical area, and an urban county is a county within a metropolitan area that has a population of 200,000 or more, or 100,000 or more if the county contains no incorporated areas.

[40] For more information about CDBG, see CRS Report R43208, *Community Development Block Grants: Funding Issues in the 113th Congress*, by Eugene Boyd.
[41] 76 *Federal Register* 75975.
[42] Ibid.
[43] U.S. Department of Housing and Urban Development, *Emergency Shelter Grants Program FY2008 Operating Instructions*, October 2008, p. 2, http://www.hudhre.info/documents/ESG_OperatingInstructions_2008.pdf.
[44] 42 U.S.C. §§5306(a) - (d).

The consolidated plan is required in order for communities to participate in four different HUD grant programs, including ESG.[45] The plan is a community's description of how it hopes to integrate decent housing, community needs, and economic needs of low- and moderate-income residents over a three- to five-year time span.[46] Consolidated plans are intended to be collaborative efforts of local government officials, representatives of for-profit and non-profit organizations, and community members. HUD may disapprove a community's consolidated plan with respect to one or more programs, although communities have 45 days to change their plans to satisfy HUD's requirements.[47] If HUD disapproves the ESG portion of the plan, the applicant community will not receive ESG funds.

If HUD approves a community's consolidated plan, the community will receive ESG funds based on its share of CDBG funds from the previous fiscal year. However, the community must have received at least 0.05% of the total CDBG allocation in order to qualify to receive ESG funds.[48] In cases where a community would receive less than 0.05% of the total ESG allocation, its share of funds goes to the state to be used in areas that do not receive their own ESG funds.[49] In FY2016, more than 360 states, cities, counties, and territories received ESG funds.[50]

After the recipient states and entitlement communities receive their ESG funds, they distribute them to local government entities, nonprofit organizations, public housing authorities, and local redevelopment

---

[45] The other programs are the Community Development Block Grant program, the HOME program, and the Housing Opportunities for Persons with AIDS (HOPWA) program. For more information about CDBG, see CRS Report R43520, *Community Development Block Grants and Related Programs: A Primer*, by Eugene Boyd, for HOME, see CRS Report R40118, *An Overview of the HOME Investment Partnerships Program*, by Katie Jones, and for HOPWA, see CRS Report RL34318, *Housing for Persons Living with HIV/AIDS*, by Libby Perl.
[46] 24 C.F.R. §91.1(a).
[47] 24 C.F.R. §91.500.
[48] 42 U.S.C. §11373.
[49] 42 U.S.C. §11373(b).
[50] HUD Office of Community Development, https://portal.hud.gov/hudportal/HUD?src=/program_offices/comm_planning/about/budget/budget16.

authorities that provide services to homeless persons.[51] These recipient organizations have been previously determined by the state or local government through an application process in which organizations submit proposals—HUD is not involved in this process. Each recipient organization must match the federal ESG funds dollar for dollar.[52] States need not match the first $100,000 that they receive, and the match does not apply to the territories.[53] The match may include funding from other federal sources and be met through the value of donated buildings, the lease value of buildings, salary paid to staff, and volunteer time.[54]

TRANSITION TO THE CONTINUUM OF CARE PROGRAM

The bulk of the funding for the Homeless Assistance Grants is awarded as competitive grants through what is now the CoC program.[55] The CoC program differs from ESG in that it focuses on the longer-term housing and services needs of homeless individuals and families. For the 20 years prior to creation of the CoC program, there were three separate competitive grants, each of which provided different services to different populations. Enactment of the HEARTH Act brought each of the three programs' functions under the umbrella of the CoC program. The programs were

- The Supportive Housing Program (SHP): The SHP provided funds for transitional housing for homeless individuals and families for up to 24 months, permanent housing for homeless individuals with disabilities, and supportive services. Eligible recipients were states, local government entities, Public Housing Authorities (PHAs),

---

[51] Until 2016, only governmental entities and private nonprofit organizations were eligible subgrantees of ESG funds. The Housing Opportunity Through Modernization Act (P.L. 114-201) added public housing authorities and local redevelopment authorities as eligible subgrantees.
[52] 42 U.S.C. §11375(a).
[53] 76 *Federal Register* 75982.
[54] 42 U.S.C. §11375(a).
[55] In FY2015, about 90% of the total amount of funds appropriated for the grant programs was set aside for the CoC program.

private nonprofit organizations, and community mental health centers. Grantees were required to meet different match requirements: acquisition, rehabilitation, or new construction with an equal amount of the grant recipient's own funds, supportive services with a 20% match, and operating expenses with a 25% match.

- The Single Room Occupancy Program (SRO): The Single Room Occupancy (SRO) program provided permanent housing to homeless individuals in efficiency units similar to dormitories, with single bedrooms, community bathrooms, and kitchen facilities. The SRO program did not require residents to have a disability and did not fund supportive services. Eligible recipients were PHAs and private nonprofit organizations. The program did not have a match requirement.
- The Shelter Plus Care (S+C) Program: The S+C program provided permanent supportive housing through rent subsidies for homeless individuals with disabilities and their families. The S+C rent subsidies could be tenant-based vouchers, project-based rental assistance, sponsor-based rental assistance, or single room occupancy housing. Eligible recipients were states, local government entities, and PHAs. The S+C program required grant recipients to match the amount of grant funds they received for rental assistance with an equal amount of funds for supportive services.

(For a more detailed description of the three programs, see the Appendix.) Applicants no longer apply for one of the three existing grants—S+C, SHP, or SRO—based on the type of housing and services they want to provide.

Instead, the new consolidated grant provides funds for all permanent housing, transitional housing, supportive services, and rehousing activities.

The Continuum of Care and Collaborative Applicants

The terminology surrounding the Continuum of Care program can be confusing. For years the term "Continuum of Care" has been used to describe three different things: (1) the way in which communities plan their response to the needs of homeless persons, (2) the local communities themselves (typically cities, counties, and combinations of both) that collaborate to arrive at a plan to address homelessness and apply to HUD for funds, and (3) the HUD process through which service providers apply for HUD funds.[56] With the advent of the HEARTH Act, the term "Continuum of Care" is also used to refer to the main program through which HUD funds homeless services providers.

Through the CoC strategy, which remains largely the same under the HEARTH Act, local communities establish CoC advisory boards made up of representatives from local government agencies, service providers, community members, and formerly homeless individuals who meet to establish local priorities and strategies to address homelessness in their communities. The CoC plan that results from this process is meant to contain elements that address the continuum of needs of homeless persons: prevention of homelessness, emergency shelter, transitional housing, permanent housing, and supportive services provided at all stages of housing.[57] The CoC system was created in 1993 as the Innovative Homeless Initiatives Demonstration Program, a grant program that

---

[56] Since the FY1996 grant application process for the competitive Homeless Assistance Grants, the CoC system has also been the vehicle through which local service providers apply for HUD competitive grants. See U.S. Department of Housing and Urban Development, "Continuum of Care Homeless Assistance; Funding Availability," *Federal Register* vol. 61, no. 52, March 15, 1996, pp. 10865-10877. The development of the Continuum of Care system is described in *Priority: Home! The Federal Plan to Break the Cycle of Homelessness*, The U.S. Department of Housing and Urban Development, 1994, pp. 73-75.

[57] Barnard-Columbia Center for Urban Policy, *The Continuum of Care: A Report on the New Federal Policy to Address Homelessness*, U.S. Department of Housing and Urban Development, December 1996, p. 9.

provided funding to communities so that they could become more cohesive in their approach to serving homeless people.[58] Since then, nearly every community in the country has become part of a CoC, with more than 400 CoCs, including those in the territories, covering most of the country.[59]

The HEARTH Act also codified the process by which the Continuum of Care body established at the community level coordinates the process of applying for CoC program funds. However, the name HUD gives to the *applicant* for the CoC program is "Collaborative Applicant."[60] The Collaborative Applicant may be any entity eligible to apply for CoC program funds, including the Continuum of Care itself. In addition, a Collaborative Applicant may choose to apply for status as a Unified Funding Agency (UFA) to apply for CoC program funds. The difference between a Collaborative Applicant and a Unified Funding Agency is that a UFA is a legal entity that has the capacity to receive CoC program funds from HUD and distribute them to each grant awardee.[61]

Features of the Continuum of Care Program

The CoC program maintains many of the aspects of the prior competitive grants, but also implements new features.[62] Below is a description of a number of aspects of the CoC program, and, where relevant, comparisons to the three programs that came before (SHP, S+C, and SRO).

---

[58] See U.S. Department of Housing and Urban Development, "Funding Availability for Fiscal Year 1994 for Innovative Project Funding Under the Innovative Homeless Initiatives Demonstration Program," *Federal Register* vol. 58, no. 243, December 21, 1993, pp. 67616-67618.

[59] "HUD-Defined CoC Names and Numbers Listed by State," Revised March 2015, https://www.hudexchange.info/resources/documents/fy-2015-continuums-of-care-names-and-numbers.pdf.

[60] 42 U.S.C. §11360(3).

[61] 42 U.S.C. §11360a(g).

[62] U.S. Department of Housing and Urban Development, "Homeless Emergency Assistance and Rapid Transition to Housing: Continuum of Care Program," 77 *Federal Register* 45422-45467, July 31, 2012.

> **Status of CoC Program Regulations**
>
> On July 31, 2012, HUD published interim regulations for the CoC program.[63] The regulations are in effect until final regulations, taking into account public comments, are published. The comment period for the interim regulations closed on November 16, 2012.[64] HUD has not yet published final regulations, and while HUD has stated that it will reopen the comment period to take account of grantee experiences in implementing the program, this has not yet happened.[65] Congress, as part of the Housing Opportunity Through Modernization Act (P.L. 114-201), directed HUD to reopen the CoC program comment period within 30 days of the law's enactment. The law was enacted on July 29, 2016. HUD reopened the CoC program interim rule for the limited purpose of proposing a new CoC formula on July 25, 2016.

Eligible Applicants

The entities eligible to administer most activities remain the same under the CoC program as under the three previous programs. These are states, local governments, instrumentalities of state or local governments (an entity created pursuant to state statute for a public purpose), PHAs, and nonprofit organizations.[66] In the HEARTH Act, entities that may administer rental assistance were initially limited to states, units of local government (e.g., cities, towns, or counties), and PHAs. However, Congress, as part of the Fixing America's Surface Transportation Act (P.L.

---

[63] U.S. Department of Housing and Urban Development, "Homeless Emergency Assistance and Rapid Transition to Housing: Continuum of Care Program: Extension of Public Comment Period," 77 *Federal Register* 59543, September 28, 2012.

[64] *Letter from Ann Oliva [Director, Office of Special Needs Assistance Programs] to Grant Recipients, CoC Leaders and Stakeholders*, July 2014, https://www.hudexchange. info/resources/documents/letter-from-ann-oliva-to-grantrecipients-coc-leaders-and-stakeholders-fy-2014.pdf.

[65] References to the Code of Federal Regulations in this section refer to Continuum of Care interim program regulations published in the Federal Register on July 31, 2012, 77 *Federal Register* 45422-45467.

[66] Note that while the CoC interim rule did not explicitly make PHAs eligible, HUD has clarified that they are eligible and that this will be clear in the final rule. See Frequently Asked Questions, "All PHAs that meet the definition of "public housing agency" in 24 C.F.R. 5.100 are eligible to apply for CoC funding (including as Collaborative Applicants) without limitation or exclusion. The CoC final rule and the CoC Fiscal Year 2012 Notice of Funding Availability (NOFA) will make explicit the eligibility of all PHAs to apply for CoC funding. Additionally, all PHAs that are current grantees may apply for renewal funding under the CoC Program."

114-94), allowed private nonprofit organizations to administer rental assistance.

Program Components and Eligible Costs

The CoC program, like those before it, consists of both program components—the types of services that grantees provide, such as permanent housing and supportive services—and the costs that CoCs incur to operate each component (e.g., entering into leases and rental assistance contracts, paying operating and administrative costs, etc.). This section discusses what CoC program grantees do, and the specific costs that go into operating each component.

Eligible Program Components

Under the CoC program, most of the program components continue to be the same as those funded under the predecessor programs. However, they are consolidated so that applicants need only apply for CoC program funds rather than one of three programs based on services provided.

- Transitional Housing: Transitional housing is housing available for up to 24 months to help homeless individuals and families transition from homelessness to permanent housing. Prior to enactment of the CoC program, transitional housing was provided through the SHP program.
- Permanent Housing: As its name indicates, the statute governing the CoC program provides that permanent housing is not time limited and may be provided with or without supportive services.[67] However, HUD, when it released interim CoC program regulations, set out two types of permanent housing that grantees may provide, refining the definition.
    - *Permanent Supportive Housing:* Pursuant to the regulations, grantees may provide permanent housing with supportive

---

[67] 42 U.S.C. §11360(15).

services to individuals with disabilities and families where an adult or child has a disability.[68]

- o *Rapid Rehousing:* The CoC program regulations allow permanent housing assistance to be provided in the context of rapid rehousing.[69] Rapid rehousing is a process targeted to assist homeless individuals and families through supportive services together with rental assistance. The hope is that, after a period of time with assistance, those experiencing homelessness will be able to maintain permanent housing on their own. Grantees may pay for short-term rental assistance (up to three months) and medium-term rental assistance (from 3 to 24 months).
- Supportive Services: The statute continues to allow the CoC program to fund an array of supportive services for homeless individuals and families.[70] The statute, augmented by the interim regulations, lists a number of authorized services. The services include case management, child care, education services, employment assistance and job training, housing search, life skills training, legal services, mental health services, outpatient health services, substance abuse treatment, transportation, and payment of moving costs and utility deposits.[71] Note, however, that a decreasing share of CoC program funds pays for supportive services. See Table 2.
- Homeless Management Information Systems (HMIS): Homeless Management Information Systems are databases established at the local level through which homeless service providers collect, organize, and store information about homeless clients who receive

---

[68] 24 C.F.R. §578.37 at 77 *Federal Register* 45450.
[69] Ibid.
[70] 42 U.S.C. §11383(a)(6). In addition to being available to individuals and families who are experiencing homelessness, supportive services are available to formerly homeless individuals and families who are living in permanent supportive housing indefinitely and those who are living in permanent housing (but not *supportive* housing) for up to six months after finding housing.
[71] 42 U.S.C. §11360(27), 24 C.F.R. §578.53 at 77 *Federal Register* 45453.

services. Prior to implementation of the HEARTH Act, communities could use SHP grants to pay for HMIS.

Eligible Costs

In the three predecessor programs to the CoC program, the methods through which grantees provided housing and services to homeless individuals (e.g., through rental assistance, construction of housing, etc.) varied based on the particular program. In the CoC program, the relevant ways of providing assistance remain the same, but there is not the same limitation based on program type.

Resident Contributions Toward Housing Costs

HUD's interim regulations for the CoC program (24 C.F.R. §578.77) set out requirements for resident contributions toward rent.

Grant recipients that sublease housing to homeless residents may charge residents for their occupancy, though they do not have to. If an occupancy charge is imposed, then it cannot exceed the greater of 30% of adjusted income, 10% of gross income, or, if a family receives welfare benefits, the portion of the benefit designated for housing costs. Residents that receive rental assistance (rather than live in leased housing) must pay rent based on 30% of adjusted income, 10% of gross income, or welfare rent.

- Acquisition, Rehabilitation, and Construction: CoC program funds can services for homeless individuals.[72] Funds can be used for construction of housing for those who are homeless (but not for a facility that would only provide supportive services).[73] These were eligible uses of funds under SHP.
- Leasing: Funds can be used to lease property in which housing and/or supportive services are made available to homeless individuals and families.[74] Grant recipients must enter into

---

[72] 42 U.S.C. §11383(a)(2). The interim regulations are at 24 C.F.R. §578.43 and §578.45, 77 *Federal Register* 45451.
[73] 42 U.S.C. §11383(a)(1), 24 C.F.R. §578.47 at 77 *Federal Register* 45451-45452.
[74] 42 U.S.C. §11383(a)(3), 24 C.F.R. §578.49 at 77 *Federal Register* 45452.

occupancy agreements or subleases with program participants, and they may impose an occupancy charge.[75] As in the SHP program, leases for housing may be for transitional or permanent housing.
- Rental Assistance: Similar to the S+C program, the HEARTH Act provides that grantees may use CoC funds for tenant-based rental assistance, project-based rental assistance, and sponsor-based rental assistance.[76] Eligible grantees are states, units of local government, Public Housing Authorities, and private nonprofit organizations.[77] With tenant-based vouchers, residents find private market housing much as they would with a Section 8 voucher; project-based assistance is provided to building owners and attached to specific units of housing (unlike a portable voucher); with sponsor-based assistance, grant recipients contract with private nonprofit housing providers or community mental health centers to provide housing. Unlike S+C, however, tenant-based rental assistance may be provided for a limited duration as rapid rehousing.[78] It can be short term (up to 3 months) or medium term (between 3 and 24 months).[79] Rental assistance may also be used for permanent housing without a time limit. Residents must pay a portion of rent in accordance with HUD rules.[80]
- Personnel Costs of Supportive Services: Grantees that provide supportive services themselves (versus contracting with outside service providers) may use CoC program funds to pay the salaries and benefits costs of staff who provide services.[81]

---

[75] 24 C.F.R. §578.77 at 77 *Federal Register* 45458.
[76] 42 U.S.C. §11383(a)(4), 24 C.F.R. §578.51 at 77 *Federal Register* 45452.
[77] Private nonprofit organizations were not initially authorized to provide rental assistance pursuant to the HEARTH Act. However, Congress amended the law as part of the Fixing America's Surface Transportation Act (P.L. 114-94) to make nonprofit organizations eligible. This brought current practice in line with what had occurred unofficially prior to the HEARTH Act.
[78] 24 C.F.R. §578.37(a)(1)(ii) at 77 *Federal Register* 45450.
[79] 24 C.F.R. §578.37(a)(1)(ii) at 77 *Federal Register* 45450.
[80] 24 C.F.R. §578.77 at 77 *Federal Register* 45458.
[81] 24 C.F.R. §578.53(e)(17) at 77 *Federal Register* 45455.

- Operating Costs: Grantees may use operating funds for transitional housing, permanent housing,[82] and facilities that provide supportive services.[83] Costs may include maintenance, taxes and insurance, reserves for replacement of major systems, security, utilities, furniture, and equipment. Funds may not be used for operating costs in cases where a property already receives rental assistance.[84]
- Administrative Costs: The percentage of funds that may be used for administrative costs increased for the CoC program compared to the three predecessor programs.
  - Individual grantees may use up to 10% of their grants for administrative expenses.[85] Administrative expenses include administrative staff salaries (as outlined in the regulations), administrative supplies, and Continuum of Care training, among other things.[86] Prior to enactment of the CoC program, SHP grant recipients could use 5% of funds for administrative purposes, and S+C recipients could use 8% of funds.[87]
  - Collaborative Applicants may use up to 3% of CoC funds for administrative expenses related to the application process for HUD funds.[88]
  - Collaborative Applicants that have the status of Unified Funding Agencies, and are able to receive and distribute the CoC program funds awarded to the Continuum of Care, may use an additional 3% of funds for fund distribution, ensuring that grant recipients develop fiscal control and accounting

---

[82] 42 U.S.C. §11383(a)(5).
[83] 24 C.F.R. §578.53(a) at 77 *Federal Register* 45453.
[84] 24 C.F.R. §578.55 at 77 *Federal Register* 45455.
[85] 42 U.S.C. §11383(a)(12).
[86] 24 C.F.R. §578.59 at 77 *Federal Register* 45455-45456.
[87] The SHP and S+C regulations set limits for administrative costs. These were at 24 C.F.R. §583.135 and 24 C.F.R. §582.105. SRO funding was through the project-based Section 8 program and PHAs received administrative expenses as part of the Housing Assistance Payments contract.
[88] 42 U.S.C. §11383(a)(10).

procedures, and arranging for annual audits or evaluations of each project.[89]

Incentives and Bonuses

The HEARTH Act expanded the way in which competitive grant funds can be used by giving more flexibility to communities that are successful in reducing homelessness.

High-Performing Communities

The HEARTH Act instituted a new program to allow certain high-performing communities to have greater flexibility in the way that they use their funds.[90] A Collaborative Applicant will be designated high-performing if the Continuum of Care it represents meets all requirements regarding[91]

1) the average length of homelessness in their communities (fewer than 20 days or a reduction of 10% from preceding year),
2) repeat instances of homelessness (less than 5% of those who leave homelessness become homeless again in the next two years or a 20% reduction in repeat episodes),
3) submission of data (80% of housing and service providers submit data to Homeless Management Information Systems),
4) outcomes among homeless families and youth defined as homeless under other federal programs (95% do not become homeless again within a two-year period and 85% achieve independent living in permanent housing),
5) comprehensive outreach plans (all communities within a CoC have an outreach plan), and
6) success in preventing homelessness for communities previously designated high-performing.

---

[89] 42 U.S.C. §11383(a)(11).
[90] 42 U.S.C. §11384.
[91] 42 U.S.C. §11384(d), 24 C.F.R. §578.65 at 77 *Federal Register* 45456-45457.

Collaborative Applicants designated high-performing will be able to use their grant awards for any eligible activity under the CoC program as well as for rental assistance or rapid rehousing to assist those at risk of homelessness.[92]

Incentives for Proven Strategies to Reduce Homelessness

Continuums of Care are to ensure that certain percentages of funds are used to provide permanent supportive housing for those experiencing chronic homelessness, as well as homeless families with children. The HEARTH Act provides that the HUD Secretary "shall provide bonuses and other incentives" to Continuums of Care that are successful in reducing or eliminating homelessness in general or among certain subpopulations through permanent housing, are successful at preventing homelessness, or that are successful at achieving independent living for families with children or youth defined as homeless under other federal statutes.[93]

The Grant Application Process

In consolidating the competitive grants, the HEARTH Act maintained many aspects of the current Continuum of Care application system and codified the system in law. Previously, much of the application system had been established through the grant funding process. HUD reviews one application for CoC program funds submitted by Collaborative Applicants. HUD continues to use its current practice of distributing funds directly to individual project applicants unless a Collaborative Applicant has the status of Unified Funding Agency.

Formula

Leading up to enactment of the HEARTH Act, HUD used the Community Development Block Grant (CDBG) program formula as a way to measure community need for competitive homeless assistance funds. (For more information, see "The Role of the Community Development Block Grant Formula.") The HEARTH Act required HUD to develop a

---

[92] 42 U.S.C. §11384(c), 24 C.F.R. §578.71 at 77 *Federal Register* 45457.
[93] 42 U.S.C. §11386b(d).

formula for determining need within two years of the bill's enactment using "factors that are appropriate to allocate funds to meet the goals and objectives of 'the Continuum of Care program.'"[94] P.L. 111-22 gave the HUD Secretary the authority to adjust the formula to ensure that Collaborative Applicants have sufficient funds to renew existing contracts for one year. When HUD released interim CoC program regulations, it continued to use the CDBG formula as the method for determining a CoC's level of need. However, in July 2016, HUD released a proposal to change the CoC formula so that the CDBG formula is no longer used. A later section in this report, "HUD Determination of Community Need," goes into more detail about the interaction of the CDBG formula and community need as well as HUD's proposal to change the formula.

Matching Requirement

Prior to enactment of the HEARTH Act, matching requirements were fulfilled at the individual grant level depending on both the type of grant (SHP, S+C, or SRO) as well as, in the case of SHP, which activities grantees participated in. The CoC program has a unified match requirement where each recipient *community* (vs. grantee) must match the total grant funds with 25% in funds from other sources (including other federal grants) or in-kind contributions.[95] The exception is funds for leasing, which does not require a match. In cases where third-party services are used to meet the match requirement, they must be documented by a memorandum of understanding.[96]

Who May Be Served

The HEARTH Act expanded the way in which communities may choose to serve people who are experiencing homelessness through the CoC program. In the programs that existed prior to the HEARTH Act, most permanent housing was designated either for unaccompanied individuals, with or without disabilities, although families of an adult with

---

[94] 42 U.S.C. §11386a(b)(2)(B)(i).
[95] 42 U.S.C. §11386d, 24 C.F.R. §578.73 at 77 *Federal Register* 45457.
[96] 24 C.F.R. §578.73 at 77 *Federal Register* 45457.

a disability were eligible for housing through the S+C program. None of the three programs provided permanent housing for families with non-disabled adults. In addition, families that might have been considered homeless under other federal programs were not necessarily eligible for assistance. The HEARTH Act made changes that made more people eligible for more services.

- Homeless Adults with Disabilities and Their Families: Prior to enactment of the HEARTH Act, nearly all funding for permanent housing was dedicated to persons with disabilities and, in some cases, their families. SHP served unaccompanied individuals with disabilities and the S+C program served persons with disabilities and their families. The HEARTH Act continues to require that at least 30% of amounts provided for both the ESG and CoC programs (not including those for permanent housing renewals) must be used through the CoC program to provide permanent supportive housing to individuals with disabilities or families with an adult head of household (or youth in the absence of an adult) who has a disability.[97] This requirement will be reduced proportionately as communities increase permanent housing units for this population, and will end when HUD determines that a total of 150,000 permanent housing units have been provided for homeless persons with disabilities since 2001.
- Homeless Families with Children: Prior to enactment of the HEARTH Act, in absence of a disability, homeless families with children did not qualify for permanent housing under the SHP, S+C, or SRO programs. Pursuant to the HEARTH Act, at least 10% of the amounts made available for both the ESG and CoC programs must be used to provide permanent housing for families with children through the CoC program.

---

[97] 42 U.S.C. §11386b(a).

Table 1. Characteristics of the SHP, S+C, SRO, and CoC Programs

Program Characteristics	Supportive Housing Program (SHP)	Shelter Plus Care (S+C)	Single Room Occupancy (SRO)	Continuum of Care Program (CoC)
Program Components	Transitional Housing Permanent Housing Supportive Services HMIS	Permanent Housing	Permanent Housing	Transitional Housing Permanent Housing *Rapid Rehousing* Supportive Services HMIS
Eligible Activities	Acquisition, Rehabilitation, Construction Leasing Operating Costs Administrative Costs	Rental Assistance Administrative Costs	Rental Assistance	Acquisition, Rehabilitation, Construction Rental Assistance Leasing Operating Costs Administrative Costs
Eligible Applicants	State Government Local Government PHAs Private Nonprofits Community Mental Health Centers	State Government Local Government PHAs	PHAs Private Nonprofits	State Government Local Government Instrumentalities of State and Local Governments PHAs Private Nonprofits
Eligible Populations	Unaccompanied individuals (transitional housing and services only) Unaccompanied individuals with disabilities Individuals with disabilities and their families (transitional housing and services only) Families with children (transitional housing and services only)	Individuals with disabilities and their families	Unaccompanied individuals	Unaccompanied individuals Unaccompanied individuals with disabilities Individuals with disabilities and their families Families with children Families with children and youth defined as homeless under other federal programs (generally limited to 10% of CoC funds)

Table 1. (Continued)

Program Characteristics	Supportive Housing Program (SHP)	Shelter Plus Care (S+C)	Single Room Occupancy (SRO)	Continuum of Care Program (CoC)
Match Requirements	Dollar for Dollar (acquisition, rehabilitation, or construction) 20% (services) 25% (operating expenses)	Equal amount of funds for services	No match requirement	Match of 25% at the CoC level

Source: The McKinney-Vento Homeless Assistance Act, Title IV, Subtitles C, E, and F, both prior to and after enactment of the HEARTH Act.

- Families with Children and Youth Certified as Homeless under Other Federal Programs: Up to 10% of CoC program funds can be used to serve homeless families with children and unaccompanied youth defined as homeless under other federal programs.[98] If a community has a rate of homelessness less than one-tenth of 1% of the total population, then the 10% limitation does not apply. (For more information on these programs, see "Other Federal Definitions.") These groups were not previously eligible for housing or services.
- Unaccompanied Homeless Individuals without Disabilities: Nothing in the HEARTH Act prohibits communities from serving homeless individuals who do not have disabilities. However, given the requirement that Continuums of Care use a portion of funds to serve homeless families with children and individuals with disabilities, communities may choose not to prioritize this group.

---

[98] 42 U.S.C. §11382(j).

DISTRIBUTION OF CONTINUUM OF CARE PROGRAM FUNDS

The way in which HUD awards CoC program grants did not change significantly with enactment of the HEARTH Act, and, in fact, the HEARTH Act served, in part, to codify the way in which the funds are distributed.

The CoC program funds, like those for the three competitive grants before it, are distributed to eligible applicant organizations through a process that involves both formula and competitive elements. HUD first uses the Community Development Block Grant (CDBG) program formula to determine the need levels of Continuums of Care; the need level sets a baseline for the amount of funding that a community can receive. HUD then determines through a competition whether applicant organizations that provide services to homeless persons qualify for funds.

HUD Determination of Community Need

Even prior to enactment of the HEARTH Act, HUD determined community need for homeless services as a way of allocating funds. The CoC program continues this process.[99] HUD goes through a process where it calculates each community's "pro rata need." Pro rata need is meant to represent the dollar amount that each community (city, county, or combination of both) needs in order to address homelessness. There are several steps in the need-determination process.

Preliminary Pro Rata Need (PPRN)

Pursuant to its interim regulations, HUD uses the CDBG formula to determine a Continuum of Care's "preliminary pro rata need" as a starting

---

[99] 42 U.S.C. §11386a(b)(2).

point for its need for homeless services.[100] This is the percentage of funds a community received (or would receive if they do not qualify for CDBG grants) from the CDBG formula multiplied by the amount of funds available to the CoC program. HUD adds together the PPRN amount for each community in a Continuum of Care to arrive at PPRN for the entire Continuum.

Annual Renewal Demand (ARD)

Next, PPRN may be adjusted by a Continuum of Care's "annual renewal demand" (i.e., the amount of funds needed to renew existing contracts that are up for renewal in a given fiscal year).

Final Pro Rata Need (FPRN)

This is the higher of PPRN or ARD.

Maximum Award Amount

Although FPRN is technically the maximum for which a Continuum of Care may qualify, a Continuum of Care may qualify for more than the FPRN level based on changes to fair market rents, planning costs of the Collaborative Applicant or Unified Funding Agency, and any bonus funding that might be available.

Competitive Process

Continuums of Care do not automatically qualify for their maximum award amount. The CoC program competition determines total funding levels. The competition consists of threshold review of both new and renewal grants, and a competitive process where points are awarded to applicants for new grants.

---

[100] 24 C.F.R. §578.17 at 77 *Federal Register* 45446-45447. Unlike the CDBG formula, however, 75% of funds are allocated to metropolitan cities and urban counties that have been funded under the ESG program in any year since FY2004 and the remainder goes to areas that have not received ESG funds during that time period.

Threshold Requirements

For existing projects, there is a renewal threshold in order to qualify to have contracts renewed. This primarily involves the organization's performance in administering its grant in prior years. For new projects, HUD ensures that every participant in the proposed projects (from applicant organizations to clients who will be served) is eligible for the CoC program, that the project quality fulfills HUD requirements, and that proposed projects meet civil rights and fair housing standards.

Competition for Funds

Collaborative Applicants are also scored based on criteria established by the HEARTH Act.[101] Most of these criteria had been used as part of the Continuum of Care competition established by HUD prior to enactment of the HEARTH Act and were made part of the law. The criteria include

- the Continuum of Care's performance (including outcomes for homeless clients and reducing homelessness);
- the Continuum of Care's planning process to address homelessness in its community (including how it will address homelessness among various subpopulations);
- how the Continuum of Care determined funding priorities;
- the amount leveraged from other funding sources (including mainstream programs);
- coordination of the Continuum of Care with other entities serving those who are homeless and at risk of homelessness in the planning process; and
- for those Continuums of Care serving families with children and youth defined as homeless under other federal programs, their success in preventing homelessness and achieving independent living.

---

[101] 42 U.S.C. §11386a.

To these factors, HUD has added via regulation the extent to which a Continuum of Care has a functioning Homeless Management Information System and whether it conducts an annual point-in-time count of those experiencing homelessness.

The competitive process also allows Continuums of Care to reallocate funds from an existing project to a new one if they decide that a new project would be more beneficial than an existing one. Continuums of Care that score enough points may receive funding for new projects whose costs are within the amount made available in the competition.

Features of the FY2017 Competitive Process

The specific scoring of the competition for the CoC program may differ from year to year based on available appropriations and HUD priorities. In addition, HUD may also change the ways in which CoCs can use funds for new and reallocated projects.

In FY2017, approximately $2 billion is available for the CoC program.[102] Because HUD is unsure if the amount is sufficient to renew existing grants, it continues to use a tiered scoring process that was introduced in the FY2012 competition.[103] HUD employs a two-tiered funding approach whereby Collaborative Applicants are to prioritize and rank projects in a way to ensure funding for their most important projects.

In the FY2017 competition for funds, the tiered funding process works as follows:

- Tier 1: The amount available to CoCs within tier 1 is the higher of (1) the amount needed to renew all permanent housing (including rapid rehousing) and HMIS projects or (2) 94% of ARD.[104]

---

[102] U.S. Department of Housing and Urban Development, *Notice of Funding Availability for the FY2017 Continuum of Care Program Competition*, July 14, 2017, p. 2, https://www.hudexchange.info/resources/documents/FY-2017-CoCProgram-Competition-NOFA.pdf (hereinafter, FY2017 NOFA).

[103] HUD initiated the two-tiered process because in FY2012 it was initially estimated that appropriations would not be sufficient to renew all existing contracts.

[104] FY2017 NOFA, p. 15.

- Tier 2: Projects that cannot be funded in tier 1 are to be ranked within tier 2. The amount potentially available is the remainder of a CoC's ARD plus an amount for a permanent housing bonus.[105]

Projects in tier 1 must pass threshold review and are scored on a 200-point scale using factors like those described in the previous, "Competitive Process," section of this report.[106] Tier 2 projects are scored on a 100-point scale, with 50 points based on the CoC application score, 40 points based on the way in which CoCs rank their projects (with higher-ranked projects receiving higher scores), and 10 points for a project's commitment either to housing first (if it is permanent housing) or to low-barrier housing and attaining permanent housing (if it is not permanent housing).[107] Unlike previous years, HUD is not awarding points based on type of housing (e.g., permanent supportive housing, rapid rehousing, transitional housing).

Funds in the CoC competition are largely used to renew existing grants, but Continuums of Care may also create new projects by reallocating funds from existing projects, and, depending on available resources, may compete for funding for new projects. In FY2017, HUD is allowing applicants to apply for new projects at up to 6% of FPRN (though funding for new projects is not guaranteed).[108]

HUD limits the ways in which new and reallocated projects can address homelessness. Both new and reallocated projects can provide the following enumerated types of housing to serve specific populations.[109] In addition, reallocated funds can be used for new HMIS and coordinated assessment systems.

- Permanent Supportive Housing (PSH) projects: new and reallocated funds can be targeted to projects
    o serving chronically homeless individuals and families, or

---

[105] Ibid., pp. 15-16.
[106] Ibid., pp. 42-54.
[107] Ibid., p. 16.
[108] Ibid., p. 11.
[109] Ibid., pp. 10-11.

- serving individuals with a disability or families with an adult or child who has a disability who also meet certain criteria established by HUD. In previous years, PSH had to be targeted to individuals and families experiencing chronic homelessness. Chronic homelessness requires that an adult have a disability and that the length of homelessness extends for 12 consecutive months, or for a total of at least 12 months on four or more occasions over the course of three years. In the FY2017 competition, HUD has expanded the circumstances in which individuals and families with disabilities may qualify for PSH. HUD refers to this housing as "DedicatedPLUS." For example, individuals and families residing in transitional housing may qualify for PSH if they had previously been considered chronically homeless, or individuals and families who have experienced homelessness for at least 12 months over the last three years, but not on four separate occasions (as is required by the definition of chronic homelessness). In addition, veterans receiving assistance through VA homeless programs who otherwise meet homeless status criteria qualify for DedicatedPLUS housing.
- Rapid Rehousing (RR) projects: new and reallocated funds can be used for rapid rehousing projects serving homeless individuals and families, including unaccompanied youth.
- Joint Transitional Housing (TH) and RR projects: new and reallocated funds can be used for joint TH-RR projects serving homeless individuals and families. FY2017 is the first year that HUD has allowed funds to be used for this joint project model where funds can be used for both types of housing. Joint TH-RR projects are expected to focus on residents obtaining and retaining permanent housing.[110]

---

[110] Ibid., pp. 32-33.

- Expansion of Existing Projects: new and reallocated funds can be used to increase units in an existing project and/or increase the number of people served.[111]

FY2017 applications are due to HUD on September 28, 2017.[112]

Features of the FY2016 Competitive Process

In FY2016, the tiered funding process worked as follows:[113]

- Tier 1: The amount available to CoCs within tier 1 was 93% of ARD.[114]
- Tier 2: Projects that could not be funded in tier 1 were to be placed in tier 2. The amount available in tier 2 was the remainder of a CoC's ARD plus 5% of FPRN for a permanent housing bonus.[115]

Projects proposed for funding in tier 1 had to pass threshold review, and were scored based on the criteria listed in the previous section describing the competitive process. A CoC could place a tier 1 project partially in tier 1, but if it did not receive tier 2 funding, then HUD was to determine if the project was still feasible with partial funding.

Tier 2 projects were scored on a 100 point scale. Up to 50 points were available based on the CoC competition score used to score tier 1 projects. Up to 35 points were available based on the way in which CoCs ranked their projects.

---

[111] Ibid., p. 12.
[112] Ibid., p. 1.
[113] U.S. Department of Housing and Urban Development, *Notice of Funding Availability for the FY2016 Continuum of Care Program Competition*, June 28, 2016, https://www.hudexchange.info/resources/documents/FY-2016-CoCProgram-NOFA.pdf.
[114] A table listing each Continuum of Care's ARD at 93% is available on HUD's website at https://www.hudexchange.info/resources/documents/FY-2016-CoC-Program-Competition-Final-ARD-Report.pdf.
[115] See Ibid. for a list of each Continuum of Care's permanent housing bonus.

The more highly ranked a project, the more points it received. Up to five points were available based on the project type, with permanent supportive housing, rapid rehousing, safe havens, coordinated assessment, and transitional housing for homeless youth eligible for all five points. Finally, up to 10 points were available for the extent to which projects apply housing first and low barrier to assistance housing principals.

Given this system, the ability of projects to be funded depended on several factors:

- The tier within which a Continuum of Care ranked a project.
- The number of points scored by an applicant in the Continuum of Care program competition.
- The order within which projects were ranked in tier 2, and the type of project; the higher the ranking, the greater the number of points available. In addition, renewal transitional housing and supportive services only projects were at a slight disadvantage, with only three and one point available based on project type compared to other projects, which receive five points.

HUD announced tier 1 and tier 2 funding awards together on December 20, 2016.[116] A total of $1.95 billion was distributed to more than 7,600 providers across the states and territories. Of this amount, $139 million funded new projects, and $103 million was reallocated from existing to new projects.[117] For a breakdown of awards among housing types and between new and existing projects, see Table 2.

---

[116] U.S. Department of Housing and Urban Development, "HUD Awards Nearly $2 Billion for Local Homeless Programs," press release, December 20, 2016, https://portal.hud.gov/hudportal/HUD?src=/press/press_releases_media_advisories/2016/HUDNo_16-194.

[117] Email from HUD, December 20, 2016.

Table 2. Continuum of Care Program Awards by Type FY2012-FY2016

Award Type	FY2012 $ in Thousands	FY2012 % of Total	FY2013 $ in Thousands	FY2013 % of Total	FY2014 $ in Thousands	FY2014 % of Total	FY2015 $ in Thousands	FY2015 % of Total	FY2016 $ in Thousands	FY2016 % of Total
Renewal Project Awards	$1,614,540	96.5%	$1,595,236	93.7%	$1,692,093	93.5%	$1,646,340	84.7%	$1,763,357	90.1%
Permanent Supportive Housing	993,844	59.4	1,063,148	62.4	1,169,101	64.6	1,273,492	65.5	1,361,019	69.5
Rapid Rehousing	6,275	0.4	8,997	0.5	67,957	3.8	105,897	5.4	196,113	10.0
Transitional Housing	417,158	24.9	371,494	21.8	325,548	18.0	172,253	8.9	108,067	5.5
Supportive Services Only	123,269	7.4	80,090	4.7	59,191	3.3	29,647	1.5	35,417	1.8
Safe Havens	33,159	2.0	29,418	1.7	26,648	1.5	23,780	1.2	17,579	0.9
HMIS	40,834	2.4	42,090	2.5	43,648	2.4	41,270	2.1	45,160	2.3
New Project Awards	$46,683	2.8%	$96,843	5.7%	$102,127	5.6%	$248,819	12.8%	$141,959	7.3%
Permanent Supportive Housing	33,656	2.0	69,477	4.1	71,336	3.9	133,529	6.9	73,252	3.7
Rapid Rehousing	6,958	0.4	27,367	1.6	30,791	1.7	92,482	4.8	53,630	2.7
Transitional Housing	299	0.0	—	—	—	—	—	—	—	—
Supportive Services Only	3,429	0.2	—	—	—	—	18,785[a]	1.0	11,649	0.6
HMIS	2,341	0.2	—	—	—	—	4,044	0.2	3,428	0.2
Administrative Costs	$12,025	0.7%	$10,705	0.6%	$16,339	0.9%	$48,158	2.5%	$52,122	2.7
CoC Planning Costs	12,025	0.7	10,670	0.6	16,258	0.9	47,554	2.4	51,426	2.6
Unified Funding	—	—	35	<1	82	<1	604	<1	696	<1
Agency Costs										
Total	$1,673,248		$1,702,784		$1,810,560		$1,943,317		$1,957,438	

Source: U.S. Department of Housing and Urban Development, 2012-2016 CoC Awards by Program Component, All States, Territories, Puerto Rico, and DC, available at https:///www.hudexchange.info/coc/awards-by-component/.

Note: Percentages may not add to 100% due to rounding. New projects include those created by reallocating funds for existing projects.

[a]. In the FY2015 and FY2016 competitions, new Supportive Services Only funds could be used for a centralized or coordinated assessment system within a Continuum of Care. Funds could not be used for new projects to provide services to people experiencing homelessness.

Rural Housing Stability Assistance Program

In the area of rural homelessness, the HEARTH Act retained portions of McKinney-Vento's rural homelessness grant program (Title IV, Subtitle G of McKinney-Vento, a program that was never implemented or funded after it was authorized as part of P.L. 102-550) as the Rural Housing Stability Assistance Program. The grants themselves are referred to as the Rural Housing Stability (RHS) grants. As of the date of this report, HUD had released proposed regulations, but had not yet made funds available through the RHS grants.

The program allows rural communities to apply separately for funds that otherwise would be awarded as part of the Continuum of Care program. The HEARTH Act provides that not less than 5% of Continuum of Care Program funds be set aside for rural communities.[118] If the funds are not used, then they are to be returned for use by the CoC program.

What Is a Rural Community?

The law defines a rural community as falling into one of three different categories,[119] which HUD further refined in its proposed regulation.[120] Under the statute and regulations, a rural community is

- a county where no part is contained within a metropolitan statistical area,
- a county located within a metropolitan statistical area, but where at least 75% of the county population is in nonurban Census blocks, or

---

[118] 42 U.S.C. §11408(*l*).
[119] 42 U.S.C. §11408.
[120] U.S. Department of Housing and Urban Development, "Homeless Emergency Assistance and Rapid Transition to Housing: Rural Housing Stability Assistance Program and Revisions to the Definition of 'Chronically Homeless'," 78 *Federal Register* 18726-18761, March 27, 2013. The statute refers to geographies as an "area or community" which the proposed regulations have defined as a county.

- a county located in a state where the population density is less than 30 people per square mile, and at least 1.25% of the acreage in the state is under federal jurisdiction. However, under this definition, no metropolitan city in the state (as defined by the CDBG statute) can be the sole beneficiary of the RHS grants.

Eligible Applicants

The entities eligible to apply for and receive RHS program grants are county and local governments and private nonprofit organizations.[121] A county that meets the definition of rural community may either submit an application to HUD or designate another eligible entity to do so. Once a grant is awarded, the county or its designee may award grants to subrecipients.

Who May Be Served

Unlike the CoC program, communities that participate in the RHS program are able to serve persons who do not necessarily meet HUD's definition of "homeless individual." HUD may award grants to rural communities to be used for the following:

- Rehousing or improving the housing situation of those who are in the worst housing situations in their geographic area.[122] In its proposed regulations, HUD defines worst housing situation to mean housing with "serious health and safety defects" and that has at least one major system that has failed or is failing.[123] A major system may include structural supports; electrical, plumbing, heating, or cooling systems; or roofing, among others.

---

[121] 42 U.S.C. §11408(e).
[122] 42 U.S.C. §11408(a)(1).
[123] 24 C.F.R. §579.3 at 78 *Federal Register* 18743.

- Stabilizing the housing situation of those in imminent danger of losing housing.[124] In its proposed regulations, HUD considers those in this category as "at risk of homelessness" as defined for the ESG and CoC programs.[125]
- Improving the ability of the lowest-income residents in the community to afford stable housing.[126]

Program Components and Eligible Costs

Grantees under the RHS program may use funds to assist people who are experiencing homelessness in many of the same ways as the CoC program. These include transitional housing, permanent housing, rapid rehousing, data collection, and a range of supportive services.

In addition, however, RHS program grants can be used for

- Homelessness prevention activities such as rent, mortgage, or utility payments. Individuals and families are eligible for assistance if they have not made a payment for at least 2 months,[127] and assistance may continue for up to 12 months.[128]
- Relocation assistance for someone moving outside the county because they have found employment, have been accepted to an educational institution, or are being reunited with family. Assistance may include moving costs, a security deposit, and payment of the first month's rent.[129]
- Short-term emergency housing in motels or shelters.[130] In general, assistance is limited to three months, but with exceptions where

---

[124] 42 U.S.C. §11408(a)(2).
[125] 78 *Federal Register* 18728.
[126] 42 U.S.C. §11408(a)(3).
[127] 42 U.S.C. §11408(b)(1)(A).
[128] 24 C.F.R. §579.202 at 78 *Federal Register* 18744.
[129] 24 C.F.R. §579.204 at 78 *Federal Register* 18744.
[130] 42 U.S.C. §11408(b)(1)(C).

The HUD Homeless Assistance Grants 175

there is no other housing option available, and the participant is still at risk of homelessness or in a worst housing situation.[131]

- Home repairs that are necessary to make housing habitable for those in worst housing situations.[132] Participants must own the home and have income at or below 50% of area median income.[133] If participants move from the premises within three years of the repairs, they may have to reimburse the grantee for costs of repairs.[134]

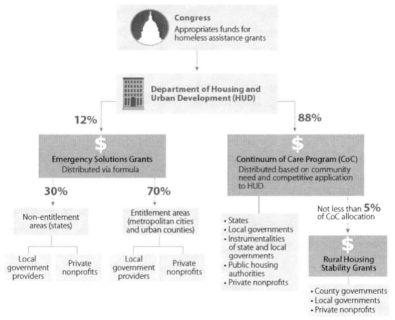

Source: Chart prepared by CRS on the basis of 42 U.S.C. §11373, §11382, and §11408. Percentages for ESG and the CoC Program are the actual percentages allocated to the programs in FY2014. Funds have not yet been made available for the RHS program, but, by statute, not less than 5% of CoC funds must be set aside for the program. RHS program proposed regulations were published on March 27, 2013.

Figure 1. Distribution of the HUD Homeless Assistance Grants.

---

[131] 24 C.F.R. §579.206 at 78 *Federal Register* 18744-18745.
[132] 42 U.S.C. §11408(b)(1)(I).
[133] 24 C.F.R. §579.220 at 78 *Federal Register* 18747.
[134] Ibid.

The eligible costs that grantees may incur in order to deliver program components are largely the same as those allowed in the CoC program. These include acquisition, rehabilitation, and construction of facilities; rental assistance; leasing costs; operating costs; and administrative costs. However, the RHS program adds that up to 20% of the grantee community's RHS funds may be used for capacity building among personnel who administer housing and services programs.[135] Eligible costs may include employee salary and benefits, education and training, and staff retention efforts.[136]

FUNDING FOR THE HOMELESS ASSISTANCE GRANTS

After creating the four Homeless Assistance Grants in 1987, Congress played a decreasing role in how funds are allocated among them. Initially, from FY1987 to FY1994, Congress appropriated funds separately for each of the four programs. However, beginning in FY1995 and continuing through FY2010, Congress appropriated one lump sum for all four programs, and HUD then determined how the funds were distributed among the ESG, SHP, S+C, and SRO programs. The way funding allocations operate changed again in FY2011, with Congress specifying in the appropriations laws a minimum amount of funds to be set aside for the ESG program in that year, and minimum amounts for the ESG, CoC, and RHS programs in FY2012 through FY2017. Table 3 shows a distribution of the grants from FY1987 through FY2017.[137]

---

[135] 42 U.S.C. §11408(b)(2).
[136] 24 C.F.R. §579.226 at 78 *Federal Register* 18749-18750.
[137] In addition to funds for the four grant programs, the congressional appropriation has at times contained funds for items like training and technical assistance, data collection, and the Interagency Council on Homelessness. These amounts make up a small percentage of the total appropriation.

Table 3. Funding for Homeless Assistance Grants, FY1987-FY2017 ($ in thousands)

	Formula Grant	Competitive Grants				
Fiscal Year	Emergency Shelter/ Solutions Grants (ESG) (a)	Single Room Occupancy (SRO) (b)	Shelter Plus Care[a] (S+C) (c)	Supportive Housing Program[b] (SHP) (d)	Continuum of Care Program (CoC) (e)	Total Funds for HUD Homeless Programs (see note) (f)
1987	60,000	35,000	—	59,000	—	195,000[c]
1988	8,000	—	—	65,000	—	72,000
1989	46,500	45,000	—	80,000	—	171,500
1990	73,164	73,185	—	126,825	—	284,004[d]
1991	73,164	104,999	—	149,988	—	339,414[e]
1992	73,164	105,000	110,533	150,000	—	449,960[f]
1993	49,496	105,000	266,550	150,443	—	571,489
1994	113,840	150,000	123,747	334,000[g]	—	822,747[h]
1995	155,218	136,000	164,000	630,000	—	1,120,000[i]
1996	113,841	48,000	89,000	606,000	—	823,000
1997	113,727	24,000	61,000	663,000	—	823,000
1998	164,993	10,000	117,000	596,000	—	823,000
1999	150,000	17,000	151,000	556,000	—	975,000
2000	150,000	20,000	95,000	784,000	—	1,020,000
2001	149,670	14,000	174,000	760,000	—	1,122,525
2002	150,000	10,400	178,700	788,200	—	1,122,525
2003	149,025	11,200	237,000	865,400	—	1,217,037
2004	159,056	12,900	322,800	906,900	—	1,259,525
2005	158,720	14,900	304,400	860,900	—	1,229,214
2006	158,400	1,600	363,000	942,200	—	1,326,600
2007	160,000	1,611	383,000	942,900	—	1,434,403
2008	160,000	2,400	405,900	1,008,000	—	1,541,081
2009	160,000	0	487,900	1,069,700	—	1,677,000
2010	160,000	2,400	521,400	1,104,100	—	1,865,000
2011	250,000	3,200	522,700	1,148,900	—	1,901,190[j]
2012	286,000	—	—	—	1,671,973	1,901,190
2013	215,000	—	—	—	1,702,784	1,933,293[k]
2014	250,000	—	—	—	1,810,659	2,105,000
2015	270,000	—	—	—	1,939,771	2,135,000
2016	270,000	—	—	—	1,953,210	2,250,000
2017	270,000l	—	—	—	—[m]	2,383,000

Sources: HUD Congressional Budget Justifications FY1988-FY2017 (all grants through FY1994; competitive grants from FY2002-FY2006, FY2008-FY2009, FY2011; and total funds for HUD homeless programs), HUD Homelessness Resource Exchange Continuum of Care Awards by Program Component (FY2007 competitive grants), HUD Community Planning and Development grantee lists FY1993-FY2017 (ESG from FY1993 through FY2017), HUD's Office of Special Needs Assistance Programs (competitive grants for FY1987 and from FY1995 through FY2001), HUD funding announcements (competitive grants for FY2010 and FY2012-FY2016), and the FY2017 Consolidated Appropriations Act (P.L. 115-31).

Note: Until FY1995, Congress separately appropriated funds for each of the four Homeless Assistance Grants. Since then, however, Congress has appropriated one amount for all of the Homeless Assistance Grants and HUD has divided the funds. Therefore, amounts in columns (a) through (d) in the years FY1987 through FY1994 represent appropriations, and those from FY1995 forward represent funds distributed to grantees. The amounts for each of the separate grant programs may add up to more or less than the amount in column (f) "Total for HUD Homeless Programs," which is the amount appropriated for HUD homeless program activities in a given fiscal year. In some years, this could be due to the use of carryover funds, recaptured funds, or reallocated funds, and in others, the sum of the separate grants may add up to less than the total due to allocations to other funds like technical assistance, data collection, or the Interagency Council on Homelessness that are not captured in the table.

[a] The S+C program was authorized in 1990 by P.L. 101-645 and first received funding in FY1992.

[b] From FY1987 to FY1993, SHP was a demonstration program. In FY1987, it was called the Transitional Housing Demonstration Program (P.L. 99-591). SHP as it currently exists was authorized in P.L. 102-550.

[c] The total includes $15 million for the Supplemental Assistance for Facilities to Assist the Homeless (SAFAH) program. In 1992, P.L. 102-550 incorporated elements of SAFAH and the Supportive Housing Demonstration Program into the new Supportive Housing Program.

[d] The total includes $10,830,000 for the SAFAH program.

[e] The total includes $11,263,000 for the SAFAH program.

[f] The total includes $11,263,000 for the SAFAH program.

[g] In P.L. 103-124, Congress provided that of the amount appropriated for SHP, an amount not to exceed $50 million could be used for the Safe Havens Demonstration Initiative and $20 million for the Rural Housing Demonstration Program.

[h] The total includes $100 million for the Innovative Homeless Initiatives Demonstration Program.

[i] The total includes $25 million for the Innovative Homeless Initiatives Demonstration Program.

[j] The FY2011 Department of Defense and Full-Year Continuing Appropriations Act (P.L. 112-10) included an across-the-board rescission of 0.2% for all discretionary programs that is reflected in the FY2011 program total.

[k] Pursuant to the FY2013 Consolidated and Further Continuing Appropriations Act (P.L. 113-6), the Homeless Assistance Grants were funded at $2.033 billion. However, after application of an across-the-board rescission of 0.2% and sequestration, the total available for the Homeless Assistance Grants was approximately $1.933 billion.

[l] The FY2017 appropriations law (P.L. 115-31) provided that $310 million be provided for ESG, of which $40 million "shall be made available, as determined by the Secretary, for grants for rapid re-housing or other critical activities in order to assist communities that lost significant capacity after January 1, 2016 to serve persons experiencing homelessness." As of the date of this report, it does not appear that HUD has awarded the additional $40 million.

[m] As of the date of this report, CoC program funds had not yet been distributed.

ISSUES REGARDING THE HOMELESS ASSISTANCE GRANTS

Despite the enactment of McKinney-Vento reauthorization legislation, there are other factors involved in the distribution of the Homeless Assistance Grants that may continue to be issues of concern to those interested in how funds are allocated. An ongoing concern has been the amount of funds required to renew existing housing and services contracts, leaving a relatively small share of funding to support new projects. (This is also an issue for the HUD budget in general.) Another issue is the way in which the CDBG formula affects the distribution of the Homeless Assistance Grants.

Contract Renewals for the CoC Program and Predecessor Programs

The cost to renew existing grants takes up a large share of Continuum of Care program funds (see Table 2). In FY2016, 90% of the CoC funds allocated went to renew existing grants.[138] HUD has made it possible for Continuums of Care to free up funds for new permanent housing projects. Beginning with the FY2005 competition for available funds, Continuums of Care can reallocate funds from an existing SHP project (now CoC project) to a new project, while still qualifying for the annual renewal demand (ARD) level that would have been required to renew the SHP/CoC projects.[139] Although this allows CoCs to defund projects that they do not think should receive grants, it does not address what CoCs can do about renewing projects they think are worth funding while also funding projects that would create new housing. HUD has allowed the reallocation of funds in all competitions since FY2005, with the exception of FY2009.

---

[138] U.S. Department of Housing and Urban Development, 2016 CoC Awards by Program Component, All States, Territories, Puerto Rico, and DC, available at https://www.hudexchange.info/coc/awards-by-component/.

[139] U.S. Department of Housing and Urban Development, "Notice of Funding Availability, Continuum of Care Homeless Assistance," *Federal Register*, vol. 70, no. 53, March 21, 2005, pp. 14283-14284.

The HEARTH Act also introduced a way in which Homeless Assistance Grant funds could be freed up for new projects. Under the new law, renewals of permanent housing rental assistance and operating cost contracts could be funded from the project-based Section 8 rental assistance account. This assumes that appropriations for the Homeless Assistance Grants would not be reduced to account for transfer of the renewals to another account. In addition, such a move would put pressure on the project-based Section 8 account, perhaps resulting in less funding for all HUD programs. To date, Congress has not renewed contracts through the project-based Section 8 account.

The Role of the Community Development Block Grant Formula

The Community Development Block Grant (CDBG) program formula has determined how ESG funds are distributed since the inception of the program in 1986, and has been used in the distribution of the competitive grants since at least FY1995. The effectiveness of using the CDBG formula to target funds to services for homeless persons has been questioned at various times. Two General Accounting Office (now Government Accountability Office) reports from the late 1980s noted that the CDBG formula might not be the best way to target funds to areas that most need homeless assistance funds.[140] Congress, too, has questioned the relationship between the formula and homelessness. In FY2001, the Senate Appropriations Committee noted that "the CDBG formula has no real nexus to homeless needs," and urged HUD to hasten its development of a method for counting homeless individuals.[141] HUD responded with a report

---

[140] U.S. General Accounting Office, *Homelessness: Implementation of Food and Shelter Programs Under the McKinney Act*. GAO/RCED-88-63. December 1987, p. 33, http://archive.gao.gov/d29t5/134578.pdf, and *Homelessness: HUD's and FEMA's Progress in Implementing the McKinney Act*. GAO/RCED-89-50. May 1989, pp. 46-48, http://archive.gao.gov/d25t7/138597.pdf.

[141] S.Rept. 106-410. The statement was made regarding the competitive Homeless Assistance Grants.

that proposed alternative methods for determining community need for homeless assistance.[142]

The HEARTH Act (P.L. 111-22) responded to these concerns, in part by directing HUD to develop a formula for determining need for the competitive Continuum of Care Program within two years of the law's enactment. In its interim regulations, HUD maintained the use of the CDBG formula for determining preliminary pro rata need (PPRN) for participating communities (see "The Grant Application Process").

The CDBG formula uses a combination of five factors to award funds to recipient communities. (The CDBG formula uses four separate methods to award funds; this report does not discuss the details of these methods.) The five factors are population, the number of persons in poverty, housing overcrowding (homes in which there are more than 1.01 persons per room), the age of housing (the number of housing structures built prior to 1940), and the extent of growth lag in a given community (the lack of population growth in a community compared to the growth rate it would have had if it had grown at the rate of other communities).[143] The factors are measured as ratios between the recipient community and all grant recipients. The CDBG formula was last changed in 1977 (P.L. 95-128).

There have been other proposals for how to determine need for the Homeless Assistance Grants. For example, legislation to reauthorize the McKinney-Vento Act that was introduced prior to enactment of the HEARTH Act gave more specific guidance as to how the HUD Secretary might determine need. The Community Partnership to End Homelessness Act of 2007 (S. 1518), as passed by the Senate Committee on Banking, Housing, and Urban Affairs, would have directed the Secretary to consider factors such as the number of homeless individuals, shortages of affordable housing, and severe housing problems among extremely low-income households. The report released by HUD in 2001 proposed a number of

---

[142] U.S. Department of Housing and Urban Development. Office of Community Planning and Development. *Report to Congress: Measuring "Need" for HUD's McKinney-Vento Homeless Competitive Grants*, 2001, https://www.onecpd.info/resources/documents/MeasuringNeed.pdf.

[143] 42 U.S.C. §5306.

potential formula factors, with an emphasis on a measure of housing affordability.[144]

In general, factors used to distribute formula funds for programs such as CDBG are based on data collected by government entities, like the Census Bureau, that do not have an interest in the way in which funds are distributed. While the best measure of community need for homeless assistance may be the number of people who are homeless in a given community, current measures of homelessness are uncertain (it is difficult to accurately collect data on people experiencing homelessness), and the entities that collect the data—the communities themselves—have an interest in the distribution of funds.

Another possible issue that could affect the distribution of the Homeless Assistance Grants is the CDBG formula itself. In past years, HUD and the Administration have proposed changes to the formula,[145] but, to date, no legislation has been introduced that would affect the distribution. For example, in the President's FY2010 budget, the Obama Administration proposed using the number of people in poverty, excluding college students; housing that is 50 years old or older and occupied by a household in poverty; female-headed households with children under the age of 18; and overcrowding.

HUD Proposed Rule to Change the CoC Program Formula

On July 25, 2016, HUD reopened the interim CoC rule to propose changes to the formula used to determine preliminary pro rata need and

---

[144] *Report to Congress: Measuring "Need" for HUD's McKinney-Vento Homeless Competitive Grants*, pp. 12-13.

[145] In 2005, HUD released a report. See Todd Richardson, *CDBG Formula Targeting to Community Development Need*, U.S. Department of Housing and Urban Development, February 2005, p. 46, http://www.huduser.org/ Publications/pdf/CDBGAssess.pdf. And the President's FY2010 budget proposed to change the CDBG formula and replace it with one of the formulas proposed in the 2005 HUD report.

solicited comments.[146] HUD proposed four alternative formulas with varying formula factors for each. HUD considered formula factors derived from data sources that have four characteristics: (1) they are relevant to measuring homelessness, (2) they are accurate, (3) they are timely, and (4) they are readily available for each jurisdiction. HUD correlated potential formula factors with the two-year average of local point-in-time counts of people experiencing homelessness in each community to determine the extent to which they might be an effective measure of homelessness. The formula factors that HUD ultimately proposed using in the four alternate formulas are population, poverty, affordability gap (gap between demand for and supply of rental housing that is affordable and available to extremely low-income renter households), rent-burdened extremely low-income households, renter-occupied units, and a hybrid factor using rent-burdened households and renter-occupied units.

HUD also published a table comparing allocations to Continuums of Care based on each alternate formula, as well as a tool that can be used to change the relative weights of each factor.[147] The comment period was open until September 23, 2016.

APPENDIX. COMPETITIVE GRANTS PRIOR TO ENACTMENT OF THE HEARTH ACT

The Supportive Housing Program (SHP)[148]

The SHP provided funds for transitional housing for homeless individuals and families for up to 24 months, permanent housing for

---

[146] U.S. Department of Housing and Urban Development, "Continuum of Care Program: Solicitation of Comment on Continuum of Care Formula," 81 *Federal Register* 48366-48369, July 25, 2016.
[147] The table and tool are available on HUD's website, https://www.hudexchange.info/resource/5092/coc-programnotice-for-further-comment-on-the-pprn-formula/.
[148] Statutory references in the sections that describe the Supportive Housing Program, Shelter Plus Care program, and Single Room Occupancy program are to sections of the U.S. Code as they existed prior to enactment of the HEARTH Act.

homeless individuals with disabilities, and supportive services. In FY2011, nearly 69% of total HUD competitive grant funds went to recipients as SHP grants.[149] Eligible applicants for SHP grants included states, local government entities, public housing authorities (PHAs), private nonprofit organizations, and community mental health centers.[150] Grant recipients could provide housing together with services, or could choose to provide services only (without a housing program component). Specifically, grantees could use funds to acquire and/or rehabilitate buildings that were used either to provide supportive housing or buildings that were used to provide supportive services only. Funds were able to be used to *construct* buildings that were used for supportive housing (but not supportive services only).[151] At least 10% of total SHP funds had to be used for supportive services, at least 25% were to be used for projects that served families with children, and at least 25% had to be used for projects that serve homeless persons with disabilities.[152]

In addition to financing physical structures, grantees could use funds to provide services like case management, health care, child care, housing assistance, nutritional counseling, and employment assistance. Grant recipients could provide these services themselves, or through contracts with outside providers. In addition, grant recipients could use funds to pay for up to 75% of their annual operating expenses and to help implement a Homeless Management Information System (HMIS) to keep records regarding the homeless individuals served within their community.

Recipients of SHP grants were required to meet match requirements. All of the matching funds had to be provided by cash sources,[153] but the level of nonfederal funds required varied with the type of activity undertaken. Funds that were used for acquisition, rehabilitation, or new construction had to be matched with an equal amount of the grant recipient's own funds.[154] SHP grantees that received funds for supportive

---

[149] FY2014 HUD Congressional Budget Justifications.
[150] 42 U.S.C. §11382(1).
[151] 42 U.S.C. §11383.
[152] 42 U.S.C. §11389(b).
[153] 24 C.F.R. §583.145.
[154] 42 U.S.C. §11386(e).

services had to provide at least a 20% match with funds from other sources, while grantees that received funds for operating expenses had to provide at least a 25% match of these funds on their own.[155]

The Single Room Occupancy Program (SRO)

The Single Room Occupancy (SRO) program provided permanent housing to homeless individuals in efficiency units similar to dormitories, with single bedrooms, community bathrooms, and kitchen facilities. In FY2011, three new competitive grants were awarded to SRO projects for a total of approximately $3.2 million.[156] The SRO program did not require homeless residents to have a disability and did not fund supportive services. Eligible applicants for SRO grants were PHAs and private nonprofit organizations.[157] SRO units were funded as part of HUD's Section 8 Moderate Rehabilitation program, which required grant recipients to spend at least $3,000 per unit to rehabilitate property to be used for SRO housing in order to bring the property into compliance with HUD's housing quality standards.[158] Grant recipients were reimbursed for the costs of rehabilitating SRO units through Section 8 rental assistance payments that they received over a 10-year contract period. The costs of rehabilitation were amortized and added to a base rental amount. The maximum amount that a building owner could spend per unit and still be reimbursed was $23,000 as of FY2011 (this amount was updated annually).[159] After the 10-year rental contracts expired, they were renewed through the Section 8 project-based rental assistance account on an annual basis rather than through the Homeless Assistance Grants.[160]

---

[155] Department of Housing and Urban Development, "Notice of Funding Availability (NOFA) for the Continuum of Care Homeless Assistance Program," August 26, 2011, p. 23, http://hudhre.info/documents/ FY2011_CoC_NOFAFinal.pdf (hereinafter, FY2011 NOFA).
[156] FY2014 HUD Congressional Budget Justifications.
[157] 42 U.S.C. §11401(j).
[158] 24 C.F.R. §882.802.
[159] See FY2011 NOFA, p. 35.
[160] Ibid.

The Shelter Plus Care Program (S+C)

The S+C program provided permanent supportive housing through rent subsidies for homeless individuals with disabilities and their families. In FY2011, approximately 40% of total competitive grant funds went to S+C grantees.[161] Eligible applicants for the S+C grants were states, local government entities, and PHAs.[162] The S+C rent subsidies could be tenant-based vouchers, project-based rental assistance, sponsor-based rental assistance, or single room occupancy housing.[163] With tenant-based vouchers, residents found private market housing much as they would with a Section 8 voucher; project-based assistance was provided to building owners and attached to specific units of housing (unlike a portable voucher); with sponsor-based assistance, grant recipients contracted with private nonprofit housing providers or community mental health centers to provide housing; and rental assistance for SROs was targeted to a particular development.[164]

The S+C program required grant recipients to match the amount of grant funds they receive for rental assistance with an equal amount of funds that they used to provide supportive services.[165] The services under S+C were similar to those provided in the SHP, and included activities like physical and mental health care, substance abuse counseling, child care services, case management, and educational and job training.[166] Grant recipients could fulfill their match requirement with cash, the value of a lease, salary expenses for employees, or the time of volunteers.

---

[161] FY2014 HUD Congressional Budget Justifications.
[162] 42 U.S.C. §11403g(2).
[163] 42 U.S.C. §§11404-11406b.
[164] U.S. Department of Housing and Urban Development, *Shelter Plus Care Resource Manual*, Section 1.2, http://www.hudhre.info/index.cfm?do=viewSpcResourceMan.
[165] 42 U.S.C. §11403b(a).
[166] 24 C.F.R. §582.5.

The HUD Homeless Assistance Grants

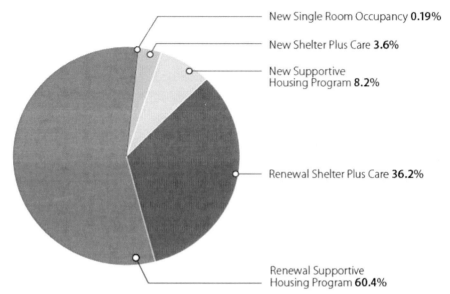

Source: HUD FY2014 Congressional Budget Justifications, available at http://portal.hud.gov/hudportal/documents/huddoc?id=HOMELESSASSTGRANTS.pdf.

Figure A-1. FY2011 Percentage Allocation of Competitive Grants.

In: A Closer Look at Grant Programs
Editor: Tabitha Reyes

ISBN: 978-1-53615-995-0
© 2019 Nova Science Publishers, Inc.

Chapter 5

COMMUNITY SERVICES BLOCK GRANTS (CSBG): BACKGROUND AND FUNDING (UPDATED)[*]

Libby Perl

ABSTRACT

Community Services Block Grants (CSBG) provide federal funds to states, territories, and tribes for distribution to local agencies to support a wide range of community-based activities to reduce poverty. These include activities to help families and individuals achieve self-sufficiency, find and retain meaningful employment, attain an adequate education, make better use of available income, obtain adequate housing, and achieve greater participation in community affairs. In addition, many local agencies receive federal funds from other sources and may administer other federal programs.

Smaller related programs—Community Economic Development (CED), Rural Community Facilities (RCF), and Individual Development Accounts (IDAs)—also support antipoverty efforts. CSBG and some of

---

[*] This is an edited, reformatted and augmented version of Congressional Research Service, Publication No. RL32872, dated January 23, 2018.

these related activities trace their roots to the War on Poverty, launched more than 50 years ago in 1964. Today, they are administered at the federal level by the Department of Health and Human Services (HHS).

Initial FY2018 funding for CSBG is provided by a series of continuing resolutions (CRs). As of the date of this report, the current CR funds most federal programs, including CSBG and related programs, at their FY2017 levels less an across-the-board rescission of 0.6791%, through February 8, 2018.

In FY2017, CSBG and related activities were funded at a total level of $742 million through the FY2017 Consolidated Appropriations Act (P.L. 115-31). This was a reduction of nearly $30 million relative to FY2016 appropriations of $770 million, though that total was more than had been appropriated in each year from FY2012-FY2015. While the block grant was funded at the FY2016 level of $715 million, funding for CED was reduced by $10 million (from $30 million to $20 million) and funding for IDAs was eliminated for the first time since the program was created as a demonstration in 1998. Funding for RCF increased slightly to $7.5 million in FY2017, compared to $6.5 million in FY2016.

Prior to enactment of the FY2018 continuing resolutions, the Administration's budget proposed to eliminate funding for CSBG, CED, and RCF, and would again have provided no funding for IDAs. Both the Senate and the House appropriations committees reported FY2018 funding bills that rejected the Administration's proposal. The House Appropriations Committee-reported bill to fund the Departments of Labor, Health and Human Services, and Education (LHHS, H.R. 3358) would provide $600 million for CSBG, $10 million for CED, $7.5 million for RCF, and no funding for IDAs. The LHHS bill approved by the Senate Appropriations Committee (S. 1771) would provide $700 million for CSBG, and maintain FY2017 funding levels for CED ($20 million) and RCF ($7.5 million). Neither the House nor the Senate committee-approved bills contain funding for IDAs. In addition, on August 16, 2017, the House passed H.R. 3354, a bill that incorporated multiple appropriations bills, as an omnibus appropriations act. However, the CR was enacted before action on H.R. 3354 was complete. Funding for CSBG and related activities in H.R. 3354 are the same as those in H.R. 3358.

The Community Services Block Grant Act was last reauthorized in 1998 by P.L. 105-285. The authorization of appropriations for CSBG and most related programs expired in FY2003, but Congress has continued to make annual appropriations each year. Legislation was introduced in the 114th Congress—with bipartisan cosponsorship—to amend and reauthorize the CSBG Act through FY2023 (H.R. 1655). Similar legislation had been introduced in the 113th Congress (H.R. 3854).

According to the most recent survey conducted by the National Association for State Community Services Programs, through a contract with HHS, the nationwide network of more than 1,000 CSBG grantees served 15.6 million people in 6.5 million low-income families in FY2015. States reported that the network spent $13.6 billion of federal, state, local, and private resources, including $637 million in federal CSBG funds.

INTRODUCTION

The Community Services Block Grant traces its roots to the War on Poverty, launched by President Lyndon Johnson more than 50 years ago when he proposed the Economic Opportunity Act of 1964. In his March 1964 message to Congress, President Johnson said the act would "give every American community the opportunity to develop a comprehensive plan to fight its own poverty—and help them to carry out their plans."[1] This was to be achieved through a new Community Action Program that would "strike poverty at its source—in the streets of our cities and on the farms of our countryside among the very young and the impoverished old."

A central feature of the new Community Action Program was that local residents would identify the unique barriers and unmet needs contributing to poverty in their individual communities and develop plans to address those needs, drawing on resources from all levels of government and the private sector. The program would be overseen by a newly created Office of Economic Opportunity, which would pay part of the costs of implementing these local plans. President Johnson signed the Economic Opportunity Act into law on August 20, 1964 (P.L. 88-452), and within a

---

[1] This was one of five "basic opportunities" that President Johnson said the act would provide. The others were to "give almost half a million young Americans the opportunity to develop skills, continue education, and find useful work;" "give dedicated Americans the opportunity to enlist as volunteers in the war against poverty;" "give many workers and farmers the opportunity to break through particular barriers which bar their escape from poverty;" and "give the entire Nation the opportunity for a concerted attack on poverty through the establishment, under [President Johnson's] direction, of the Office of Economic Opportunity, a national headquarters for the war against poverty." U.S. Congress, House, *Poverty: Message from the President of the United States*, 88th Cong., 2nd sess., March 16, 1964, Doc. No. 243 (Washington: GPO, 1964).

few years, a nationwide network of about 1,000 local Community Action Agencies was established.[2]

This report provides information on the Community Services Block Grant (CSBG), which is the modern-day program that continues to fund this network of local antipoverty agencies. The report also describes several smaller related programs that are administered by the same federal office that currently oversees the CSBG. The report begins with background information and legislative history of the CSBG and related activities ("Background"); it then summarizes the ways in which CSBG eligible entities use funds and who is served ("CSBG Program Data"). The next section discusses recent funding for CSBG ("Funding for CSBG and Related Activities"), and the final section provides an overview of legislation in the 114th Congress that would have reauthorized CSBG and related activities ("Reauthorization Proposal in the 114th Congress"). Appendix A has tables showing historical funding for CSBG and related activities dating back to the beginning of the program, in 1982, as well as a table with CSBG funding distributed to states, tribes, and territories in recent years. The most recent review of CSBG by the Government Accountability Office (GAO) is discussed in Appendix B.

BACKGROUND

Administered by the Department of Health and Human Services (HHS), the Community Services Block Grant (CSBG) provides federal funds to states, territories, and Indian tribes for distribution to local agencies in support of a variety of antipoverty activities. As noted above, the origins of the CSBG date back to 1964, when the Economic Opportunity Act (P.L. 88-452; 42 U.S.C. §2701) established the War on Poverty and authorized the Office of Economic Opportunity (OEO) as the lead agency in the federal antipoverty campaign. A centerpiece of OEO

---

[2] For a brief history of federal antipoverty policy broadly and a discussion of recurring themes, see CRS Report R43731, *Poverty: Major Themes in Past Debates and Current Proposals*, by Gene Falk and Karen Spar.

was the Community Action Program, which would directly involve low-income people in the design and administration of antipoverty activities in their communities through mandatory representation on local agency governing boards. Currently, these local agencies, generally known as Community Action Agencies (CAAs), are the primary substate grantees of the CSBG.

In 1975, OEO was renamed the Community Services Administration (CSA), but remained an independent executive branch agency. In 1981, CSA was abolished and replaced by the CSBG, to be administered by a newly created office in HHS. At the time CSA was abolished, it was administering nearly 900 CAAs, about 40 local community development corporations, and several small categorical programs that were typically operated by local CAAs. The CSBG Act was enacted as part of the Omnibus Budget Reconciliation Act of 1981 (P.L. 97-35, Title VI, §671; 42 U.S.C. §9901) as partial response to President Reagan's proposal to consolidate CSA with 11 other social service programs into a block grant to states. Congress rejected this proposal and instead created two new block grants, the Social Services Block Grant under Title XX of the Social Security Act, and the CSBG, which consisted of activities previously administered by CSA.

The CSBG Act was reauthorized in 1984 under P.L. 98-558, in 1986 under P.L. 99-425, in 1990 under P.L. 101-501, in 1994 under P.L. 103-252, and in 1998 under P.L. 105-285. The authorization of appropriations for CSBG and most related programs expired in FY2003, although Congress has continued to appropriate funds for the programs each year since then. The House and Senate passed reauthorization legislation during the 108th Congress but it was not enacted. Similar legislation was introduced in the 109th Congress but not considered. Legislation was introduced in the 113th Congress to amend and reauthorize the CSBG and related activities through FY2023 (H.R. 3854); however, no further action was taken. Similar legislation was introduced in the 114th Congress (H.R. 1655), but again received no further action. (For more details, see "Reauthorization Proposal in the 114th Congress.")

Several related national activities—Community Economic Development (CED), Rural Community Facilities (RCF), and Individual Development Accounts (IDAs)—receive appropriations separate from the block grant and offer grants to assist local low-income communities with economic development, rural housing and water management, and asset development for low-income individuals. These activities are administered at the federal level by the same Office of Community Services at HHS (part of the Administration for Children and Families) that administers the CSBG, and in some cases, are also authorized by the CSBG Act. Congress has also funded other related activities over the years, but none except CED, RCF, and IDAs have received funding since FY2011.

The Block Grant

Allocation of Funds

Of funds appropriated annually under the CSBG Act, HHS is required to reserve 1.5% for training and technical assistance and other administrative activities, and half of this set-aside must be provided to state or local entities. In addition, 0.5% of the appropriation is reserved for outlying territories (Guam, American Samoa, the U.S. Virgin Islands, and the Commonwealth of the Northern Mariana Islands). The law further requires that 9% of the total appropriation be reserved for certain related activities, which are described below, and that the remainder be allocated among the states. In practice, however, Congress typically specifies in annual appropriations laws exactly how much is to be made available for the block grant and each of the related activities. Block grant funds are allotted to states, including the District of Columbia and Puerto Rico, based on the relative amount received in each state in FY1981, under a section of the former Economic Opportunity Act. HHS may allow Indian tribes to receive their allotments directly, rather than through the state. See Table A-2 for a history of CSBG appropriations from its first year of funding (FY1982) through FY2017.

Use of Funds

CSBG funds are used for activities designed to have a "measurable and potentially major impact on causes of poverty." The law envisions a wide variety of activities undertaken on behalf of low-income families and individuals, including those who are welfare recipients, homeless, migrant or seasonal farm workers, or elderly. States must submit an application and plan to HHS, stating their intention that funds will be used for activities to help families and individuals achieve self-sufficiency, find and retain meaningful employment, attain an adequate education, make better use of available income, obtain adequate housing, and achieve greater participation in community affairs. In addition, states must ensure that funds will be used to address the needs of youth in low-income communities; coordinate with related programs, including state welfare reform efforts; and ensure that local grantees provide emergency food-related services.

State Role

At the state level, a lead agency must be designated to develop the state application and plan. States must pass through at least 90% of their federal CSBG allotment to local eligible entities.[3] States also may use up to $55,000 or 5% of their allotment, whichever is higher, for administrative costs.[4] Remaining funds may be used by the state to provide training and technical assistance, coordination and communication activities, payments to assure that funds are targeted to areas with the greatest need, supporting "asset-building" programs for low-income individuals (such as Individual Development Accounts, discussed later), supporting innovative programs and activities conducted by local organizations, or other activities consistent with the purposes of the CSBG Act. In addition, as authorized

---

[3] Under a one-time appropriation of $1 billion for the CSBG under the American Recovery and Reinvestment Act (ARRA, P.L. 111-5), states were required to pass through 99% of their allotments to local eligible entities and use the remaining 1% for benefits eligibility coordination activities.
[4] The Urban Institute conducted an evaluation of the use of CSBG administrative funds by state and local agencies, published in February 2012, which is available at http://www.urban.org/UploadedPDF/412601-Community-ServicesBlock-Grant-Administrative-Expenses.pdf.

by the 1998 amendments, states may use some CSBG funds to offset revenue losses associated with any qualified state charity tax credit.

Local Delivery System

As noted above, states are required to pass through at least 90% of their federal block grant allotments to "eligible entities"—primarily (but not exclusively) Community Action Agencies (CAAs) that had been designated prior to 1981 under the former Economic Opportunity Act. The distribution of these funds among local agencies is left to the discretion of the state, although states may not terminate funding to an eligible entity or reduce its share disproportionately without determining cause, after notice and an opportunity for a hearing.[5] There are more than 1,000 eligible entities around the country, the majority of which are private nonprofit organizations. Many of these organizations contract with others in delivering various services.

Once designated as an eligible entity for a particular community, an agency retains its designation unless it voluntarily withdraws from the program or its grant is terminated for cause. Eligible entities are monitored within a systematic schedule; return visits are made when goals are not met. In designating new or replacement entities, states may select a public agency only when no qualified private nonprofit organization is available, in accordance with the 1998 CSBG amendments.

Local activities vary depending on the needs and circumstances of the local community. Each eligible entity, or CAA, is governed by a board of directors, of which at least one-third of members are representatives of the low-income community. Under the 1998 amendments to the CSBG Act, low-income board members must live in the community that they represent. Another third of the board members must be local elected officials or their representatives, and the remaining board members represent other community interests, such as business, labor, religious

---

[5] 42 U.S.C. §9908(b)(8).The law contains four exceptions to the prohibition against states reducing funding to an eligible entity below its proportional share of funding in the previous year: changes in recent Census data, designation of a new eligible entity, severe economic dislocation, or failure of an eligible entity to comply with state requirements. See 42 U.S.C. §9908(c).

organizations, and education. A public entity must either have a governing board with low-income representation as described above, or another mechanism specified by the state to assure participation by low-income individuals in the development, planning, implementation, and evaluation of programs.

There is no typical CAA, since each agency designs its programs based on a local community needs assessment. Examples, however, of CSBG-funded services include emergency assistance, home weatherization, activities for youth and senior citizens, transportation, income management and credit counseling, domestic violence crisis assistance, parenting education, food pantries, and emergency shelters. In addition, local agencies provide information and referral to other community services, such as job training and vocational education, depending on the needs of individual clients. CAAs may also receive federal funds from other sources and may administer federal programs such as Head Start and energy assistance programs. For more information, see the "Use of Federal CSBG Funds" section of this report.

Related Activities

In addition to the block grant itself, the CSBG Act has authorized various related activities over the years that have been funded along with CSBG and administered through the Office of Community Services (OCS) within HHS. There have also been programs authorized by other laws but administered by OCS. These programs provided various types of assistance, including food and nutrition assistance and help obtaining jobs, and programs have targeted services to specific populations including migrant farmworkers and people experiencing homelessness.

Most of the related activities administered through OCS no longer receive funding, and some have not been funded for many years. See Table A-3 for programs that have been funded from FY1982 to the present. Two of these programs—CED and RCF, both authorized by the CSBG Act—continue to be funded, and have received funding in every year since

FY1982. In addition, a third program, Individual Development Accounts (IDAs), is also administered by the Office of Community Services, though it is not directly authorized by the CSBG Act.[6] IDAs were funded in every year since their creation as a demonstration program in 1998 until FY2017, when they were not funded for the first time. This section describes these three recently funded, related activities.

Community Economic Development[7]

The Community Economic Development (CED) program helps support local community development corporations (CDCs) to generate employment and business development opportunities for low-income residents. Projects must directly benefit persons living at or below the poverty level and must be completed within 12 to 60 months of the date the grant was awarded. Preferred projects are those that document public/private partnership, including the leveraging of cash and in-kind contributions; and those that are located in areas characterized by poverty, a Temporary Assistance for Needy Families (TANF) assistance rate of at least 20%, high levels of unemployment or incidences of violence, gang activity, and other indicators of socioeconomic distress.

During FY2016, HHS supported 39 grants, all of which were continuations of existing grants, plus three contracts and two interagency agreements, according to agency budget documents.[8] While HHS expected to fund the same number of grantees in FY2017, ultimately Congress reduced CED funding by $10 million (from $30 million to $20 million), so it is unclear whether the same number of grants will be funded. As of the date of this report, information on FY2017 grantees was not available.

---

[6] The Office of Community Services administers several additional programs; however, these are not considered part of the cluster of CSBG-related activities and are not discussed in this report. These programs include the Social Services Block Grant (SSBG) and the Low-Income Home Energy Assistance Program (LIHEAP).

[7] For more information on this program, see http://www.acf.hhs.gov/programs/ocs/programs/ced.

[8] U.S. Department of Health and Human Services, *FY2018 Administration for Children and Families Budget Justifications*, p. 150, https://www.acf.hhs.gov/sites/default/files/olab/acf_master_cj_508_compmay_21_2017.pdf (hereinafter *FY2018 ACF Budget Justifications*).

Healthy Food Financing Initiative

From FY2011 through FY2016, approximately $10 million per year has been set aside from the CED appropriation for the Healthy Food Financing Initiative (HFFI).[9] HFFI is a multiyear, multiagency effort through which HHS has partnered with the Departments of Agriculture (USDA) and the Treasury to make available a total of $400 million to address the lack of affordable healthy food in many urban and rural communities (areas known as "food deserts"). Under the HHS/CED component, competitive grants go to community development corporations for projects to finance grocery stores, farmers markets, and other sources of fresh nutritious food, creating employment and business opportunities in low-income communities while also providing access to healthy food options.[10] Legislation to formally authorize the program in USDA was passed by Congress as part of the 2014 "farm bill" (P.L. 113-79). As of the date of this report, information on FY2017 grantees was not available.

Rural Community Facilities[11]

Rural Community Facilities (RCF) funds are for grants to public and private nonprofit organizations for rural housing and community facilities development projects to train and offer technical assistance on the following: home repair to low-income families, water and waste water facilities management, and developing low-income rental housing units. Each year, beginning with its FY2010 budget request to Congress through FY2017, the Obama Administration proposed to terminate RCF, arguing that it does not belong in HHS. Instead, the Administration noted that federal assistance for water treatment facilities is available through two much larger programs in the Environmental Protection Agency (EPA) (i.e., the Clean Water and Drinking Water State Revolving Funds) and through

---

[9] Lists of HFFI grantees from FY2011 through FY2016 are available on the HHS website, https://www.acf.hhs.gov/ocs/programs/community-economic-development/healthy-food-financing.

[10] For more information about the HHS component of this program, see http://www.acf.hhs.gov/programs/ocs/programs/community-economic-development/healthy-food-financing.

[11] For more information about this program, also known as the Rural Community Development Program, see http://www.acf.hhs.gov/programs/ocs/programs/rcd.

loans and grants administered by USDA. The FY2018 Trump Administration budget proposed to eliminate funding for RCF, stating that "services provided are duplicative of other federal programs."[12] Notwithstanding Administration requests to stop funding RCF, Congress has continued to provide funding for this program.

During FY2016, HHS supported eight grants, all of which were continuations of existing grants, plus one contract and one interagency agreement, according to agency budget documents.[13] In FY2017, the department again expected to support eight grants, one contract, and one interagency agreement. As of the date of this report, information on FY2017 grantees was not available. HHS expected no program activity in FY2018 due to the program's proposed termination.

Individual Development Accounts[14]

The Assets for Independence Act (AFI, Title IV, P.L. 105-285), enacted in 1998, initially authorized a five-year demonstration initiative to encourage low-income people to accumulate savings through Individual Development Accounts (IDAs).[15] The Assets for Independence Act expired at the end of FY2003, although Congress continued to provide appropriations for the program under this authority through FY2016. In FY2017, Congress did not provide funding for IDAs for the first time since the demonstration program was enacted.

IDAs are dedicated savings accounts that can be used for specific purposes, such as buying a first home, paying for college, or starting a business. Contributions are matched, and participants are given financial and investment counseling. To conduct the demonstration, grants are made to public or private nonprofit organizations that can raise an amount of

---

[12] *FY2018 ACF Budget Justifications*, p. 149.
[13] Ibid., p. 151.
[14] For more information on IDAs, see http://www.acf.hhs.gov/programs/ocs/programs/afi. Also see CRS Report RS22185, *Individual Development Accounts (IDAs): Background on Federal Grant Programs to Help Low-Income Families Save*, by Gene Falk; and the most recent annual report to Congress on the program by HHS, "Assets for Independence Program: Status at the Conclusion of the Fifteenth Year," available at https://www.acf.hhs.gov/sites/default/files/ocs/fy2014_15th_afi_report_to_congress_final_8_5_16b.pdf.
[15] IDAs are codified at 42 U.S.C. §604 note.

private and public (nonfederal) funds that is equal to the federal grant; federal matches into IDAs cannot exceed the non-federal matches. The maximum federal grant is $1 million each year.

According to Administration budget documents, in FY2016 the IDA program supported 42 new grants, 6 contracts, and 3 interagency agreements. While HHS expected to support a similar number of grants, contracts and agreements in FY2017, ultimately Congress did not appropriate funds.

In the 115th Congress, a bill to amend and reauthorize IDAs, the Stephanie Tubbs Jones Assets for Independence Reauthorization Act (H.R. 271), would fund IDAs at an annual level of $75 million through FY2022. A similar bill with the same title (H.R. 3367) was introduced in the 114th Congress. Two other bills in the 114th Congress also would have reauthorized IDAs.[16]

CSBG PROGRAM DATA

Data on the programs administered and people served by CSBG local eligible entities are captured in CSBG Annual Reports. Since 1987, HHS has contracted with the National Association for State Community Services Programs (NASCSP) to collect, analyze, and publish data related to CSBG through a survey of the 50 states, the District of Columbia, and Puerto Rico.[17] HHS also produces annual CSBG Reports to Congress using the data collected for the CSBG Annual Reports.[18]

---

[16] These were the Refund to Rainy Day Savings Act (S. 2797), which would have authorized IDAs at $25 million through FY2021, and the Saving Our Next Generation Act (S. 473), which would have reauthorized the program through FY2020.

[17] See the *Community Services Block Grant Annual Report 2016*, National Association for State Community Services Programs, Washington, DC, February 2017, p. 8, available at http://www.nascsp.org/data/files/csbg_publications/annual_reports/2016/2016%20annual%20report_final_01%2017%2017_full.pdf (hereinafter *2016 CSBG Annual Report*).

[18] See, for example, *Community Services Block Grant Report to Congress, FY2013*, p. 7, https://www.acf.hhs.gov/sites/default/files/ocs/rtc_csbg_fy2013.pdf. CSBG Reports to Congress are available on the HHS website, https://www.acf.hhs.gov/ocs/resource/csbg-report-to-congress-0.

Recipients of CSBG Services

According to states responding to the survey, the CSBG network provided services to 15.6 million individuals in 6.5 million families in FY2015.[27] Of families for whom the survey captured demographic information, more than 70% had incomes at or below federal poverty guidelines and almost a third of families were "severely poor" with incomes at or below 50% of the poverty guidelines.[28] Some 47% of families reported income that indicated participation in employment. About 88% of families that reported some income included either a worker, an unemployed job-seeker, or a retired worker.[29] Almost half of the families included children; of those, 58% were headed by a single mother, 36% by two parents, and 6% by a single father.[30] Looking at participants by age, the survey found that 37% of individuals served were children age 17 or younger, and 21% were age 55 or older.[31] About 57% of individuals reported they were white and 26% were African American. Almost 19% of individuals reported their ethnicity as Hispanic or Latino, regardless of race.[32]

The survey collected information on potential barriers to self-sufficiency and reported that, of people served by the CSBG network in FY2015, approximately 27% had no health insurance (a decline from 32% in FY2013 and the same percentage without insurance as FY2014); 18% had disabilities; and 33% of participating adults older than 24 had no high school diploma or equivalency certificate.[33]

---

[27] Ibid., p. 46.
[28] Ibid.
[29] Ibid., p. 47.
[30] Ibid., p. 48.
[31] Ibid., p. 50.
[32] Ibid., p. 49.
[33] Ibid., pp. 50-51.

The most recent CSBG Annual Report summarizes data from FY2015. According to the report, the nationwide CSBG network consisted of 1,026 local eligible entities in FY2015, including 907 Community Action Agencies, 79 local government agencies, 16 "limited purpose agencies" that specialized in one or two types of programs, 16 tribes or tribal organizations,[19] 6 migrant or seasonal farmworker organizations, and 2 organizations that fell into other categories.[20]

This network of local eligible entities reported spending nearly $13.6 billion in FY2015, with funding coming from federal, state, local, and private sources. Of the total amount spent, $637 million came from the federal CSBG allotment, and another $8.3 billion came from federal programs other than CSBG.[21] Approximately $1.7 billion came from state governments, $1.5 billion came from private agencies, and nearly $1.5 billion came from local governments. In addition to these financial resources, the estimated value of volunteer hours was $298 million.

Use of Federal CSBG Funds

Based on reports from all jurisdictions, local entities spent their CSBG funds in FY2015 for a wide variety of activities, including emergency services (17%); activities to promote self-sufficiency (17%); activities to promote linkages among community groups and other government or private organizations (13%); education-related activities (12%); employment-related activities (13%); housing-related services (9%); nutrition services (7%); income management (6%); health services (3%); and other activities.[22]

Sources of Federal Non-CSBG Funds

The bulk of funds spent by local eligible entities come from federal programs other than CSBG. More than half of the funding in FY2015 was dedicated to Head Start or energy assistance.[23] Of nearly $8.3 billion in non-CSBG federal funds spent by local agencies in FY2015, 35% came from Head Start or Early Head Start. Low Income Home Energy Assistance Program (LIHEAP) fuel assistance made up 15% of federal funds spent by local agencies, and LIHEAP weatherization funding, together with funding from the Department of Energy's Weatherization Assistance Program, made up another 5% of funding.

States reported that nearly 10% of federal non-CSBG funds received by local agencies came from Agriculture Department nutrition programs, including almost 3% from the Special Supplemental Nutrition Program for Women, Infants and Children (WIC) alone.[24] Another 6% of federal non-CSBG funds came from the TANF block grant, more than 3% came from employment and training programs administered by the Labor Department, and almost 3% came from the Department of Housing and Urban Development (HUD) Section 8 program.[25] The Child Care and Development Block Grant and funding for Medicare/Medicaid each accounted for more than 2% of funding.[26]

---

[19] Tribes and tribal organizations may participate in the CSBG program as local eligible entities (i.e., substate grantees). In addition, tribes may request to receive funds directly from HHS, rather than through the state in which they are located. For example, in FY2017, 69 individual tribes or tribal organizations received direct allotments from HHS. These amounts were subtracted from the allotments of states in which the tribe or tribal organization was located. See https://www.acf.hhs.gov/sites/default/files/ocs/list_csbg_4th_quarter_allocations_fy2017.pdf.

[20] *2016 CSBG Annual Report*, p.7.

[21] Ibid., p. 52.

[22] Ibid., p. 55.

[23] Ibid., Appendix Table 23-1.

[24] Ibid., Appendix Table 23-3.

[25] Ibid., Appendix Tables 23-2, 23-4, and 23-5.

[26] Ibid., Appendix Tables 23-2 and 23-3.

FUNDING FOR CSBG AND RELATED ACTIVITIES

FY2018 Funding

As of the date of this report, FY2018 funding for CSBG has been provided via a series of continuing resolutions (CRs).[34] To date, the CRs fund most federal programs, including CSBG, at FY2017 levels less an across-the-board rescission of 0.6791%, through February 8, 2018. For CSBG, the FY2017 funding level was $715 million, while CED received $20 million and RCF $7.5 million. No funding was provided for IDAs in FY2017.

Prior to enactment of the CRs, the Administration proposed to eliminate funding for CSBG, CED, and RCF. Additionally, IDAs would have continued at zero funding under the Administration's proposal. HHS budget justifications stated that "[i]n a constrained budget environment, difficult funding decisions were made to ensure that federal funds are being spent as effectively as possible."[35]

The House Appropriations Committee approved a bill to fund the Departments of Labor, Health and Human Services, and Education (LHHS) on July 24, 2017 (H.R. 3358). The bill proposed to reduce funding for CSBG to $600 million, to reduce funding for CED to $10 million, and to maintain RCF funding at $7.5 million. Additionally, the bill would not fund IDAs. The House Appropriations Committee report (H.Rept. 115-244) would direct HHS to issue a notice of funding availability prioritizing applicants for CED funds from "rural areas with high rates of poverty, unemployment, and substance abuse."

In addition, on August 16, 2017, the full House passed a bill (H.R. 3354) that incorporated multiple FY2018 appropriations bills, including

---

[34] The Continuing Appropriations Act, 2018, and Supplemental Appropriations for Disaster Relief Requirements Act, 2017 (P.L. 115-56), enacted on September 8, 2017, funded federal programs, including CSBG, until December 8, 2017. A second CR (P.L. 115-90) extended funding through December 22, 2017, a third CR (P.L. 115-96) extended funding through January 19, 2018, and a fourth CR (H.R. 195) provided funding through February 8, 2018.

[35] *FY2018 ACF Budget Justifications*, p. 144.

that for LHHS. Funding for CSBG and related programs in H.R. 3354 was the same as the levels proposed in H.R. 3358.

The Senate Appropriations Committee reported its LHHS funding bill on September 7, 2017 (S. 1771). The bill would reduce funding for CSBG by $15 million, from $715 million to $700 million. Funding for CED and RCF would remain the same at approximately $20 million and $7.5 million, respectively, and IDAs would receive no funding. Similar to H.Rept. 115-244, the Senate Appropriations Committee report (S.Rept. 115-150) encourages CED funds to be prioritized for rural communities "to help them identify community service needs and improve upon the services provided to low-income individuals and families in such communities."

Table 1. FY2016-FY2017 Enacted and FY2018 Proposed Funding for CSBG and Related Activities (Dollars in millions)

Program	FY2016 Final (P.L. 114-113)	FY2017 Final (P.L. 115-31)	FY2018 President's Budget Proposal	FY2018 House Appropriations Committee (H.R. 3358)	FY2018 Senate Appropriations Committee (S. 1771)
Community Services Block Grant	715.00	714.65	0	600.00	700.00
Community Economic Development	29.88	19.88	0	10.00	19.88
Rural Community Facilities	6.50	7.50	0	7.50	7.50
Individual Development Accounts	18.95	0	0	0	0
Total for CSBG and Related Activities	**770.33**	**742.38**	**0**	**617.50**	**727.38**

Source: Prepared by the Congressional Research Service (CRS). Sources of data are agency budget justifications and congressional appropriations documents.

FY2017 Funding[36]

Final FY2017 Funding

For FY2017, Congress provided just over $742 million for CSBG and related activities as part of the FY2017 Consolidated Appropriations Act (P.L. 115-31), enacted on May 5, 2017. Prior to enactment of P.L. 115-31, CSBG and most federal programs had been funded pursuant to a series of continuing resolutions.[37] Of the amount appropriated, nearly $715 million went to the block grant, the same amount that was appropriated in FY2016. Funding for CED was reduced compared to FY2016, from $30 million to $20 million. Funding for RCF increased by $1 million compared to FY2016, from $6.5 million to $7.5 million. For the first time since IDAs were created in 1998, they received no funding. The accompanying Explanatory Statement did not provide a reason for eliminating funding for IDAs. The Senate Appropriations Committee-reported bill (described below) recommended no funding for IDAs, but the House Appropriations Committee-reported bill would have provided level funding of approximately $19 million.

House Committee Action

The House Appropriations Committee reported its FY2017 spending bill for the Departments of Labor, HHS, Education, and related agencies on July 22, 2016 (H.R. 5926, H.Rept. 114-699). The bill included level funding for CSBG and all related programs, except for Rural Community Facilities, which the House committee proposed to increase by $1 million. Recommended spending for CSBG and related activities in FY2017 would have totaled $771 million under H.R. 5926, compared to FY2016 spending of $770 million.

In its report accompanying the FY2017 spending bill, the House committee expressed concern that block grant funds "are not reaching local

---

[36] For background on FY2017 funding for HHS and related agencies, see CRS Report R44478, *Status of FY2017 Labor-HHS-Education Appropriations*, by Jessica Tollestrup, Karen E. Lynch, and David H. Bradley.

[37] P.L. 114-223 provided funding through December 9, 2017, P.L. 114-254 through April 28, 2017, and P.L. 115-30 through May 5, 2017.

agencies and community residents promptly." The report contained language urging HHS to "take all necessary action" to ensure funds are allocated and made available in a timely way, and also to "engage with stakeholders" on new data collection and federal reporting initiatives. The committee further stated that it wanted an update on these efforts.

The report also explained the House committee's decision to continue funding for CED (which the Obama Administration, as described below, proposed to zero out). The report stated that CED, which requires that low-income individuals fill at least 75% of jobs created, is the only federal economic development program with such highly targeted job creation. Likewise, the committee would have maintained and increased funding for RCF, despite the Obama Administration's request for zero funding, explaining that some of the small rural communities served by the program may not be eligible for larger programs administered by the Department of Agriculture or the Environmental Protection Agency.

Finally, the House committee, like the Senate committee and as requested by the Obama Administration (see below), would have required the Secretary to issue performance standards for states and territories receiving block grant funds, and would have required the states and territories to implement these standards by September 30, 2017, and report on their progress. This language built upon language in previous appropriations laws and reflected actions underway at HHS.

Additional statutory provisions requested by the Obama Administration, described below, were not included in the recommended House bill language.

Senate Committee Action

The Senate Appropriations Committee reported its FY2017 Labor-HHS-ED spending bill on June 9, 2016 (S. 3040, S.Rept. 114-274), recommending $715 million for the block grant (the same as the House recommendation and the FY2016 level) and no funding for any of the related activities. The committee agreed with the Obama Administration that both CED and RCF are similar to programs administered by the Department of Agriculture and Environmental Protection Agency. The committee further stated that IDAs began in 1998 as a demonstration program and, thus, no further funding is recommended.

As noted above, the Senate committee, like the House committee, would have included legislative language requested by the Obama Administration related to the issuance and implementation of performance standards for states and territories. However, the Senate language did not include the Obama Administration's other proposed statutory provisions.

Obama Administration Budget and Legislative Proposals

President Obama submitted his FY2017 budget to Congress in February 2016, requesting a total of $693 million for CSBG and related activities. This amount included $674 million for the block grant, nothing for either CED or RCF, and level funding ($19 million) for IDAs. The amount requested for the block grant was the same as provided in FY2015, but was $41 million less than appropriated for FY2016.

As mentioned above, the Obama Administration requested certain legislative language to be included in the FY2017 appropriations bill, including provisions requiring states and territories to implement national performance standards. This language built on provisions in the FY2016 appropriations law requiring the Secretary to issue such national standards, and was part of a larger effort to establish a new performance management framework for CSBG.

In the FY2017 budget request, the Obama Administration also requested language that would provide flexibility in FY2017 and FY2018 for states to exceed the authorizing law's 5% cap on state administrative costs, as long as the excess funds were used for modernization of data systems and integration with other social services programs.

REAUTHORIZATION PROPOSAL IN THE 114TH CONGRESS

The authorization of appropriations for CSBG and related activities expired at the end of FY2003, although Congress has continued to fund these programs through the annual appropriations process. Until 2014, no reauthorization attempt had been made since the 109th Congress, when legislation was introduced, but not considered, in the House (H.R. 341). That legislation was largely identical to a bill that was passed by the House during the 108th Congress (H.R. 3030). The Senate also passed a reauthorization bill during the 108th Congress (S. 1786), but conferees never met to resolve differences between the House and Senate bills.

In both the 113th and 114th Congresses, for the first time since the 109th Congress, legislation was introduced in the House to reauthorize CSBG and certain related activities. In the 113th Congress, Representative Fitzpatrick introduced the Community Economic Opportunity Act, with bipartisan support, on January 13, 2014 (H.R. 3854). The bill was referred to the House Education and the Workforce Committee, but no further action occurred. Representative Fitzpatrick reintroduced a mostly identical version of the bill (with some changes) in the 114th Congress (H.R. 1655), where it was again referred to the House Education and the Workforce Committee but received no further action.[38]

H.R. 1655 would have made numerous changes in language throughout the statute, with more specific provisions regarding the roles and responsibilities of the federal Office of Community Services, state lead agencies, and local agency governing boards. The bill would have required federal, state, and local entities to establish performance requirements and benchmarks, and included provisions intended to increase accountability for the use of federal funds and to ensure timely distribution and expenditure of these funds. The bill had extensive provisions on monitoring of state and local compliance with applicable law and regulations, corrective action, and withholding, reduction, or elimination of federal funds.

H.R. 1655 proposed to authorize appropriations of $850 million per year for FY2014-FY2018, with "such sums as necessary" authorized for

---

[38] In addition to H.R. 1655, the multi-purpose Saving Our Next Generation Act (S. 473) was also introduced in the 114th Congress. It would have reauthorized CSBG with no changes through FY2014, and was referred to the Senate Finance Committee.

FY2019-FY2023.[39] Like current law, the bill would have required the Secretary to reserve 0.5% of appropriations for grants to territories, but would have increased the amount reserved for training and technical assistance from 1.5% to 2%. Remaining funds would have been allocated among states (including DC and Puerto Rico). While no change would have been made in the basic state allocation formula, the minimum allotment would have increased to one-half of 1% or, if appropriations exceeded $850 million in a given year, to three-quarters of 1%. Under current law, each state gets at least one-quarter of 1% or, if appropriations exceed $345 million, one-half of 1%. Current law provisions that hold states harmless at their FY1990 levels, and that establish a maximum allotment percentage, would have been eliminated under the bill.

The bill would have required states to reserve at least 2% of block grant funds received for a new Community Action Innovations Program. These funds would have gone to local eligible entities or their associations to carry out innovative projects that test or replicate promising practices to reduce poverty conditions, and to disseminate the results of these projects. These funds could have been used to satisfy nonfederal matching requirements when used in conjunction with other federal programs that have such requirements, and could have been used to serve participants with incomes up to 80% of area median income.

State applications and plans would have been subject to the Secretary's approval under H.R. 1655, a change from current law. Likewise, local community action plans would have been newly subject to the state's approval. Like the 113th Congress version of the bill (H.R. 3854), H.R. 1655 would have allowed states to request waivers from the Secretary to increase the income eligibility level for CSBG activities. However, H.R. 1655 also included a provision found in current law that allows states to increase eligibility to 125% of the poverty line whenever the state determines the change serves the objectives of the program, without the need for a waiver. This provision had not been included in H.R. 3854.

---

[39] The most recent CSBG *authorization* law (P.L. 105-285) did not specify an amount but authorized "such sums as necessary" for FY1999 through FY2003. The most recent *appropriations* law (P.L. 115-31) provided $715 million for the block grant in FY2017.

In designating new or replacement eligible entities, H.R. 1655 would have given priority to existing Community Action Agencies (which would have been explicitly defined for the first time) and public agencies could no longer be designated unless they were already serving as an eligible entity. H.R. 3854 would have allowed two or more local eligible entities to propose a merger, subject to state approval, if they determined their local service areas would be better served by a single agency. If approved, these agencies would have been eligible to receive Merger Incentive Funds from amounts reserved by the Secretary. H.R. 1655 had the same language with regard to mergers, but also would have allowed states to approve "privatization" proposals from public organizations that determined they could serve their areas more effectively as private eligible entities.

Current law provisions affecting the participation of religious organizations in CSBG-funded activities would have been retained by H.R. 1655. These provisions require federal, state, or local governments to consider religious organizations on the same basis as other nongovernmental organizations, and prohibit discrimination against such organizations on the basis of their religious character. Like current law, the pending legislation would have provided that a religious organization's exemption under Section 702 of the Civil Rights Act of 1964, regarding its employment practices, is not affected by participating in or receiving funds from programs under the CSBG Act. The bill also would have established a new provision, prohibiting religious organizations that provide assistance under the act from discriminating against a program beneficiary or prospective beneficiary on the basis of that person's religion or religious belief.

The bill would have separately authorized "such sums as necessary" for related federal activities, including Community Economic Development and Rural Community Facilities, during FY2014- FY2023. Current law requires that 9% of total appropriations be set aside for these related activities; however, this has never occurred in practice and the bill would have eliminated this language.[40]

---

[40] Most recently, P.L. 115-31 appropriated $20 million for Community Economic Development and $7.5 million for Rural Community Facilities in FY2017. (See the section of this report

private and public (nonfederal) funds that is equal to the federal grant; federal matches into IDAs cannot exceed the non-federal matches. The maximum federal grant is $1 million each year.

According to Administration budget documents, in FY2016 the IDA program supported 42 new grants, 6 contracts, and 3 interagency agreements. While HHS expected to support a similar number of grants, contracts and agreements in FY2017, ultimately Congress did not appropriate funds.

In the 115th Congress, a bill to amend and reauthorize IDAs, the Stephanie Tubbs Jones Assets for Independence Reauthorization Act (H.R. 271), would fund IDAs at an annual level of $75 million through FY2022. A similar bill with the same title (H.R. 3367) was introduced in the 114th Congress. Two other bills in the 114th Congress also would have reauthorized IDAs.[16]

CSBG PROGRAM DATA

Data on the programs administered and people served by CSBG local eligible entities are captured in CSBG Annual Reports. Since 1987, HHS has contracted with the National Association for State Community Services Programs (NASCSP) to collect, analyze, and publish data related to CSBG through a survey of the 50 states, the District of Columbia, and Puerto Rico.[17] HHS also produces annual CSBG Reports to Congress using the data collected for the CSBG Annual Reports.[18]

---

[16] These were the Refund to Rainy Day Savings Act (S. 2797), which would have authorized IDAs at $25 million through FY2021, and the Saving Our Next Generation Act (S. 473), which would have reauthorized the program through FY2020.

[17] See the *Community Services Block Grant Annual Report 2016*, National Association for State Community Services Programs, Washington, DC, February 2017, p. 8, available at http://www.nascsp.org/data/files/csbg_publications/annual_reports/2016/2016%20annual%20report_final_01%2017%2017_full.pdf (hereinafter *2016 CSBG Annual Report*).

[18] See, for example, *Community Services Block Grant Report to Congress, FY2013*, p. 7, https://www.acf.hhs.gov/sites/ default/files/ocs/rtc_csbg_fy2013.pdf. CSBG Reports to Congress are available on the HHS website, https://www.acf.hhs.gov/ocs/resource/csbg-report-to-congress-0.

The most recent CSBG Annual Report summarizes data from FY2015. According to the report, the nationwide CSBG network consisted of 1,026 local eligible entities in FY2015, including 907 Community Action Agencies, 79 local government agencies, 16 "limited purpose agencies" that specialized in one or two types of programs, 16 tribes or tribal organizations,[19] 6 migrant or seasonal farmworker organizations, and 2 organizations that fell into other categories.[20]

This network of local eligible entities reported spending nearly $13.6 billion in FY2015, with funding coming from federal, state, local, and private sources. Of the total amount spent, $637 million came from the federal CSBG allotment, and another $8.3 billion came from federal programs other than CSBG.[21] Approximately $1.7 billion came from state governments, $1.5 billion came from private agencies, and nearly $1.5 billion came from local governments. In addition to these financial resources, the estimated value of volunteer hours was $298 million.

Use of Federal CSBG Funds

Based on reports from all jurisdictions, local entities spent their CSBG funds in FY2015 for a wide variety of activities, including emergency services (17%); activities to promote self-sufficiency (17%); activities to promote linkages among community groups and other government or private organizations (13%); education-related activities (12%); employment-related activities (13%); housing-related services (9%);

---

[19] Tribes and tribal organizations may participate in the CSBG program as local eligible entities (i.e., substate grantees). In addition, tribes may request to receive funds directly from HHS, rather than through the state in which they are located. For example, in FY2017, 69 individual tribes or tribal organizations received direct allotments from HHS. These amounts were subtracted from the allotments of states in which the tribe or tribal organization was located. See https://www.acf.hhs.gov/sites/default/files/ocs/list_csbg_4th_quarter_allocations_fy2017.pdf.
[20] *2016 CSBG Annual Report*, p.7.
[21] Ibid., p. 52.

nutrition services (7%); income management (6%); health services (3%); and other activities.[22]

Sources of Federal Non-CSBG Funds

The bulk of funds spent by local eligible entities come from federal programs other than CSBG. More than half of the funding in FY2015 was dedicated to Head Start or energy assistance.[23] Of nearly $8.3 billion in non-CSBG federal funds spent by local agencies in FY2015, 35% came from Head Start or Early Head Start. Low Income Home Energy Assistance Program (LIHEAP) fuel assistance made up 15% of federal funds spent by local agencies, and LIHEAP weatherization funding, together with funding from the Department of Energy's **Weatherization Assistance Program**, made up another 5% of funding.

States reported that nearly 10% of federal non-CSBG funds received by local agencies came from Agriculture Department nutrition programs, including almost 3% from the Special Supplemental Nutrition Program for Women, Infants and Children (WIC) alone.[24] Another 6% of federal non-CSBG funds came from the TANF block grant, more than 3% came from employment and training programs administered by the Labor Department, and almost 3% came from the Department of Housing and Urban Development (HUD) Section 8 program.[25] The Child Care and Development Block Grant and funding for Medicare/Medicaid each accounted for more than 2% of funding.[26]

---

[22] Ibid., p. 55.
[23] Ibid., Appendix Table 23-1.
[24] Ibid., Appendix Table 23-3.
[25] Ibid., Appendix Tables 23-2, 23-4, and 23-5.
[26] Ibid., Appendix Tables 23-2 and 23-3.

Recipients of CSBG Services

According to states responding to the survey, the CSBG network provided services to 15.6 million individuals in 6.5 million families in FY2015.[27] Of families for whom the survey captured demographic information, more than 70% had incomes at or below federal poverty guidelines and almost a third of families were "severely poor" with incomes at or below 50% of the poverty guidelines.[28] Some 47% of families reported income that indicated participation in employment. About 88% of families that reported some income included either a worker, an unemployed job-seeker, or a retired worker.[29] Almost half of the families included children; of those, 58% were headed by a single mother, 36% by two parents, and 6% by a single father.[30] Looking at participants by age, the survey found that 37% of individuals served were children age 17 or younger, and 21% were age 55 or older.[31] About 57% of individuals reported they were white and 26% were African American. Almost 19% of individuals reported their ethnicity as Hispanic or Latino, regardless of race.[32]

The survey collected information on potential barriers to self-sufficiency and reported that, of people served by the CSBG network in FY2015, approximately 27% had no health insurance (a decline from 32% in FY2013 and the same percentage without insurance as FY2014); 18% had disabilities; and 33% of participating adults older than 24 had no high school diploma or equivalency certificate.[33]

---

[27] Ibid., p. 46.
[28] Ibid.
[29] Ibid., p. 47.
[30] Ibid., p. 48.
[31] Ibid., p. 50.
[32] Ibid., p. 49.
[33] Ibid., pp. 50-51.

FUNDING FOR CSBG AND RELATED ACTIVITIES

FY2018 Funding

As of the date of this report, FY2018 funding for CSBG has been provided via a series of continuing resolutions (CRs).[34] To date, the CRs fund most federal programs, including CSBG, at FY2017 levels less an across-the-board rescission of 0.6791%, through February 8, 2018. For CSBG, the FY2017 funding level was $715 million, while CED received $20 million and RCF $7.5 million. No funding was provided for IDAs in FY2017.

Prior to enactment of the CRs, the Administration proposed to eliminate funding for CSBG, CED, and RCF. Additionally, IDAs would have continued at zero funding under the Administration's proposal. HHS budget justifications stated that "[i]n a constrained budget environment, difficult funding decisions were made to ensure that federal funds are being spent as effectively as possible."[35]

The House Appropriations Committee approved a bill to fund the Departments of Labor, Health and Human Services, and Education (LHHS) on July 24, 2017 (H.R. 3358). The bill proposed to reduce funding for CSBG to $600 million, to reduce funding for CED to $10 million, and to maintain RCF funding at $7.5 million. Additionally, the bill would not fund IDAs. The House Appropriations Committee report (H.Rept. 115-244) would direct HHS to issue a notice of funding availability prioritizing applicants for CED funds from "rural areas with high rates of poverty, unemployment, and substance abuse."

In addition, on August 16, 2017, the full House passed a bill (H.R. 3354) that incorporated multiple FY2018 appropriations bills, including

---

[34] The Continuing Appropriations Act, 2018, and Supplemental Appropriations for Disaster Relief Requirements Act, 2017 (P.L. 115-56), enacted on September 8, 2017, funded federal programs, including CSBG, until December 8, 2017. A second CR (P.L. 115-90) extended funding through December 22, 2017, a third CR (P.L. 115-96) extended funding through January 19, 2018, and a fourth CR (H.R. 195) provided funding through February 8, 2018.

[35] *FY2018 ACF Budget Justifications*, p. 144.

that for LHHS. Funding for CSBG and related programs in H.R. 3354 was the same as the levels proposed in H.R. 3358.

The Senate Appropriations Committee reported its LHHS funding bill on September 7, 2017 (S. 1771). The bill would reduce funding for CSBG by $15 million, from $715 million to $700 million. Funding for CED and RCF would remain the same at approximately $20 million and $7.5 million, respectively, and IDAs would receive no funding. Similar to H.Rept. 115-244, the Senate Appropriations Committee report (S.Rept. 115-150) encourages CED funds to be prioritized for rural communities "to help them identify community service needs and improve upon the services provided to low-income individuals and families in such communities."

Table 1. FY2016-FY2017 Enacted and FY2018 Proposed Funding for CSBG and Related Activities (Dollars in millions)

Program	FY2016 Final (P.L. 114-113)	FY2017 Final (P.L. 115-31)	FY2018 President's Budget Proposal	FY2018 House Appropriations Committee (H.R. 3358)	FY2018 Senate Appropriations Committee (S. 1771)
Community Services Block Grant	715.00	714.65	0	600.00	700.00
Community Economic Development	29.88	19.88	0	10.00	19.88
Rural Community Facilities	6.50	7.50	0	7.50	7.50
Individual Development Accounts	18.95	0	0	0	0
Total for CSBG and Related Activities	**770.33**	**742.38**	**0**	**617.50**	**727.38**

Source: Prepared by the Congressional Research Service (CRS). Sources of data are agency budget justifications and congressional appropriations documents.

FY2017 Funding[36]

Final FY2017 Funding

For FY2017, Congress provided just over $742 million for CSBG and related activities as part of the FY2017 Consolidated Appropriations Act (P.L. 115-31), enacted on May 5, 2017. Prior to enactment of P.L. 115-31, CSBG and most federal programs had been funded pursuant to a series of continuing resolutions.[37] Of the amount appropriated, nearly $715 million went to the block grant, the same amount that was appropriated in FY2016. Funding for CED was reduced compared to FY2016, from $30 million to $20 million. Funding for RCF increased by $1 million compared to FY2016, from $6.5 million to $7.5 million. For the first time since IDAs were created in 1998, they received no funding. The accompanying Explanatory Statement did not provide a reason for eliminating funding for IDAs. The Senate Appropriations Committee-reported bill (described below) recommended no funding for IDAs, but the House Appropriations Committee-reported bill would have provided level funding of approximately $19 million.

House Committee Action

The House Appropriations Committee reported its FY2017 spending bill for the Departments of Labor, HHS, Education, and related agencies on July 22, 2016 (H.R. 5926, H.Rept. 114-699). The bill included level funding for CSBG and all related programs, except for Rural Community Facilities, which the House committee proposed to increase by $1 million. Recommended spending for CSBG and related activities in FY2017 would have totaled $771 million under H.R. 5926, compared to FY2016 spending of $770 million.

In its report accompanying the FY2017 spending bill, the House committee expressed concern that block grant funds "are not reaching local

---

[36] For background on FY2017 funding for HHS and related agencies, see CRS Report R44478, *Status of FY2017 Labor-HHS-Education Appropriations*, by Jessica Tollestrup, Karen E. Lynch, and David H. Bradley.

[37] P.L. 114-223 provided funding through December 9, 2017, P.L. 114-254 through April 28, 2017, and P.L. 115-30 through May 5, 2017.

agencies and community residents promptly." The report contained language urging HHS to "take all necessary action" to ensure funds are allocated and made available in a timely way, and also to "engage with stakeholders" on new data collection and federal reporting initiatives. The committee further stated that it wanted an update on these efforts.

The report also explained the House committee's decision to continue funding for CED (which the Obama Administration, as described below, proposed to zero out). The report stated that CED, which requires that low-income individuals fill at least 75% of jobs created, is the only federal economic development program with such highly targeted job creation. Likewise, the committee would have maintained and increased funding for RCF, despite the Obama Administration's request for zero funding, explaining that some of the small rural communities served by the program may not be eligible for larger programs administered by the Department of Agriculture or the Environmental Protection Agency.

Finally, the House committee, like the Senate committee and as requested by the Obama Administration (see below), would have required the Secretary to issue performance standards for states and territories receiving block grant funds, and would have required the states and territories to implement these standards by September 30, 2017, and report on their progress. This language built upon language in previous appropriations laws and reflected actions underway at HHS.

Additional statutory provisions requested by the Obama Administration, described below, were not included in the recommended House bill language.

Senate Committee Action

The Senate Appropriations Committee reported its FY2017 Labor-HHS-ED spending bill on June 9, 2016 (S. 3040, S.Rept. 114-274), recommending $715 million for the block grant (the same as the House recommendation and the FY2016 level) and no funding for any of the related activities. The committee agreed with the Obama Administration that both CED and RCF are similar to programs administered by the Department of Agriculture and Environmental Protection Agency. The committee further stated that IDAs began in 1998 as a demonstration program and, thus, no further funding is recommended.

As noted above, the Senate committee, like the House committee, would have included legislative language requested by the Obama Administration related to the issuance and implementation of performance standards for states and territories. However, the Senate language did not include the Obama Administration's other proposed statutory provisions.

Obama Administration Budget and Legislative Proposals

President Obama submitted his FY2017 budget to Congress in February 2016, requesting a total of $693 million for CSBG and related activities. This amount included $674 million for the block grant, nothing for either CED or RCF, and level funding ($19 million) for IDAs. The amount requested for the block grant was the same as provided in FY2015, but was $41 million less than appropriated for FY2016.

As mentioned above, the Obama Administration requested certain legislative language to be included in the FY2017 appropriations bill, including provisions requiring states and territories to implement national performance standards. This language built on provisions in the FY2016 appropriations law requiring the Secretary to issue such national standards, and was part of a larger effort to establish a new performance management framework for CSBG.

In the FY2017 budget request, the Obama Administration also requested language that would provide flexibility in FY2017 and FY2018 for states to exceed the authorizing law's 5% cap on state administrative costs, as long as the excess funds were used for modernization of data systems and integration with other social services programs.

REAUTHORIZATION PROPOSAL IN THE 114TH CONGRESS

The authorization of appropriations for CSBG and related activities expired at the end of FY2003, although Congress has continued to fund these programs through the annual appropriations process. Until 2014, no reauthorization attempt had been made since the 109th Congress, when legislation was introduced, but not considered, in the House (H.R. 341). That legislation was largely identical to a bill that was passed by the House during the 108th Congress (H.R. 3030). The Senate also passed a reauthorization bill during the 108th Congress (S. 1786), but conferees never met to resolve differences between the House and Senate bills.

In both the 113th and 114th Congresses, for the first time since the 109th Congress, legislation was introduced in the House to reauthorize CSBG and certain related activities. In the 113th Congress, Representative Fitzpatrick introduced the Community Economic Opportunity Act, with bipartisan support, on January 13, 2014 (H.R. 3854). The bill was referred to the House Education and the Workforce Committee, but no further action occurred. Representative Fitzpatrick reintroduced a mostly identical version of the bill (with some changes) in the 114th Congress (H.R. 1655), where it was again referred to the House Education and the Workforce Committee but received no further action.[38]

H.R. 1655 would have made numerous changes in language throughout the statute, with more specific provisions regarding the roles and responsibilities of the federal Office of Community Services, state lead agencies, and local agency governing boards. The bill would have required federal, state, and local entities to establish performance requirements and benchmarks, and included provisions intended to increase accountability for the use of federal funds and to ensure timely distribution and expenditure of these funds. The bill had extensive provisions on monitoring of state and local compliance with applicable law and regulations, corrective action, and withholding, reduction, or elimination of federal funds.

H.R. 1655 proposed to authorize appropriations of $850 million per year for FY2014-FY2018, with "such sums as necessary" authorized for

---

[38] In addition to H.R. 1655, the multi-purpose Saving Our Next Generation Act (S. 473) was also introduced in the 114th Congress. It would have reauthorized CSBG with no changes through FY2014, and was referred to the Senate Finance Committee.

FY2019-FY2023.[39] Like current law, the bill would have required the Secretary to reserve 0.5% of appropriations for grants to territories, but would have increased the amount reserved for training and technical assistance from 1.5% to 2%. Remaining funds would have been allocated among states (including DC and Puerto Rico). While no change would have been made in the basic state allocation formula, the minimum allotment would have increased to one-half of 1% or, if appropriations exceeded $850 million in a given year, to three-quarters of 1%. Under current law, each state gets at least one-quarter of 1% or, if appropriations exceed $345 million, one-half of 1%. Current law provisions that hold states harmless at their FY1990 levels, and that establish a maximum allotment percentage, would have been eliminated under the bill.

The bill would have required states to reserve at least 2% of block grant funds received for a new Community Action Innovations Program. These funds would have gone to local eligible entities or their associations to carry out innovative projects that test or replicate promising practices to reduce poverty conditions, and to disseminate the results of these projects. These funds could have been used to satisfy nonfederal matching requirements when used in conjunction with other federal programs that have such requirements, and could have been used to serve participants with incomes up to 80% of area median income.

State applications and plans would have been subject to the Secretary's approval under H.R. 1655, a change from current law. Likewise, local community action plans would have been newly subject to the state's approval. Like the 113th Congress version of the bill (H.R. 3854), H.R. 1655 would have allowed states to request waivers from the Secretary to increase the income eligibility level for CSBG activities. However, H.R. 1655 also included a provision found in current law that allows states to increase eligibility to 125% of the poverty line whenever the state determines the change serves the objectives of the program, without the need for a waiver. This provision had not been included in H.R. 3854.

---

[39] The most recent CSBG *authorization* law (P.L. 105-285) did not specify an amount but authorized "such sums as necessary" for FY1999 through FY2003. The most recent *appropriations* law (P.L. 115-31) provided $715 million for the block grant in FY2017.

In designating new or replacement eligible entities, H.R. 1655 would have given priority to existing Community Action Agencies (which would have been explicitly defined for the first time) and public agencies could no longer be designated unless they were already serving as an eligible entity. H.R. 3854 would have allowed two or more local eligible entities to propose a merger, subject to state approval, if they determined their local service areas would be better served by a single agency. If approved, these agencies would have been eligible to receive Merger Incentive Funds from amounts reserved by the Secretary. H.R. 1655 had the same language with regard to mergers, but also would have allowed states to approve "privatization" proposals from public organizations that determined they could serve their areas more effectively as private eligible entities.

Current law provisions affecting the participation of religious organizations in CSBG-funded activities would have been retained by H.R. 1655. These provisions require federal, state, or local governments to consider religious organizations on the same basis as other nongovernmental organizations, and prohibit discrimination against such organizations on the basis of their religious character. Like current law, the pending legislation would have provided that a religious organization's exemption under Section 702 of the Civil Rights Act of 1964, regarding its employment practices, is not affected by participating in or receiving funds from programs under the CSBG Act. The bill also would have established a new provision, prohibiting religious organizations that provide assistance under the act from discriminating against a program beneficiary or prospective beneficiary on the basis of that person's religion or religious belief.

The bill would have separately authorized "such sums as necessary" for related federal activities, including Community Economic Development and Rural Community Facilities, during FY2014- FY2023. Current law requires that 9% of total appropriations be set aside for these related activities; however, this has never occurred in practice and the bill would have eliminated this language.[40]

---

[40] Most recently, P.L. 115-31 appropriated $20 million for Community Economic Development and $7.5 million for Rural Community Facilities in FY2017. (See the section of this report

Appendix A. Additional Funding Information

This appendix provides additional funding information for Community Services Block Grants and related activities.

- Table A-1 shows funding amounts distributed to the states, tribes, and territories from FY2013 through FY2017.

Table A-1. Community Services Block Grant Funding Distributed to States, Tribes, and Territories FY2013-FY2017 (Dollars in millions)

	FY2013	FY2014	FY2015	FY2016	FY2017
Alabama	11.596	12.190	12.300	13.052	12.926
Alaska	2.467	2.498	2.522	2.668	2.610
Arizona	5.163	5.428	5.476	5.811	5.760
Arkansas	8.598	9.039	9.120	9.678	9.592
California	56.380	59.271	59.802	63.459	62.895
Colorado	5.492	5.774	5.826	6.182	6.127
Connecticut	7.627	8.006	8.077	8.571	8.495
Delaware	3.340	3.517	3.552	3.757	3.675
District of Columbia	10.389	10.922	11.020	11.693	11.590
Florida	18.378	19.321	19.494	20.686	20.502
Georgia	17.010	17.882	18.042	19.145	18.975
Hawaii	3.340	3.517	3.552	3.757	3.675
Idaho	3.304	3.479	3.513	3.716	3.635
Illinois	29.871	31.402	31.684	33.621	33.322
Indiana	9.207	9.679	9.766	10.363	10.271
Iowa	6.844	7.195	7.259	7.703	7.634
Kansas	5.161	5.426	5.475	5.809	5.758
Kentucky	10.660	11.207	11.308	11.999	11.892
Louisiana	14.845	15.606	15.746	16.475	16.329
Maine	3.334	3.510	3.545	3.750	3.699
Maryland	8.677	9.122	9.203	9.766	9.679
Massachusetts	15.755	16.472	16.620	17.636	17.479
Michigan	23.236	24.404	24.623	26.128	25.896
Minnesota	7.609	8.000	8.071	8.565	8.489
Mississippi	10.057	10.573	10.668	11.320	11.220

on funding activity.) The third currently funded "related activity"—Individual Development Accounts—is not authorized under the Community Services Block Grant Act, and would not have been reauthorized by H.R. 1655.

Table A-1. (Continued)

	FY2013	FY2014	FY2015	FY2016	FY2017
Missouri	17.498	18.395	18.560	19.695	19.520
Montana	3.070	3.232	3.264	3.453	3.377
Nebraska	4.408	4.634	4.675	4.961	4.917
Nevada	3.340	3.517	3.552	3.757	3.675
New Hampshire	3.340	3.517	3.552	3.757	3.675
New Jersey	17.323	18.211	18.375	19.498	19.325
New Mexico	3.467	3.645	3.678	3.902	3.868
New York	54.882	57.696	58.213	61.772	61.223
North Carolina	16.580	17.448	17.604	18.680	18.514
North Dakota	3.055	3.217	3.208	3.393	3.319
Ohio	24.649	25.913	26.145	27.744	27.497
Oklahoma	7.557	7.955	7.872	8.320	8.246
Oregon	5.042	5.300	5.348	5.675	5.625
Pennsylvania	26.772	28.144	28.397	30.133	29.865
Puerto Rico	26.639	28.005	28.256	29.983	29.717
Rhode Island	3.496	3.675	3.708	3.934	3.899
South Carolina	9.716	10.214	10.306	10.936	10.839
South Dakota	2.746	2.892	2.878	3.044	2.977
Tennessee	12.457	13.096	13.213	14.021	13.897
Texas	30.421	31.980	32.267	34.240	33.936
Utah	3.264	3.437	3.471	3.671	3.591
Vermont	3.340	3.517	3.552	3.754	3.672
Virginia	10.124	10.643	10.738	11.395	11.294
Washington	7.493	7.878	7.948	8.434	8.359
West Virginia	7.079	7.442	7.508	7.968	7.897
Wisconsin	7.694	8.088	8.161	8.660	8.583
Wyoming	3.340	3.517	3.327	3.519	3.442
Subtotal to States	*617.133*	*648.649*	*654.042*	*693.610*	*686.873*
American Samoa	0.868	0.914	0.923	0.977	0.955
Guam	0.822	0.865	0.874	0.924	0.904
Commonwealth of the Northern Mariana Islands	0.515	0.542	0.547	0.579	0.566
U.S. Virgin Islands	1.135	1.195	1.207	1.277	1.249
Subtotal to Territories	*3.340*	*3.517*	*3.552*	*3.757*	*3.675*
Subtotal to Tribes	*4.790*	*5.239*	*5.750*	*6.363*	*6.278*
Total to States, Territories, and Tribes	625.263	657.405	663.344	703.729	696.826

Source: Data are from Department of Health and Human Services, Administration for Children and Families, Office of Community Services funding announcements available at https://www.acf.hhs.gov/ocs/resource/csbgdear-colleague-letters.

- Table A-2 shows funding for CSBG (not including related activities) from its first year in FY1982 through FY2017.
- Table A-3 shows funding for the various related activities that have been funded at different times from FY1982 to FY2017.

Table A-2. Community Services Block Grant Appropriations History FY1982-FY2017 (Dollars in millions)

Fiscal Year	Authorization Level	President's Request	Appropriation
FY1982	389.38[a]	—	314.50
FY1983	389.38[a]	100.00[b]	341.68[c]
FY1984	389.38[a]	2.85[d]	316.68
FY1985	400.00[e]	2.92[f]	335.00
FY1986	415.00[e]	3.86[g]	320.60
FY1987	390.00[h]	3.61	335.00
FY1988	409.50[h]	310.00[i]	325.52
FY1989	430.00[h]	310.00[i]	318.63
FY1990	451.50[h]	0[j]	322.09
FY1991	451.50[k]	0[l]	349.37
FY1992	460.00[k]	0[m]	360.00
FY1993	480.00[k]	0[n]	372.00
FY1994	500.00[k]	372.00	397.00
FY1995	525.00[o]	399.62	389.60
FY1996	such sums as necessary (ssn)[o]	391.50	389.60
FY1997	ssn[o]	387.59	489.60
FY1998	ssn[o]	414.72	489.69
FY1999	ssn[p]	490.60	499.83
FY2000	ssn[p]	500.00	527.62
FY2001	ssn[p]	510.00	599.99
FY2002	ssn[p]	599.99	649.97
FY2003	ssn[p]	570.00	645.76
FY2004	—[q]	494.96	641.94
FY2005	—	494.95	636.79
FY2006	—	0[r]	629.99
FY2007	—	0[s]	630.44
FY2008[t]	—	0[u]	653.80
FY2009[v]	—	0[w]	699.98
FY2010	—	700.00	700.00
FY2011[x]	—	700.00	678.64
FY2012[y]	—	350.00	677.35

Table A-2. (Continued)

Fiscal Year	Authorization Level	President's Request	Appropriation
FY2013[z]	—	346.30	635.28
FY2014	—	350.00	667.96
FY2015	—	344.75	673.99
FY2016	—	674.00	714.99
FY2017	—	674.00	714.65
FY2018		0[aa]	

Source: Prepared by the Congressional Research Service (CRS), based on information in Department of Health and Human Services congressional budget justifications, the budget appendix, enacted appropriations laws and accompanying committee reports and tables, and archived CRS reports. It is possible that there are years in which rescissions occurred that are not accounted for in the table.

Notes: In addition to amounts shown for FY2009 and FY2010, the American Recovery and Reinvestment Act (ARRA, P.L. 111-5) included a one-time appropriation of $1 billion for CSBG, which was available for obligation in those two years.

[a] From FY1982 through FY1984, CSBG was authorized as part of the Omnibus Budget Reconciliation Act of 1981 (P.L. 97-35).

[b] Of the amount requested by the President in FY1983, $9 million would have come from a transfer from the Rural Development Loan Fund. In addition, the President's budget proposed to close out the CSBG program.

[c] In addition to annual appropriations for CSBG in FY1983 (P.L. 97-377), Congress appropriated $25 million as part of a supplemental appropriations act (P.L. 98-8).

[d] The FY1984 budget recommended funding sufficient to terminate and close out the CSBG program.

[e] In FY1985 and FY1986, CSBG was authorized as part of the Human Services Reauthorization Act (P.L. 98-558).

[f] The FY1985 budget recommended no funding for CSBG, stating that it duplicated other programs. The appropriation would have funded staff salaries for an "orderly closeout" of the program.

[g] The FY1986 budget proposed sufficient funds to close out the CSBG program.

[h] From FY1987 through FY1990, CSBG was authorized as part of the Human Services Reauthorization Act of 1986 (P.L. 99-425).

[i] The FY1988 and FY1989 President's budgets proposed to phase out the CSBG program over a four-year period starting in the subsequent fiscal year.

[j] The FY1990 budget proposed no new funding for CSBG, stating that "[t]his action is necessary given current budget constraints and the need for more effective control of the Federal budget deficit. State and local governments must assume a greater share of responsibility for providing the assistance previously made available by the CSBG program."

[k] From FY1991 through FY1994, CSBG was authorized as part of the Augustus F. Hawkins Human Services Reauthorization Act of 1990 (P.L. 101-501).

[l] The FY1991 President's budget proposed no new funding for CSBG. The budget justifications stated that it "proposes to fund CAA [Community Action Agency] administrative and other costs through allocations included in the appropriations for the various Federal programs which are partially administered by CAA's [sic]."

[m] In FY1992, the President's budget recommended no new funding for CSBG. The budget justifications stated "[t]he Community Action Agencies and other local organizations that

historically have received Community Services and discretionary funds have been successful in obtaining funding from other sources. In general, Community Services funds now represent a small fraction of the operating budgets of most of these organizations. Thus the more successful of these organizations no longer are dependent on Community Services funding."

[n] The FY1993 President's budget proposed no funding for CSBG. Budget justifications observed that since the creation of CSBG, funding had increased for other activities to support low-income people, and that "services will continue to be provided through funds from other federal resources, as well as State and local resources."

[o] From FY1995 through FY1998, CSBG was authorized as part of the Human Services Amendments of 1994 (P.L. 103-252).

[p] From FY1999 through FY2003, CSBG was authorized as part of the Community Opportunities, Accountability, and Training and Educational Services Act of 1998 (P.L. 105-285).

[q] From FY2004 through the present fiscal year, CSBG has not been authorized.

[r] According to the FY2006 budget justifications for CSBG, the President's budget proposed "to focus economic and community development activities through a more targeted and unified program to be administered by the Department of Commerce."

[s] According to the FY2007 budget justifications for CSBG, the President's budget proposed no new funding for CSBG "because it lacks performance measures, does not award grants on a competitive basis nor hold grantees accountable for program results."

[t] Funding reflects a 1.747% across-the-board reduction, as mandated by the Consolidated Appropriations Act, 2008 (P.L. 110-161).

[u] The FY2008 President's budget would have provided no funding for CSBG because "it does not award grants on a competitive basis and states cannot hold their grantees accountable for program results as reflected in their low PART [Program Assessment Rating Tool] assessment."

[v] Funding levels shown for FY2009 were included in the FY2009 Omnibus Appropriations Act (P.L. 111-8) and do not include the additional $1 billion provided to the CSBG under the American Recovery and Reinvestment Act (ARRA, P.L. 111-5).

[w] The FY2009 President's budget proposed no new funding for CSBG because "the program does not award grants on a competitive basis and states cannot hold their grantees accountable for program results as reflected in the program's PART assessment of Results Not Demonstrated."

[x] Funding reflects a 0.2% across-the-board rescission as mandated by the FY2011 Department of Defense and Full-Year Continuing Appropriations Act (P.L. 112-10).

[y] The Consolidated Appropriations Act, 2012 (P.L. 112-74) mandated that appropriated amounts were subject to an across-the-board rescission of 0.189%. Amounts shown in this table reflect that rescission, as implemented by HHS and displayed in the FY2013 justifications for the Administration for Children and Families.

[z] The source for numbers shown for FY2013 is the "all-purpose table" published by the Administration for Children and Families at HHS on May 20, 2013. Numbers shown reflect funding provided by the FY2013 Consolidated and Further Continuing Appropriations Act (P.L. 113-6) and the effects of budget sequestration and an across-the-board rescission of 0.2%.

[aa] The President's FY2018 budget requested no funding for CSBG. The budget justifications stated that "[i]n a constrained budget environment, difficult funding decisions were made to ensure that federal funds are being spent as effectively as possible. The CSBG accounts for approximately five percent of total funding received by local agencies that benefit from these funds. Although states have discretion to reduce or terminate funding to local agencies that do not meet state-established performance standards, CSBG continues to be distributed by a formula not tied directly to the local agency performance."

Table A-3. Appropriations for CSBG Related Activities FY1982–FY2017 (Dollars in millions)

Fiscal Year	Migrant and Seasonal Farm-workers Assistance[a]	Demonstration Partnership Program[b]	Emergency Community Services for the Homeless[c]	National Youth Sports[a]	Community Food and Nutrition[d]	Job Opportunities for Low-Income Individuals[e]	Individual Development Accounts[f]	Rural Community Facilities[a]	Community Economic Development[a]
FY1982	3.00	—	—	6.00	—	—	—	4.00	19.63
FY1983	2.88	—	—	5.76	—	—	—	3.84	18.84
FY1984	2.88	—	—	5.76	—	—	—	3.84	18.84
FY1985	3.04	—	—	6.13	—	—	—	4.05	19.92
FY1986[g]	2.70	—	—	5.9	—	—	—	3.60	17.60
FY1987	2.69	1.00	—	5.87	2.50	—	—	3.57	17.61
FY1988	2.97	2.87	19.10	6.32	2.39	—	—	3.93	18.91
FY1989	2.95	3.51	18.92	9.67	2.42	—	—	4.01	20.25
FY1990	2.95	3.50	21.86	10.62	2.41	3.50[h]	—	4.01	20.25
FY1991	3.03	4.05	25.00	10.83	2.44	4.50[i]	—	4.10	20.49
FY1992	3.03j	4.05	25.00	12.00[j]	7.00	k	—	4.10[j]	22.00[j]
FY1993	2.95	3.80	19.84	9.42	6.94	5.00[l]	—	4.96	20.73
FY1994	2.95	7.995	19.84	12.00	7.94	5.50[l]	—	5.46	22.23
FY1995	—	—	19.75	12.00	8.68	5.50[l]	—	3.27	23.69
FY1996	—	—	—	11.52	4.00	5.50[m]	—	3.01	27.33[m]
FY1997	—	—	—	12.00	4.00	5.50[m]	—	3.50	27.33[m]
FY1998	—	—	—	14.00	3.99	5.50[m]	—	3.49	30.01[m]
FY1999	—	—	—	15.00	5.00	5.50[m]	9.99	3.50	30.04[m]
FY2000	—	—	—	15.00	6.31	8.33	10.00	5.31	21.71
FY2001	—	—	—	16.00	6.31	5.50	24.89	5.32	24.53

Fiscal Year	Migrant and Seasonal Farm-workers Assistance[a]	Demonstration Partnership Program[b]	Emergency Community Services for the Homeless[c]	National Youth Sports[a]	Community Food and Nutrition[d]	Job Opportunities for Low-Income Individuals[e]	Individual Development Accounts[f]	Rural Community Facilities[a]	Community Economic Development[a]
FY2002	—	—	—	17.00	7.31	5.50	24.94	7.00	26.98
FY2003	—	—	—	16.89	7.28	5.46	24.83	7.20	27.08
FY2004	—	—	—	17.89	7.24	5.43	24.70	7.18	26.91
FY2005	—	—	—	17.86	7.18	5.44	24.70	7.24	27.30
FY2006	—	—	—	—	—	5.38	24.44	7.29	27.00
FY2007	—	—	—	—	—	5.38	24.45	7.29	27.02
FY2008[n]	—	—	—	—	—	5.29	24.02	7.89	31.47
FY2009	—	—	—	—	—	5.29	24.02	10.00	36.00
FY2010	—	—	—	—	—	2.64	23.91	10.00	36.00
FY2011[o]	—	—	—	—	—	1.64	23.98	4.99	17.96
FY2012[p]	—	—	—	—	—	—	19.87	4.98	29.94
FY2013[q]	—	—	—	—	—	—	18.59	4.67	28.08
FY2014	—	—	—	—	—	—	19.00	5.97	29.88
FY2015	—	—	—	—	—	—	18.95	6.50	29.88
FY2016	—	—	—	—	—	—	18.95	6.50	29.88
FY2017	—	—	—	—	—	—	—	7.50	19.88

Source: The table was compiled by CRS using various sources: congressional budget justifications, budget appendices, appropriations materials including appropriations bills and committee reports and tables, and archived CRS reports. It is possible that there are years in which rescissions occurred that are not accounted for in the table.

[a] Authorization of assistance for Migrant and Seasonal Farmworkers, National Youth Sports, Rural Community Facilities, and Community Economic Development was provided as part of the original CSBG Act (included in the Omnibus Budget Reconciliation Act of 1981, P.L. 97-35, Section 681).

[b] The Demonstration Partnership Program was authorized by Section 408 of P.L. 99-425, the Human Resources Reauthorization Act of 1986.

[c] Emergency Community Services for the Homeless was authorized by the McKinney-Vento Homeless Assistance Act (P.L. 100-77), Title VII, Subtitle D.

d. Community Food and Nutrition was originally authorized as part of the Economic Opportunity Act of 1964 (P.L. 88-452). It was repealed at the end of FY1981, but then reauthorized in FY1985 as an activity of the Office of Community Services in HHS as part of the Human Services Reauthorization Act (P.L. 98-558). Between FY1981 and FY1987, the program did not receive funding.

e. Job Opportunities for Low-Income Individuals was initially authorized as a demonstration program as part of the Family Support Act of 1988 (P.L. 100-485), Section 505. It was amended by the Personal Responsibility and Work Opportunity Reconciliation Act of 1996 (P.L. 104-193), Section 112.

f. Individual Development Accounts were authorized as a demonstration program as part of the Assets for Independence Act, which was included in the Coats Human Services Reauthorization Act of 1998 (P.L. 105-285), Title IV.

g. Funding for FY1986 is from the archived CRS Report, "Community Services Block Grants: History, Funding, Program Data," by Karen Spar and Kimberly T. Henderson, September 1, 1987. Appropriated funding was reduced to levels presented in the table pursuant to the Gramm-Rudman-Hollings deficit reduction law. CRS could not identify a source that showed final funding levels to the same decimal place as other funding levels in the table.

h. According to the Senate report accompanying the FY1991 appropriations bill for the Departments of Labor, Health and Human Services, and Education (H.R. 5257, S.Rept. 101-516), $3.5 million "is being awarded in fiscal year 1990 for 3-year grants to nonprofit organizations such as community development corporations" for programs authorized under Section 505 of the Family Support Act.

i. The FY1991 funding level for Job Opportunities for Low-Income Individuals (JOLI) was in Conference Report (H.Rept. 101-908) to accompany the FY1991 Departments of Labor, Health and Human Services, and Education Appropriations Act (H.R. 5257, P.L. 101-517).

j. Funding for FY1992 is in the Conference Report (H.Rept. 102-282) accompanying the FY1992 appropriations act (P.L. 102-170).

k. CRS could not locate a funding level for JOLI in FY1992.

l. From FY1993-FY1995, funds for JOLI were set aside within the Social Services Research Account.

m. From FY1996-FY1999, JOLI funds were provided as a set-aside within Community Economic Development (CED).

n. Funding reflects a 1.747% across-the-board reduction, as mandated by the Consolidated Appropriations Act, 2008 (P.L. 110-161).

o. Funding reflects a 0.2% across-the-board rescission, as mandated by P.L. 112-10, the FY2011 Department of Defense and Full-Year Continuing Appropriations Act.

p. The Consolidated Appropriations Act, 2012 (P.L. 112-74) mandated that appropriated amounts were subject to an across-the-board rescission of 0.189%. Amounts shown in this table reflect that rescission, as implemented by HHS and displayed in the FY2013 justifications for the Administration for Children and Families.

q. The source for numbers shown in FY2013 is the "all-purpose table" published by the Administration for Children and Families at HHS on May 20, 2013. Numbers shown reflect funding provided by the FY2013 Consolidated and Further Continuing Appropriations Act (P.L. 113-6) and the effects of budget sequestration and an across-the-board rescission of 0.2%.

APPENDIX B. GOVERNMENT ACCOUNTABILITY OFFICE (GAO) REVIEW

The Government Accountability Office (GAO) released a report on the CSBG program in July 2006, in response to a request by the House Education and the Workforce Committee. GAO's review focused on three topics related to program monitoring and training and technical assistance: (1) HHS compliance with legal requirements and standards governing its oversight of state efforts to monitor local CSBG grantees; (2) efforts by states to monitor local grantee compliance with fiscal requirements and performance standards; and (3) targeting by HHS of its training and technical assistance funds and the impact of such assistance on grantee performance.[41]

GAO concluded that the Office of Community Services (OCS) lacked "effective policies, procedures, and controls" to ensure its own compliance with legal requirements for monitoring states and with federal internal control standards. GAO found that OCS had visited states as mandated by law but failed to issue reports to the states after the visits or annual reports to Congress, which also are mandated by law. OCS failed to meet internal control standards because their monitoring teams lacked adequate financial expertise; moreover, OCS lost the documentation from the monitoring visits to states. Finally, OCS was not systematic in its selection of states to visit, and did not use available information on state performance or collect other data to allow more effective targeting of its limited monitoring resources on states at highest risk of management problems.

---

[41] *Community Services Block Grant Program: HHS Should Improve Oversight by Focusing Monitoring and Assistance Efforts on Areas of High Risk*, GAO-06-627, U.S. Government Accountability Office, June 2006. GAO had revealed some of the findings of this review in February 2006 in a letter submitted to HHS ("Community Services Block Grant Program: HHS Needs to Improve Monitoring of State Grantees," GAO-06-373R, letter to Wade F. Horn, Assistant Secretary for Children and Families, Department of Health and Human Services, from the U.S. Government Accountability Office, February 7, 2006).

In connection with its assessment of state efforts to monitor local grantees, GAO visited five states and found wide variation in the frequency with which they conducted on-site monitoring of local grantees, although officials in all states said they visited agencies with identified problems more often. States also varied in their interpretation of the law's requirement that they visit local grantees at least once in a three-year period, and GAO noted that OCS had issued no guidance on this requirement. States reported varying capacities to conduct on-site monitoring and some states cited staff shortages; however, the states all performed other forms of oversight in addition to on-site visits, such as review of local agency reports (e.g., local agency plans, goals, performance data, and financial reports) and review of annual Single Audits where relevant. Several states coordinated local oversight with other federal and state programs, and also used state associations of Community Action Agencies to help provide technical assistance.

GAO found, with regard to federal training and technical assistance funds, that OCS targeted at least some of these funds toward local agencies with identified financial and program management problems, but generally was not strategic in allocating these funds and had only limited information on the outcome of providing such training and technical assistance.

GAO made five recommendations to OCS in its report (and HHS indicated its agreement and intent to act upon these recommendations). GAO recommended that OCS should

- conduct a risk-based assessment of states by systematically collecting and using information;
- establish policies and procedures to ensure monitoring is focused on the highest-risk states;
- issue guidance to states on complying with the requirement that they monitor local agencies during each three-year period;
- establish reporting guidance for training and technical assistance grants so that OCS receives information on the outcomes for local agencies that receive such training or technical assistance; and

- implement a strategic plan for targeting training and technical assistance in areas where states feel the greatest need.

HHS Response

HHS took a series of steps in response to the GAO report. On October 10, 2006, HHS issued an information memorandum to state agencies responding to GAO's third recommendation and providing guidance on compliance with the statutory requirement that states conduct a full on-site review of each eligible entity at least once during every three-year period.[42] Subsequently, on March 1, 2007, HHS issued another information memorandum, responding to GAO's first two recommendations and providing a schedule of states that would receive federal monitoring in each of the next three years (FY2007-FY2009).[43]

The October 2006 memorandum explained that states were selected through a process intended to identify states that would receive the most benefit from federal monitoring visits. This process considered the extent to which eligible entities in the state were considered vulnerable or in crisis; the physical size of the state, its number of eligible entities, and the number of state personnel assigned to the CSBG program; the extent of poverty in the state compared to the number of eligible entities and state CSBG personnel; the number of clients served compared to the number of eligible entities and state CSBG personnel; evidence of past audit problems; and tardiness by the state in submitting CSBG state plans to HHS or responses to information surveys conducted by the National Association of State Community Services Programs.[44]

---

[42] Office of Community Services (OCS) Information Memorandum, Transmittal No. 97, dated 10/10/06: http://www.acf.hhs.gov/programs/ocs/resource/im-no-97-guidance-on-the-csbg-requirement-to-monitor-eligibleentities.

[43] Office of Community Services (OCS) Information Memorandum, Transmittal No. 98, dated 3/1/07: http://www.acf.hhs.gov/programs/ocs/resource/im-no-1. The most recent monitoring schedule was provided in OCS Information Memorandum Transmittal No. 117, dated August 25, 2010, and covers FY2011-FY2013: http://www.acf.hhs.gov/programs/ocs/resource/no-117-three-year-csbg-monitoring-schedule-ffy-2011-ffy-2013.

[44] See discussion of this survey earlier in this report.

HHS developed a CSBG state assessment tool to help states prepare for federal monitoring,[45] and on August 24, 2007, issued a strategic plan for the CSBG program, which was intended to describe training, technical assistance, and capacity-building activities and promote accountability within the CSBG.[46] As discussed in Appendix A of this report, HHS began funding the national community economic development training and capacity development initiative in FY2009. More recently, HHS issued an information memorandum on May 4, 2011, announcing a reorganization and new "strategy for excellence" in the CSBG training and technical assistance program for FY2011.[47]

---

[45] Office of Community Services (OCS) Information Memorandum, Transmittal No. 102: http://www.acf.hhs.gov/sites/ default/files/ocs/im_no_102_csbg_monitoring_checklist.pdf.
[46] Office of Community Services (OCS) Information Memorandum, Transmittal No. 103, dated 8/24/07: http://www.acf.hhs.gov/sites/default/files/ocs/im_no_103_csbg_strategic_plan_final_strategic_plan.pdf.
[47] Office of Community Services (OCS) Information Memorandum, Transmittal No. 123, dated 5/4/11: http://www.acf.hhs.gov/programs/ocs/resource/reorganization-of-csbg-t-ta-resources-a-new-strategy-for-excellence.

In: A Closer Look at Grant Programs
Editor: Tabitha Reyes

ISBN: 978-1-53615-995-0
© 2019 Nova Science Publishers, Inc.

Chapter 6

PROJECT SAFE NEIGHBORHOODS GRANT PROGRAM AUTHORIZATION ACT OF 2017[*]

Committee on the Judiciary

Mr. Goodlatte
From the Committee on the Judiciary submitted the following report together with additional views.
[To accompany H.R. 3249]
[Including cost estimate of the Congressional Budget Office]

The Committee on the Judiciary, to whom was referred the bill (H.R. 3249) to authorize the Project Safe Neighborhoods Grant Program, and for other purposes, having considered the same, report favorably thereon with an amendment and recommend that the bill as amended do pass.

---

[*] This is an edited, reformatted and augmented version of House of Representatives Report to the Committee of the Whole House on the State of the Union and ordered to be printed, Publication No. 115–597, dated March 14, 2018.

THE AMENDMENT

The amendment is as follows:
Strike all after the enacting clause and insert the following:

Section 1. Short Title

This Act may be cited as the "Project Safe Neighborhoods Grant Program Authorization Act of 2017".

Section 2. Definitions

For the purposes of this Act—

1. the term "criminal street gangs" has the meaning given such term in section 521 of title 18, United States Code;
2. the term "gang crime" means a felony or misdemeanor crime, under State or Federal law, committed by one or more persons who are a member of, or directly affiliated with, a criminal street gang;
3. the term "transnational organized crime group" has the meaning given such term in section 36(k)(6) of the State Department Basic Authorities Act of 1956 (22 U.S.C. 2708(k)(6));
4. the term "transnational organized crime" has the meaning given such term in section 36(k)(5) of the State Department Basic Authorities Act of 1956 (22 U.S.C. 2708(k)(5)); and
5. the term 'firearms offenses" means an offense under section 922 or 924 of title 18, United States Code.

Section 3. Establishment

The Attorney General of the United States is authorized to establish and carry out a program, to be known as the "Project Safe Neighborhoods Block Grant Program" or, in this Act, as the "Program", within the Office of Justice Programs at the Department of Justice.

Section 4. Purpose

The purpose of the Project Safe Neighborhoods Block Grant Program is to foster and improve existing partnerships between Federal, State, and local agencies, including the United States Attorney in each Federal judicial district, to create safer neighborhoods through sustained reductions in violent crimes by—

1. developing and executing strategic plans to assist law enforcement agencies in combating gang crimes, including the enforcement of gun laws and drug interdiction; and
2. developing intervention and prevention initiatives, including juvenile justice projects and activities which may include street-level outreach, conflict mediation, and the changing of community norms, in order to reduce violence.

Section 5. Rules and Regulations

(a) IN GENERAL.—The Attorney General shall, not later than 60 days after the date of enactment of this Act, make rules to create, carry out, and administer the Program in accordance with this section.
(b) FUNDS TO BE DIRECTED TO LOCAL CONTROL.—Amounts made available as grants under the Program shall be, to the greatest

extent practicable, locally controlled to address problems that are identified locally

(c) REGIONAL GANG TASK FORCES.—30 percent of the amounts made available as grants under the Program each fiscal year shall be granted to established Regional Gang Task Forces in regions experiencing a significant or increased presence of, or high levels of activity from, transnational organized crime groups posing threats to community safety in terms of violent crime, firearms offenses, human trafficking, trafficking and distribution of illegal opioids and heroin, and other crimes.

Section 6. Authorization of Appropriations; Consolidation of Programs

(a) AUTHORIZATION OF APPROPRIATIONS.—There is authorized to be appropriated for the Program under this Act $50,000,000 for each of fiscal years 2018 through 2020.

(b) CONSOLIDATION OF PROGRAMS.—For each of fiscal years 2018 through 2022, no funds are authorized to be separately appropriated to the Department of Justice Office of Justice Programs for—
1. competitive and evidence-based programs to reduce gun crime and gang violence;
2. an Edward Byrne Memorial criminal justice innovation program;
3. community-based violence prevention initiatives; or
4. gang and youth violence education, prevention and intervention, and related activities.

PURPOSE AND SUMMARY

H.R. 3249, the "Project Safe Neighborhoods Grant Program Authorization Act of 2017," officially authorizes the Project Safe Neighborhoods ("PSN") Block Grant Program. The activities the Program will cover were previously only authorized through appropriations of other grants.

The bill permits the Attorney General to authorize the PSN Block Grant Program for the purpose of combating violent gang crimes, by facilitating partnerships between Federal, State, and local agencies, including the United States Attorney in each Federal judicial district. The Program grants will be used to develop strategic initiatives to combat crime and also for developing prevention initiatives, such as community outreach. The legislation provides the localities receiving grants with control, to the extent practicable, over how the funds are to be used to ensure local law enforcement has the flexibility to put funds toward problems they have identified. It also allocates 30 percent of the funds to go toward regional task forces in areas with a significant or increased presence of criminal activity caused by gangs. The bill further consolidates programs within the Department of Justice's Office of Justice Programs to be funded through the PSN Block Grant Program.

BACKGROUND AND NEED FOR THE LEGISLATION

Street gang activity in the United States is on the rise. Gangs are actively recruiting middle and high school aged children across the country. Specifically, the FBI has pointed to transnational gangs, such as MS–13, as becoming an increasingly troublesome problem. While MS–13 is not the largest gang in the country, it is increasingly the most violent and well-organized. With leadership based in El Salvador and Honduras, it is clear that our local law enforcement agencies need additional resources to confront this organization and others, including the option to participate in regional anti-gang task forces.

In recent years, it has been increasingly difficult for law enforcement agencies across the nation to obtain grants to adequately fund these task forces. For instance, in Northern Virginia, the Regional Gang Task Force has gone from an annual budget of $3 million in 2012 to $325,000 today.

During that same time, gangs have seen a surge in recruitment, and the public has seen an increasing amount of gang-related violent crime. Working with members of the community, including teachers, guidance counselors, and parents, law enforcement personnel are able to recognize at-risk youths and offer help and guidance on how to avoid getting involved with a gang in the first place.

Project Safe Neighborhoods was established in 2001 as an initiative within the Department of Justice's Bureau of Justice Assistance. The program, which was based in part on Richmond, Virginia's Project Exile,[1] represented a nationwide commitment to reduce gun and gang crime in America by networking existing local programs that target gun crime and provided these programs with the tools necessary to be successful. In recent years, however, fund- ing for the program has dwindled. The Attorney General recently announced his intent to rejuvenate this program.[2] This legislation will help the Department of Justice achieve this goal.

HEARINGS

The Subcommittee on Crime held a hearing on gang violence on July 20, 2017. Testimony was received from Mr. Kenneth Blanco, Acting Assistant Attorney General of the Criminal Division, U.S. Department of

---

[1] See "Project Exile, U.S. Attorney's Office— Eastern District of Virginia, available at https://www.ojjdp.gov/pubs/gun violence/profile38.html.
[2] "Attorney General Sessions Announces Reinvigoration of Project Safe Neighborhoods and Other Actions to Reduce Rising Tide of Violent Crime," U.S. Department of Justice, October 5, 2017, available at *https://www.justice.gov/opa/pr/attorney-general-sessions-announces-reinvigoration-project-safe-neighborhoods-and-other.*

Justice; Mr. Marc Vanek, Board Advisory Member, Midwest Gang Investigators Association, Illinois Chapter; Captain Chris Marks, Los Angeles County Sheriff's Department; and, Dr. Gary Slutkin, Founder, Cure Violence.

COMMITTEE CONSIDERATION

On November 2, 2017, the Committee met in open session and ordered the bill (H.R. 3249) favorably reported, with an amendment, by voice vote, a quorum being present.

COMMITTEE VOTES

In compliance with clause 3(b) of rule XIII of the Rules of the House of Representatives, the Committee advises that the following roll call votes occurred during the Committee's consideration of H.R. 3249.

1. An Amendment, offered by Ms. Jackson-Lee to strike the consolidation of programs within the Department of Justice's Office of Justice Programs. The amendment was defeated by a roll call vote of 12 to 16.

Rollcall No. 1

	Ayes	Nays	Present
Mr. Goodlatte (VA), Chairman		X	
Mr. Sensenbrenner, Jr. (WI)		X	
Mr. Smith (TX)			
Mr. Chabot (OH)		X	
Mr. Issa (CA)		X	
Mr. King (IA)			
Mr. Franks (AZ)		X	
Mr. Gohmert (TX)		X	
Mr. Jordan (OH)			
Mr. Poe (TX)			
Mr. Marino (PA)		X	
Mr. Gowdy (SC)			
Mr. Labrador (ID)		X	
Mr. Farenthold (TX)			
Mr. Collins (GA)		X	
Mr. DeSantis (FL)			
Mr. Buck (CO)		X	
Mr. Ratcliffe (TX)		X	

Ms. Roby (AL)		
Mr. Gaetz (FL)		X
Mr. Johnson (LA)		X
Mr. Biggs (AZ)		X
Mr. Rutherford (FL)		X
Ms. Handel (GA)		X
Mr. Conyers, Jr. (MI), Ranking Member	X	
Mr. Nadler (NY)	X	
Ms. Lofgren (CA)	X	
Ms. Jackson Lee (TX)	X	
Mr. Cohen (TN)	X	
Mr. Johnson (GA)	X	
Mr. Deutch (FL)	X	
Mr. Gutierrez (IL)		
Ms. Bass (CA)	X	
Mr. Richmond (LA)		
Mr. Jeffries (NY)		
Mr. Cicilline (RI)	X	
Mr. Swalwell (CA)		
Mr. Lieu (CA)		
Mr. Raskin (MD)	X	
Ms. Jayapal (WA)	X	
Mr. Schneider (IL)	X	
Total	12	16

2. An Amendment, offered by Chairman Goodlatte to clarify the purpose of the Program includes prevention programs, increase funding to regional task forces, and lower the authorization level to $50 million to comply with House Rules. The amendment was approved by a roll call vote of 15 to 11.

Rollcall No. 2

	Ayes	Nays	Present
Mr. Goodlatte (VA), Chairman	X		
Mr. Sensenbrenner, Jr. (WI)	X		
Mr. Smith (TX)			
Mr. Chabot (OH)	X		
Mr. Issa (CA)	X		
Mr. King (IA)			
Mr. Franks (AZ)	X		
Mr. Gohmert (TX)	X		
Mr. Jordan (OH)			
Mr. Poe (TX)			
Mr. Marino (PA)	X		
Mr. Gowdy (SC)			
Mr. Labrador (ID)	X		
Mr. Farenthold (TX)			
Mr. Collins (GA)		X	

Mr. DeSantis (FL)		
Mr. Buck (CO)	X	
Mr. Ratcliffe (TX)	X	
Ms. Roby (AL)		
Mr. Gaetz (FL)	X	
Mr. Johnson (LA)	X	
Mr. Biggs (AZ)		
Mr. Rutherford (FL)	X	
Ms. Handel (GA)	X	
Mr. Conyers, Jr. (MI), Ranking Member		X
Mr. Nadler (NY)		X
Ms. Lofgren (CA)		X
Ms. Jackson Lee (TX)		X
Mr. Cohen (TN)		X
Mr. Johnson (GA)		X
Mr. Deutch (FL)		X
Mr. Gutierrez (IL)		
Ms. Bass (CA)		
Mr. Richmond (LA)		
Mr. Jeffries (NY)		
Mr. Cicilline (RI)		X
Mr. Swalwell (CA)		
Mr. Lieu (CA)		
Mr. Raskin (MD)		X
Ms. Jayapal (WA)		X
Mr. Schneider (IL)		X
Total	15	11

COMMITTEE OVERSIGHT FINDINGS

In compliance with clause 3(c)(1) of rule XIII of the Rules of the House of Representatives, the Committee advises that the findings and recommendations of the Committee, based on oversight activities under clause 2(b)(1) of rule X of the Rules of the House of Representatives, are incorporated in the descriptive portions of this report.

NEW BUDGET AUTHORITY AND TAX EXPENDITURES

Clause 3(c)(2) of rule XIII of the Rules of the House of Representatives is inapplicable because this legislation does not provide new budgetary authority or increased tax expenditures.

CONGRESSIONAL BUDGET OFFICE COST ESTIMATE

In compliance with clause 3(c)(3) of rule XIII of the Rules of the House of Representatives, the Committee sets forth, with respect to the bill, H.R. 3249, the following estimate and comparison prepared by the Director of the Congressional Budget Office under section 402 of the Congressional Budget Act of 1974:

U.S. Congress,
Congressional Budget Office,
Washington, DC, November 20, 2017.

Hon. BOB GOODLATTE,
Chairman, Committee on the Judiciary, House of Representatives, Washington, DC.

DEAR MR. CHAIRMAN: The Congressional Budget Office has prepared the enclosed cost estimate for H.R. 3249, the Project Safe Neighborhoods Grant Program Authorization Act of 2017.

If you wish further details on this estimate, we will be pleased to provide them. The CBO staff contact is Mark Grabowicz.

Sincerely,

Keith Hall.

Enclosure.
cc: Honorable John Conyers Jr. Ranking Member

H.R. 3249—Project Safe Neighborhoods Grant Program Authorization Act of 2017

As ordered reported by the House Committee on the Judiciary on November 2, 2017

H.R. 3249 would authorize the appropriation of $50 million annually over the 2018–2020 period for the Department of Justice to make grants to state and local governments to support intergovernmental partnerships that would aim to reduce violent crime, including that perpetrated by street gangs. Assuming appropriation of the authorized amounts, CBO estimates that implementing H.R. 3249 would cost $130 million over the 2018–2022 period, with the remaining amounts spent in subsequent years.

The costs of the bill fall within budget function 750 (administration of justice) and are shown in the following table. Estimated outlays are based on the historical rate of spending for similar programs.

	2018	2019	2020	2021	2022	2018–2022
By fiscal year, in millions of dollars						
INCREASES IN SPENDING SUBJECT TO APPROPRIATION						
Authorization Level	50	50	50	0	0	150
Estimated Outlays	11	26	36	33	24	130

Enacting H.R. 3249 would not affect direct spending or revenues; therefore, pay-as-you-go procedures do not apply. CBO estimates that enacting H.R. 3249 would not increase net direct spending or on-budget deficits in any of the four consecutive 10-year periods beginning in 2028.

H.R. 3249 contains no intergovernmental or private-sector mandates as defined in the Unfunded Mandates Reform Act.

The CBO staff contact for this estimate is Mark Grabowicz. The estimate was approved by H. Samuel Papenfuss, Deputy Assistant Director for Budget Analysis.

DUPLICATION OF FEDERAL PROGRAMS

No provision of H.R. 3249 establishes or reauthorizes a program of the Federal government known to be duplicative of another Federal program, a program that was included in any report from the Government Accountability Office to Congress pursuant to section 21 of Public Law 111–139, or a program related to a program identified in the most recent Catalog of Federal Domestic Assistance.

Disclosure of Directed Rule Makings

The Committee states that H.R. 3249 specifically directs the Attorney General to conduct one rule making within the meaning of 5 U.S.C. § 551. The rulemaking directs the Attorney General to by rule create rules and regulations to carry out the program created by the bill within 60 days of the date of enactment.

Performance Goals and Objectives

The Committee states that pursuant to clause 3(c)(4) of rule XIII of the Rules of the House of Representatives, H.R. 3249 authorizes the Project Safe Neighborhoods Block Grant Program for the purpose of combating violent gang crimes by facilitating partnerships between federal, state, and local agencies, including the United States Attorney in each federal judicial district, so they may develop strategic plans to combat crimes and develop initiatives for crime prevention.

Advisory on Earmarks

In accordance with clause 9 of rule XXI of the Rules of the House of Representatives, H.R. 3249 does not contain any congressional earmarks, limited tax benefits, or limited tariff benefits as defined in clause 9(e), 9(f), or 9(g) of rule XXI.

Section-by-Section Analysis

The following discussion describes the bill as reported by the Committee.

- *Section 1. Short title.* Section 1 sets forth the short title of the bill as the "Project Safe Neighborhoods Grant Program Authorization Act of 2017"
- *Sec. 2. Definitions.* This section defines certain terms involving gangs and organized crimes, using other provisions of the United States Code.
- *Sec. 3. Establishment.* This section authorizes the Attorney General to establish and operate the "Project Safe Neighborhoods Block Grant Program" within the Office of Justice Programs.
- *Sec. 4. Purpose.* This section states that the purpose of this program is to improve existing partnerships between Federal, State, and local agencies, to create safer neighborhoods through sustained reductions in crimes, especially violent crimes committed by gangs, by developing strategic plans to assist law enforcement in combating gang violence and by developing intervention and prevention initiatives that reduce violence.
- *Sec. 5. Rules and regulations.* This section:
   (a) Requires the Attorney General to create rules and regulations to carry out the program within 60 days of the enactment of the bill;
   (b) Directs that the funds, to the extent possible, be locally controlled; and
   (c) Mandates that 30 percent of the amounts allocated be used to create regional task forces in regions with a significant or increased presence of criminal activity caused by gangs. Sec. 6. Authorization of appropriations; Consolidation of programs. This section authorizes $50 million for this program for fiscal years between 2018–2020. It further consolidates programs within the Department of Justice's Office of Justice Programs to fall within the PSN Program.

Additional Views

We support providing additional resources to help local jurisdictions prevent and fight crime in their communities, and therefore support H.R. 3249, the "Project Safe Neighborhoods Grant Program Authorization Act of 2017." The bill would authorize the Attorney General to establish and implement a program, to be known as the "Project Safe Neighborhoods Block Grant Program" (Program), within the Office of Justice Programs (OJP) at the Department of Justice (DOJ), thereby providing a formal authorization for the Project Safe Neighborhoods Program currently implemented by DOJ. A portion of the funding awards under the Program would be allocated to fighting gang-related crime. Although we support authorizing this Program, we write separately to highlight two concerns.

First, a substantial portion of the funding under this bill would be dedicated to anti-gang task forces. We support preventing and fighting crime no matter who the perpetrator may be, but we must be careful to avoid targeting groups of young people who are not engaged in crime, and also avoid using law enforcement as a means to target anyone because of their ethnicity or national origin. Too often, the rhetoric of fighting gangs has been laced with racial bias. We cannot ignore that unfortunate reality of current times. Therefore, we must be vigilant in conducting oversight of the use of Program funds and in protecting against such possible abuse.

Second, we have serious concerns about the provisions of the bill that would prevent funding for certain programs, for fiscal years 2018 through 2022. The bill would prevent funding for (1) competitive and evidence-based programs to reduce gun crime and gang violence; (2) an Edward Byrne Memorial criminal justice innovation program; (3) community-based violence prevention initiatives; and (4) gang and youth violence education, prevention and intervention, and related activities.

Although the Majority proposes these funding prohibitions to comply with House Republican "cut-go" requirements so that $50 million may be authorized for the Program, we reject the false choice that other equally worthy initiatives must be sacrificed in order to authorize the Program.

The Program would be but one facet of DOJ's efforts to address gun and gang violence at the local, state, and tribal levels. We should view it as an effort to supplement, not supplant, other DOJ efforts that may employ different approaches to combatting gun and gang violence. None of the funding prohibitions would serve the interests of public safety. For instance, the bill would eliminate the Byrne Criminal Justice Innovation Program (BCJI) which, when implemented, helps local governments develop crime reduction strategies to address crime "hot spots" that generate a significant amount of crime within the larger community or jurisdiction. BCJI is a community-based strategy that aims to prevent and control violent crime, drug abuse, and gang activity in high crime neighborhoods by providing funding to support partnerships between law enforcement agencies and community-based organizations that balance targeted enforcement with prevention, intervention, and neighborhood restoration services. In the past, OJP has coordinated the efforts of this program with related efforts to promote neighborhood revitalization by the Departments of Housing and Urban Development and Education.[3] We see no reason to eliminate funding for this program, which is a very useful additional strategy to making our communities safer.

During the Committee's consideration of the H.R. 3249, we expressed these funding concerns in response to an amendment offered by Chairman Bob Goodlatte (R–VA). Representative Sheila Jackson Lee (D–TX) offered an amendment to the Goodlatte amendment, in an effort to eliminate these funding restrictions, but the amendment failed on a party line vote of 12 to 16. The Goodlatte amendment was then adopted by a party line vote of 15 to 11. As the bill progresses to the floor, we urge that these funding prohibitions be eliminated.

For these reasons, we support providing a formal authorization for the Project Safe Neighborhoods Program, but we caution against its possible abuse and believe restricting the funding of alternative public safety programs is unnecessary and counterproductive.

---

[3] U.S. Department of Justice, Office of Justice Programs, "FY 2017 Budget Request at a Glance" *available at* https://www.justice.gov/jmd/file/822111/download.

In: A Closer Look at Grant Programs
Editor: Tabitha Reyes

ISBN: 978-1-53615-995-0
© 2019 Nova Science Publishers, Inc.

Chapter 7

MATERNAL AND CHILD HEALTH SERVICES BLOCK GRANT: BACKGROUND AND FUNDING[*]

Victoria L. Elliott

ABSTRACT

The Maternal and Child Health (MCH) Services Block Grant is a federal-state partnership program that aims to improve the health of low-income pregnant women, mothers, and children. In addition, the program aims to connect low-income families with other services and programs, such as Medicaid and the State Children's Health Insurance Program (CHIP). This federal-state partnership is composed of three programs. First, formula-based block grants are provided to states and territories (collectively referred to as *states* in this report). Second, competitive grants are available through the Special Projects of Regional and National Significance (SPRANS) program. Third, competitive grants are available through the Community Integrated Service Systems (CISS) program. As a whole, these programs are administered by the Maternal and Child

---

[*] This is an edited, reformatted and augmented version of Congressional Research Service, Publication No. R44929, dated August 28, 2017.

Health Bureau (MCHB) of the Health Resources and Services Administration (HRSA) in the Department of Health and Human Services (HHS). This block grant was authorized under Title V of the Social Security Act (SSA).

Appropriations. The MCH Services Block Grant received an appropriation of $638.2 million in FY2016. Of that amount, approximately $550.8 million (86.31%) was for block grants to states, $77.1 million (12.08%) was for SPRANS, and $10.3 million (1.61%) was for CISS. Congress provided $20 million in supplemental funding to the SPRANS program to help territories respond to the Zika virus.

Eligible Population. Although the MCH Services Block Grant program primarily serves low-income pregnant women, mothers, and children, individuals who are not from low-income families are also eligible to receive services. Such recipients may include nonpregnant women who are over 21 years of age.

Program Services. MCH Services Block Grant funds are distributed for the purpose of funding core public health services provided by maternal and child health agencies. These core services are often divided into four categories: (1) direct health care, (2) enabling services, (3) population-based services, and (4) infrastructure building. Within these categories, the MCH Services Block Grant supports a wide array of programs, including newborn screening, health services for children with special health care needs (CSHCNs), and immunization programs.

Topics Covered in This Report. This report provides background and funding information on the MCH Services Block Grant. It also includes select program and health expenditure data to provide context on issues that Congress and HRSA have sought to address through this block grant program.

INTRODUCTION

The Maternal and Child Health (MCH) Services Block Grant is administered by the Maternal and Child Health Bureau (MCHB) of the Health Resources and Services Administration (HRSA) in the Department of Health and Human Services (HHS). This block grant is intended to improve the well-being of the low-income maternal and child population. According to HRSA, the MCH Services Block Grant serves as a "safety-net provider for the [maternal and child health] population by providing gap-filling health care services, as well as essential public health services, to the [maternal and child health] population."[1] Generally, these services are provided to pregnant women, mothers, children, and children with special health care needs (CSHCNs), some of whom are also eligible for and receive services from Medicaid[2] or the State Children's Health Insurance Program (CHIP).[3]

The MCH Services Block Grant is composed of three funding programs. The first is a block grant and is the largest of the three funding programs. It is provided to states and territories (referred to collectively as *states* in this report)[4] to enable them to coordinate programs, develop systems, and provide a broad range of health services.[5] The second funding program is the Special Projects of Regional and National Significance (SPRANS) program. SPRANS is a competitive grant program that funds research and training projects that focus on low-income pregnant women, mothers, and children, including CSHCNs. The third funding program is the Community Integrated Service Systems (CISS) program. CISS is a competitive grant program that funds projects that support the development and expansion of integrated services at the community level.

The MCH Services Block Grant is the oldest *federal-state partnership* program.[6] A federal-state partnership is a program that joins a federal agency with a state or jurisdiction, in order for the two to address a certain

---

[1] Health Resources and Services Administration, Title V Maternal and Child Health Services Block Grant to States Program - Guidance and Forms for the Title V Application/Annual Report, OMB NO: 0915-0172, 2017, p. 2, https://mchb.tvisdata.hrsa.gov/uploadedfiles/Documents/blockgrantguidance.pdf. This guidance expires on December 31, 2017.

[2] To learn more about Medicaid, see CRS Report R43357, *Medicaid: An Overview*, coordinated by Alison Mitchell.

[3] To learn more about the State Children's Health Insurance Program, see CRS Report R43627, *State Children's Health Insurance Program: An Overview*, by Evelyne P. Baumrucker and Alison Mitchell.

[4] Referred to collectively as "states" in this report, all 50 states and nine jurisdictions are eligible to apply for the MCH Services Block Grant. The nine jurisdictions consist of (1) American Samoa, (2) District of Columbia, (3) Federated States of Micronesia, (4) Guam, (5) Marshall Islands, (6) Northern Mariana Islands, (7) Palau, (8) Puerto Rico, and (9) U.S. Virgin Islands.

[5] Health Resources and Services Administration, *Understanding Title V of the Social Security Act*, p. iii, http://www.amchp.org/AboutTitleV/Documents/UnderstandingTitleV.pdf.

[6] Health Resources and Services Administration, *Title V Maternal and Child Health Services Block Grant Program*, https://mchb.hrsa.gov/maternal-child-health-initiatives/title-v-maternal-and-child-health-services-block-grant-program.

issue. Under this federal-state partnership, states make available federal and nonfederal funds to provide health care services to their maternal and child health populations (see the "Requirements of Block Grant Allocation and Distribution" section of this report). The FY2015 dollar amounts from these sources, the latest available, are presented in Table A-1. Congress established this block grant under Title V of the Social Security Act (SSA, P.L. 74-271, as amended).

PROGRAM HISTORY

The MCH Services Block Grant was established to serve as a single block grant under the previous SSA statutory heading, "Title V – Grants to States for Maternal and Child Welfare";[7] which was referred to as "Title V." In 1981, Congress combined the MCH Services Block Grant with other maternal and child health services and programs.[8] Such services and programs aimed to improve the health of mothers and children, particularly those in low-income households.[9] They included maternal and child health services, services for disabled children, child welfare services, and vocational rehabilitation services. Title V services included activities related to abstinence, postpartum depression, and personal responsibility educational services and programs.

---

[7] Social Security Administration, *Legislative History: Social Security Act of 1935*, https://www.ssa.gov/history/ 35actv.html.

[8] The programs that were consolidated by P.L. 97-35 were maternal and child health and services for children with special health needs; supplemental security income for children with disabilities; lead-based paint poisoning prevention programs; genetic disease programs; sudden infant death syndrome programs; hemophilia treatment centers; and adolescent pregnancy prevention grants. (Health Resources and Services Administration, *Understanding Title V of the Social Security Act*, p. 1.).

[9] For purposes of the MCH Services Block Grant program, "low-income" is defined as income that is below the federal poverty level, as defined by the Office of Management and Budget (OMB). (42 U.S.C. §701(b)(2).) In practice, the poverty guidelines are issued annually by the Department of Health and Human Services (HHS) rather than OMB. See HHS Office of the Secretary, "Annual Update of the HHS Poverty Guidelines," 82 *Federal Register* 8832, January 31, 2017, https://www.federalregister.gov/d/2017-02076/p-20.

The 97th Congress named this consolidation the MCH Services Block Grant and renamed it in statute as the "Title V MCH Services Block Grant," which is commonly referred to as "Title V." This change was implemented by the Omnibus Budget Reconciliation Act (OBRA)[10] of 1981 (P.L. 97-35), as amended.[11] The 1981 OBRA gave states more flexibility in determining how to use federal funds to address maternal and child health needs. In addition, the 1981 OBRA required that each state receive, at a minimum, the combined funding of the programs consolidated under it.

Congress made additional changes to the MCH Services Block Grant under the Omnibus Budget Reconciliation Act of 1989 (P.L. 101-239). These changes increased the authorization of appropriations; called for greater accountability; and created stricter rules for application and reporting requirements for states, including a statewide needs assessment requirement. Over time, additional programs targeting CSHCNs and low-income women and children were added to the SSA and the Public Health Service Act (PHSA).[12] Title V also supports services that are offered by the Maternal, Infant, and Early Childhood Home Visiting (MIECHV) program and the state-based CSHCNs program.[13]

---

[10] Omnibus reconciliation bills are drafted within the budget reconciliation process. To learn about the budget reconciliation process, see CRS Report RL30458, *The Budget Reconciliation Process: Timing of Legislative Action*, by Megan S. Lynch.
[11] 42 U.S.C. §701.
[12] The additional programs that were added to the Social Security Act (SSA) and the Public Health Service Act (PHSA) include certain services for children with disabilities who receive Supplemental Security Income (SSI, P.L. 106-170); lead-based paint poisoning prevention programs (P.L. 97-35); genetic disease programs (P.L. 97-35); sudden infant death syndrome programs (P.L. 97-35); hemophilia treatment centers (P.L. 97-35); and adolescent pregnancy grants (P.L. 95-626).
[13] To learn more about the Maternal, Infant, and Early Childhood Home Visiting (MIECHV) program, see CRS Report R43930, *Maternal and Infant Early Childhood Home Visiting (MIECHV) Program: Background and Funding*, by Adrienne L. Fernandes-Alcantara. To learn more about the state-based Children and Youth with Special Health Care Needs (CSHCNs) program, see Health Resources and Services Administration, Children with Special Health Care Needs, https://mchb.hrsa.gov/maternal-child-health-topics/children-and-youth-special-health-needs.

THE MATERNAL AND CHILD HEALTH SERVICES BLOCK GRANT

Purpose

The MCH Services Block Grant program creates partnerships between the federal government and states. The aim of the federal-state partnerships is to give attention to the health care needs of the maternal and child health populations.[14] The MCH Services Block Grant enables states to

- ensure that quality health care is provided to mothers and children, particularly to those with low incomes or limited availability of care;
- reduce the number of infant deaths, preventable diseases, and handicapping conditions among children;
- reduce hospital inpatient and long-term care services;
- increase the number of low-income children who receive health assessments and follow-up diagnostic and treatment services;
- provide *perinatal care*[15] to low-income, at-risk women and provide preventive and primary care services to low-income children;
- provide rehabilitation services that are not under subchapter XIX[16] of the SSA to blind and disabled children who are under the age of 16 and who are beneficiaries under subchapter XVI[17] of the SSA;
- provide family-centered, community-based, and care-coordinated services; and

---

[14] Health Resources and Services Administration, *Explore the Title V Federal-State Partnership*, https://mchb.tvisdata.hrsa.gov/Home.

[15] Perinatal care is delivered to a woman when she is at least 28 weeks pregnant and up to no more than seven days after she delivers her child. See Health Resources and Services Administration, *Glossary*, https://mchb.tvisdata.hrsa.gov/Home/Glossary.

[16] Title XIX of the SSA (Medicaid) provides grants to states for their medical assistance programs. To learn more about Medicaid, see CRS In Focus IF10322, *Medicaid Primer*, by Alison Mitchell.

[17] Title XVI of the SSA (Supplemental Security Income, SSI) provisions describes hospital insurance benefits for elderly and disabled individuals. To learn more about SSI, see CRS In Focus IF10482, *Supplemental Security Income (SSI)*, by William R. Morton.

- enable the development of community-based systems for CSHCNs.[18]

Population Served

The population served by the MCH Services Block Grant consists of pregnant women, infants, children, CSHCNs, and others. HRSA defines these as follows:

- Pregnant Women. Pregnant women are served from the date of conception to 60 days after the child or fetus is delivered or "expulsion of the fetus" happens.[19] Expulsion may occur, for example, when a miscarriage takes place.
- Infants. Infants are babies aged one year and less.[20]
- Children. Children are served from the age of one year, up to the day before their 22nd birthday. If a female child becomes pregnant, HRSA classifies her as a pregnant woman rather than as a child.
- Children with Special Health Care Needs. CSHCNs are infants and children who have or are at risk of having a disability, chronic illness/condition, or educational/behavioral issue.[21]
- Others. This category includes women who are over 21 years of age (referred to by HRSA as child-bearing age) and other

---

[18] This list was summarized and adapted from 42 U.S.C. §701.
[19] Ibid.
[20] For budgetary purposes only, HRSA classifies an infant with a disability as a child with special health care needs, such as an infant who is born with a developmental delay. See Health Resources and Services Administration, *Glossary*, https://mchb.tvisdata.hrsa.gov/Home/Glossary.
[21] For budgetary purposes only, states determine the infants and children to serve, from birth through their 21st year. For planning and systems development, children who have or are at risk of having chronic behavioral, developmental, emotional, or physical conditions and who generally require more intensive types or an increased volume of services than other children are considered as children with special health care needs. See Health Resources and Services Administration, *Glossary*, https://mchb.tvisdata.hrsa.gov/Home/Glossary.

individuals who are not defined by a state as being in one of the categories above.[22]

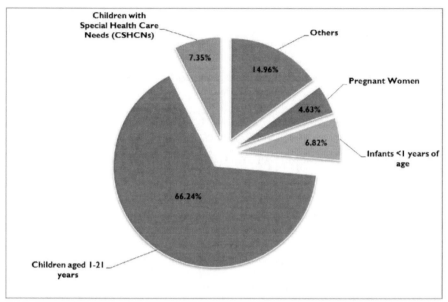

Source: Health Resources and Services Administration, "Explore the Title V Federal-Partnership," https://mchb.tvisdata.hrsa.gov/.

Note: "Others" includes women of childbearing age and any others who are not classified by the state. Individuals who received direct and enabling services were counted for each health care service that was provided to them.

Figure 1. Percentage of Individuals Served Under the MCH Services Block Grant, by Classification, FY2015.

In FY2015 (the year in which the most recent data are available), 57,064,187 individuals were served by programs funded by the MCH Services Block Grant (see Figure 1). Of the total served, 2,640,078 were pregnant women, 3,891,644 were infants, 37,797,789 were children, 4,195,464 were CSHCNs, and 8,539,212 were "others" (women of childbearing age and any others who are not classified by the state).[23]

---

[22] This list was adapted from Health Resources and Services Administration, *Glossary*, https://mchb.tvisdata.hrsa.gov/ Home/Glossary.

[23] Individuals who received direct and enabling services were counted for each health care service that was provided to them. HRSA requests that states submit an unduplicated

PROGRAMS AND SERVICES

The primary use of funds under the MCH Services Block Grant, including formula grants to states, competitive grants for Special Projects of Regional and National Significance (SPRANS), and competitive grants for projects through the Community Integrated Services Systems (CISS) program, is to provide core public health services for low-income mothers and children. Projects funded by SPRANS include maternal and child health workforce development, genetic services, and diagnostic and treatment services for hemophilia. CISS grants fund projects that support integrated maternal and child health services at the community level.

Block Grants to States

Block grant funds are to be used by the states "to provide and to assure mothers and children (in particular those with low income or with limited availability of health services) access to quality maternal and child health services."[24] States determine the actual services provided under the block grant. For example, such services may include

- counseling services,
- dental care,
- family planning,

---

number for direct and enabling services; however, states may count an individual for each service that is received under the MCH Services Block Grant program. For information about the different service levels, see "Types of Funded Services" in this report. Health Resources and Services Administration, *Title V Maternal and Child Health Services Block Grant to States Program - Guidance and Forms for the Title V Application/Annual Report*, OMB NO: 0915-0172, 2017, p. 55, https://mchb.tvisdata.hrsa.gov/ uploadedfiles/ Documents/blockgrantguidance.pdf. This guidance expires on December 31, 2017. See also Health Resources and Services Administration, *Explore the Title V Federal-Partnership*, https://mchb.tvisdata.hrsa.gov/.

[24] SSA, §501(a)(1)(A).

- immunization,
- inpatient services,
- prenatal care,
- screening services for lead-based poisoning,
- support for community health centers,
- vision and hearing screening services, and
- well-child care.[25]

Participation

All 50 states and nine jurisdictions[26] may apply for the MCH Services Block Grant.[27] In FY2015 (the year in which the most recent data are available), block grant funding to each of the states and nine jurisdictions ranged from $154,000 to $38,909,810 (see Table A-1).[28] According to HRSA, "within each state, the state health agency is responsible for the administration (or supervision of the administration) of programs carried out with Title V allotments."[29] States are organized within the 10 general regions of HHS (see Figure 2).

---

[25] This list was adapted from Health Resources and Services Administration, Title V Maternal and Child Health Services Block Grant to States Program - Guidance and Forms for the Title V Application/Annual Report-Appendix of Supporting Documents, https://mchb.hrsa.gov/sites/default/files/mchb/MaternalChildHealthInitiatives/TitleV/blockgrantguidanceappendix.pdf.

[26] The following nine jurisdictions may receive the block grant: American Samoa, District of Columbia, Federated States of Micronesia, Guam, Marshall Islands, Northern Mariana Islands, Palau, Puerto Rico, and U.S. Virgin Islands.

[27] For a listing of the 59 states and territories, see the drop down menu "Title V in Your State" at the bottom of the webpage at Health Resources and Services Administration, *Title V Maternal and Child Health Services Block Grant Program*, https://mchb.hrsa.gov/maternal-child-health-initiatives/title-v-maternal-and-child-health-services-blockgrant-program.

[28] In FY2015, Palau received the smallest ($154,000) and New York received the largest ($38.9 million) allocation of federal dollars. See Health Resources and Services Administration, *Explore the Title V Federal-State Partnership*, https://mchb.tvisdata.hrsa.gov/Home.

[29] Health Resources and Services Administration, *Title V Maternal and Child Health Services Block Grant to States Program - Guidance and Forms for the Title V Application/Annual Report*, OMB NO: 0915-0172, 2017, p. 12, https://mchb.tvisdata.hrsa.gov/uploadedfiles/Documents/blockgrantguidance.pdf. This guidance expires on December 31, 2017.

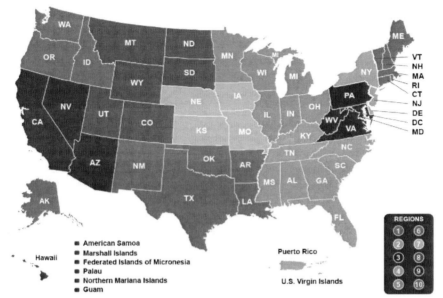

Source: Figure prepared by CRS based on information from Health Resources and Services Administration, *MCH Public Health 101*, https://mchb.hrsa.gov/about/timeline/in-depth-1-mchph101.asp.

Notes: This figure illustrates the general regions of the Department of Health and Human Services (HHS). See Department of Health and Human Services, *Regional Offices*, https://www.hhs.gov/about/agencies/iea/regionaloffices/.

Figure 2. MCH Services Block Grant Designated Regions.

Types of Funded Services

There are four types of funded services: (1) direct health care services, (2) enabling services, (3) population-based services, and (4) infrastructure building services. Generally, these core services are presented as a four-level pyramid (see Figure 3).[30]

Although states deliver four types of services, direct health care services incurred the largest proportion (57.62%) of expenditures under the MCH Services Block Grant program in FY2015.[31] Direct health care

---

[30] Health Resources and Services Administration, *Maternal and Child Health*, http://mchb.hrsa.gov/programs/.
[31] The most recent available data presented on the Title V Information System (TVIS) is from FY2015; see Health Resources and Services Administration, "Explore the Title V Federal-Partnership," https://mchb.tvisdata.hrsa.gov/.

services are intended to fill the gaps in primary and preventive health care that are not otherwise available through other funding sources or providers, such as private insurance, Medicaid, or CHIP. In FY2015, approximately $3.87 billion went to direct services.[32] In that same fiscal year, the MCH Services Block Grant program incurred $6.29 billion in expenditures (see Table A-1 in Appendix A). Other federal and nonfederal funds combine with the actual (appropriated) funding level of the block grant to yield the larger figure, reflecting the nature of the grant's federal-state partnership.

Source: Figure prepared by CRS based on information from Health Resources and Services Administration, MCH Public Health 101, https://mchb.hrsa.gov/about/timeline/in-depth-1-mchph101.asp.

Notes: Under the enabling services category, WIC stands for the Special Supplemental Nutrition Program for Women, Infants, and Children and Education refers to the Department of Education.

Figure 3. Four-Level Pyramid of Core Maternal and Child Health Services.

---

[32] Health Resources and Services Administration, *Funding by Services Level*, https://mchb.tvisdata.hrsa.gov/Financial/ FundingByServiceLevel.

Permitted Service Use

States may use their block grants "to provide and to assure [that] mothers and children (in particular those with low income or with limited availability of health services) [have] access to quality maternal and child health services."[33] States determine the actual services provided under the block grant. For example, a state may provide medical services in sectors where public and private health insurers offer limited coverage options, such as coverage for dental and durable medical equipment (e.g., wheelchairs and oxygen equipment). In addition, states may use their MCH Services Block Grant to support the following activities:

- expand the capacity of state and local health care systems;
- engage in community capacity building to deliver enabling services, such as transportation, nutrition counseling, and care coordination;
- offer education and outreach programs, technical assistance, and provider training;
- increase newborn screening and genetic services, as well as injury and lead poisoning prevention;
- promote health care and safety in child care settings; and
- provide additional support for CSHCNs.[34]

According to HRSA's *FY2017 Annual Performance Report*, "the MCH Services Block Grant program also serves as the payer of last resort. In cases where no resources or services are available, states use their block grants to fund direct care services, such as prenatal care, pediatric specialty care, or services for children with special health care needs."[35]

---

[33] SSA, §501(a)(1)(A).
[34] Ibid.
[35] Health Resources and Services Administration, Department of Health and Human Services, *FY 2017 Annual Performance Report*, p. 34, .https://hrsa.gov/about/budget/fy17annual performancereport.pdf.

Prohibited Service Use

Certain uses of block grant funds are prohibited under Section 504 of the SSA:[36]

- Funds may not be used to pay for inpatient services, other than for children with special health care needs, high-risk pregnant women, and infants (unless approved by the Secretary of HHS).
- States may not use the block grant funds to provide cash payments to recipients of health services, or for the purchase of land, facilities, or major medical equipment.
- States may not use funds to satisfy any requirement for the expenditure of nonfederal funds, and may not transfer block grant funds to any other program.
- Block grant funds may not be used for research or training at a private, for-profit entity.

In addition, block grant funds are subject to any restrictions that are included in Division H of the Consolidated Appropriations Act, 2017 (P.L. 115-31). For example, funds from the MCH Services Block Grant may not be used to promote or advocate for gun control.[37]

Requirements to Receive Funds

To receive block grant funds, states must submit to the Secretary of HHS an application that includes a statewide needs assessment (to be conducted once every five years) and a plan for meeting the needs that were identified in the needs assessment. The needs assessment must identify statewide goals that intend to meet national health objectives; the need for preventive and primary care services for pregnant women, mothers, infants, and children; and services for CSHCNs.[38] The plan to

---

[36] 42 U.S.C. §704.
[37] Section 210 of the Consolidated Appropriations Act, 2017 (P.L. 115-31).
[38] Health Resources and Services Administration, Title V Maternal and Child Health Services Block Grant to States Program - Guidance and Forms for the Title V Application/Annual Report, OMB NO: 0915-0172, 2017, pp. 16-25, https://mchb.tvisdata.hrsa.gov/

address those needs must describe how and where block grant funds will be used within the state.

Coordination with Related Programs

State block grant administrators must coordinate with other related programs, including the state's **Medicaid** program (specifically the Early Periodic Screening, Diagnosis, and Treatment [EPSDT] Program);[39] the Special Supplemental Nutrition Program for Women, Infants, and Children (WIC);[40] related education programs; and other health, developmental disability, and family planning programs. The primary purpose of this coordination effort is to make Medicaid services accessible, to enroll those who are eligible, and to avoid duplication of effort among the programs. Coordination varies among states and jurisdictions.[41]

Some state Medicaid and maternal and child health agencies have created interagency agreements that outline the expected areas and levels of coordination between the programs. Within these agreements, some states specify the services that are provided by each agency. Generally, the Title V agency contracts with health providers to provide the services, and the agency administering the state's Medicaid program assumes responsibility for reimbursing those services, when possible. HRSA performed an analysis of the coordination efforts between state Medicaid and maternal and child health agencies in 2008. This analysis showed a

---

uploadedfiles/Documents/blockgrantguidance.pdf. This guidance expires on December 31, 2017.

[39] The Early Periodic Screening, Diagnosis, and Treatment (EPSDT) Program is a Medicaid benefit for children and adolescents, up to the age of 21 years. For more information about the EPSDT program, see CRS Report R43627, *State Children's Health Insurance Program: An Overview*, by Evelyne P. Baumrucker and Alison Mitchell. For additional information on the EPSDT program and MCH Services Block Grant program coordination requirements, see Health Resources and Services Administration, *Early Periodic Screening, Diagnosis, and Treatment*, https://mchb.hrsa.gov/ maternal-child-health-initiatives/mchb-programs/early-periodic-screening-diagnosis-and-treatment.

[40] To learn more about the Special Supplemental Nutrition Program for Women, Infants, and Children (WIC), see CRS Report R44115, *A Primer on WIC: The Special Supplemental Nutrition Program for Women, Infants, and Children*, by Randy Alison Aussenberg.

[41] Health Resources and Services Administration, *State MCH-Medicaid Coordination: A Review of Title V and Title XIX Interagency Agreements (2nd Ed)*, 2008, p. 27, https://www.ncemch.org/IAA/resources/ State_MCH_Medicaid_Coord.pdf.

wide variety in the scope and level of formality among interagency agreements.[42]

Special Projects of Regional and National Significance (SPRANS)

The SPRANS program is a competitive grant for research and training programs and services related to maternal and child health and children with special health care needs. SPRANS may be used for genetic disease testing, counseling, and information development and dissemination programs; for grants relating to hemophilia without regard to age; for the screening of newborns for sickle cell anemia and other genetic disorders; and for follow-up services.[43] Eligible grantees include (1) public or nonprofit private institutions of higher learning that train health care and maternal and child health personnel and (2) public or nonprofit private organizations or institutions of higher learning that conduct maternal and child health research. Preference is given to applicants who carry out their projects in areas with a high infant mortality rate.[44]

A *high infant mortality rate* is defined as an infant mortality rate that is higher than the average national infant mortality rate or higher than the average infant mortality rate within a state.[45] For example, the national infant mortality rate was 5.82 for every 1,000 live births in 2014.[46]

---

[42] Ibid.
[43] Health Resources and Services Administration, Title V Maternal and Child Health Services Block Grant to States Program - Guidance and Forms for the Title V Application/Annual Report-Appendix of Supporting Documents, p. 3, https://mchb.hrsa.gov/sites/default/files/mchb/MaternalChildHealthInitiatives/TitleV/blockgrantguidanceappendix.pdf.
[44] An *infant mortality* is defined as an infant who dies before his or her first birthday. To determine the magnitude of infant deaths, the Centers for Disease Control and Prevention (CDC) calculates the *infant mortality rate* for the United States. The infant mortality rate is the comparison of the number of infant deaths against 1,000 live births in a given year.
[45] Section 502(b)(2)(A) of the Social Security Act (U.S.C. 42 §702(b)(2)(A)).
[46] National Center for Health Statistics, *Deaths: Final Data for 2014*, June 30, 2016, p. 101, Table 22, https://www.cdc.gov/nchs/data/nvsr/nvsr65/nvsr65_04.pdf.

As reported by the Centers for Disease Control and Prevention (CDC), Indiana's infant mortality rate in 2014 was 7.08.[47] Accordingly, relative to the national average, Indiana had a high infant mortality rate in 2014. That same year in Indiana, the infant mortality rate for black infants was 14.34, more than twice as much as the state's infant mortality rate of 7.08.[48] As a result, compared with the state's overall infant mortality rate, the rate for black infants was high in Indiana, in 2014.

Community Integrated Service Systems (CISS)

CISS is a competitive grant program that funds projects that support the development and expansion of integrated services at the community level. Public and private organizations or institutions are eligible for these grants. CISS projects must "seek to increase service delivery capacity" at the local level and promote community-based health systems for mothers and children, particularly for children in rural areas and those with special health care needs.[49] Section 502 of the SSA authorizes CISS funds to be made available for various programs, such as the MIECHV program, community-based health service programs for CSHCNs, and programs for the maternal and child health population that reside in rural areas. CISS funds may also be made available for various activities, such as integrating maternal and child health systems and increasing the participation of obstetricians and pediatricians under Medicaid and the Title X Family Planning program.

---

[47] Ibid.
[48] Ibid.
[49] Health Resources and Services Administration, Title V Maternal and Child Health Services Block Grant to States Program - Guidance and Forms for the Title V Application/Annual Report-Appendix of Supporting Documents, p. 3, https://mchb.hrsa.gov/sites/default/files/mchb/MaternalChildHealthInitiatives/TitleV/blockgrantguidanceappendix.pdf.

FUNDING BY PROGRAM

The MCH Services Block Grant is allocated by formula. The following allocation requirements are provided by 42 U.S.C §702(a):

- SPRANS: 15% of the appropriation that does not exceed $600 million, and 15% of funds remaining above $600 million after CISS funds are set aside.
- CISS: 12.75% of the appropriation that is above 600 million.
- Block grants to states: remainder of the total appropriation.

These allocation requirements have not always been implemented; for example, they were not implemented for the FY2016 funding (see the "Appropriations History" section of this report).

Block Grants to States

Individual state allocations are determined by a formula that compares the proportion of low-income children in a state with the total number of low-income children within all states. Specifically, the first $422 million of the amount appropriated is distributed to each state based on the amount the state received under the consolidated maternal and child health programs in 1983.[50] Any funds above that amount are distributed based on the number of children in each state who are at or below 100% of the federal poverty level (FPL)[51] as a proportion of the total number of children at or below 100% of the FPL for all states.[52]

---

[50] This amount is the sum of the funding for the individual programs consolidated into the MCH Services Block Grant, under OBRA 1981 (P.L. 97-35).

[51] The federal poverty level (FPL) is an income-based measurement used to determine eligibility for certain programs and benefits. It is issued by the Department of Health and Human Services (HHS) and calculated annually. To learn more about FPL, see Department of Health and Human Services, *Federal Poverty Level (FPL)*, https://www.healthcare.gov/glossary/federal-poverty-level-FPL/.

[52] Historically, the state MCH Services Block Grant allocations were calculated based on the child poverty data reported in the U.S. Census Bureau's decennial census. The American

State matching funds and other sources of maternal and child health funding are not required to follow the allocation requirements of federal funds, giving the states flexibility to direct those funds where they are needed. Similarly, state funds are not required to be directed toward specific populations in the same proportions as the federal block grant allocation.

Block grant funds are awarded each fiscal year in quarterly installments and remain available for spending in the current and subsequent fiscal year.[53] Table A-1 shows the federal allocation and state match for FY2015, by state.

Requirements of Block Grant Allocation and Distribution

For the purposes of allocating block grant funds for this program, low-income mothers and children are defined as those with family income below 100% of federal poverty guidelines.[54]

However, due to the broad reach of Title V programs and services, this definition is used only in the allocation formula, and not as a criterion for receiving Title V-funded services. There is no federally prescribed means test for recipients of services funded by the block grants to states.

States are required to use at least 30% of their block grant allocations for the population of CSHCNs, 30% for services for preventive and primary care services for children, and 40% for services for either of these groups or for other appropriate maternal and child health activities. However, states may use no more than 10% of their federal allocations for

---

Community Survey (ACS) has replaced the decennial census long form as the source for annual state-specific child poverty statistics. Beginning in FY2013, data from the ACS are being used as the reference data for calculating the annual state MCH Services Block Grant formula allocations.

[53] Section 503(b) of the Social Security Act (42 U.S.C. §703(b)).

[54] For purposes of the MCH Services Block Grant program, *low-income* is defined as income that is below the federal poverty level, as defined by the Office of Management and Budget (OMB). (42 USC §701(b)(2).) In practice, the federal poverty guidelines are issued annually by the Department of Health and Human Services (HHS) rather than OMB. In the 48 contiguous states, the 2017 federal poverty guideline for a four-member family is an annual income at $24,600. For more information, see Health and Human Services, *Annual 2017 Poverty Guidelines for the 48 Contiguous States*, https://aspe.hhs.gov/poverty-guidelines.

administrative costs.[55] Beyond these broad requirements, states determine the actual services provided under the block grant.

A state that partners with the federal government under this program must sustain a level of state funding for its maternal and child health programs and services that matches, at a minimum, its FY1989 level of state funding.[56] HRSA categorizes the funding for federal-state partnerships as coming from five sources:[57]

1. Federal allocation is the funding that a state receives from the federal government.
2. Local MCH funds are from local jurisdictions within a state.
3. Other funds include, but are not limited to, funds from the Centers for Disease Control and Prevention (CDC); Emergency Medical Services for Children (EMSC); Healthy Start; and the Special Supplemental Nutrition Program for Women, Infants and Children (WIC).
4. Program income funds are collected by state maternal and child health agencies that include health maintenance organization (HMO) payments, insurance payments, and Medicaid reimbursements.
5. State MCH funds are the funds that states match to their federal allocations. States are required to match at least $3 for every $4 given by the federal government.

In FY2015, the federal-state partnership was funded at $6.3 billion (see Figure 4).[58] Two sources—State MCH funds and program income—accounted for more than 78% of combined federal and state spending.

---

[55] Section 504(d) of the Social Security Act (42 U.S.C. §704(d)).
[56] Section 505(a)(4) of the Social Security Act (42 U.S.C. §705(a)(4)).
[57] Health Resources and Services Administration, *Glossary*, https://mchb.tvisdata.hrsa.gov/Home/Glossary.
[58] Health Resources and Services Administration, *Explore the Title V Federal-Partnership*, https://mchb.tvisdata.hrsa.gov/.

Maternal and Child Health Services Block Grant 261

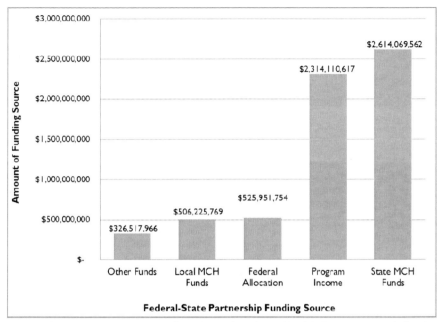

Source: Figure prepared by CRS based on data from Health Resources and Services Administration, Funding by Source, https://mchb.tvisdata.hrsa.gov/Financial/FundingBySource.

Figure 4. Federal-State Partnership Funding, by Source, FY2015.

Nonuse of Funds

If a state chooses not to apply for block grant funds, is not qualified for such funds, or indicates that it does not plan to use its full allotment, that state's allotment is redistributed among the remaining states in the proportion otherwise allotted to the state.[59]

SPRANS

By law, of the amount appropriated to the MCH Services Block Grant (up to $600 million), 15% is awarded on a competitive basis to public and private not-for-profit organizations for SPRANS. Congress has directed

---

[59] Section 502(d)(1) of the Social Security Act (42 U.S.C. §702(d)(1)).

some SPRANS funds through authorizations and appropriations for specific programs. The program also receives 15% of funds remaining above $600 million after CISS funds are set aside.

Generally, the priority for funding SPRANS projects is determined by HRSA. However, Congress has sometimes provided specific directives for certain programs, including set-asides. For example, the FY2017 Consolidated Appropriations Act included appropriations language that provided SPRANS set-aside funds for oral health ($5.25 million, an increase of 5% from FY2016), epilepsy ($3.64 million, same allocation from FY2016), sickle cell ($3.00 million, an increase of 1.35% from FY2016), and fetal alcohol syndrome ($0.48 million, same allocation as FY2016).[60] In FY2016, these congressional directives comprised about 16% of SPRANS funding.[61] Additionally and under the Continuing Appropriations and Military Construction, Veterans Affairs, and Related Agencies Appropriations Act, 2017, and Zika Response and Preparedness Act (P.L. 114-223), Congress provided $20 million in supplemental funding to the SPRANS program to help territories respond to the Zika virus.[62] In FY2016, HRSA awarded $17 million to American Samoa, U.S. Virgin Islands, and Puerto Rico under the SPRANS program, to help the territories address the Zika virus.[63]

Currently, SPRANS has additional funding of $5 million to develop Family-to-Family Health Information Centers (F2F HICs) through FY2017. (See Appendix B for the appropriation history of F2F HICs.) The F2F HICs program funds family-staffed and family-run centers[64] in 50

---

[60] "Title II-Department of Health and Human Services," House of Representatives, *Congressional Record*, vol. 163, no. 76 (May 3, 2017), p. H3950; and "Title II-Department of Health and Human Services," House of Representatives, *Congressional Record*, vol. 161, no. 184 (December 2015), p. H10282.
[61] Ibid.
[62] 130 Stat. 903.
[63] Health Resources and Services Administration, "HRSA Awards $17 Million to Reach Populations in U.S. Territories Affected by Zika," press release, December 15, 2016, https://www.hrsa.gov/about/news/press-releases/2016-12-15-territories-affected-by-zika.html.
[64] A family-staffed and family-run center is a nonprofit organization that is staffed and/or managed by family leaders who have children with special health care needs. To learn more about family-staffed and family-run centers, see Health Resources and Services Administration, "HRSA Awards $5 Million to Support Families of Children with Special

states and the District of Columbia.[65] The F2F HICs provide information, education, technical assistance, and peer support to families of children (including youth) with special health care needs and health professionals who serve such families. In addition, the centers help ensure that families and health professionals are partners in decisionmaking at all levels of care and service delivery.

CISS

The SSA requires Congress to appropriate over $600 million to the MCH Services Block Grant in order to initiate any funding for the CISS program. The CISS program will receive a set-aside of 12.75% of any amount appropriated over $600 million.[66] Since HRSA began providing CISS competitive grants in 1996, Congress has not appropriated any amount less than $600 million to the MCH Services Block Grant program.[67] Funds are distributed on a competitive basis to public and private nonprofit organizations, with preference given to entities that propose activities focusing on areas with high infant mortality rates.[68]

Appropriations History

In FY2016, HRSA received $638.2 million for the MCH Services Block Grant program. This funding was allocated differently from what is stated in 42 U.S.C. §702(a) (as described in the "Funding by Program"

Health Care Needs," press release, May 14, 2015, https://www.hrsa.gov/about/news/pressreleases/ 150514familytofamily.html.

[65] SSA, §501(c).
[66] Section 502(b)(1)(A) of the Social Security Act (U.S.C. 42 §702(b)(1)(A)).
[67] Health Resources and Services Administration, "Special Project Grants; Maternal and Child Health (MCH) Services; Community Integrated Service Systems (CISS) Set-Aside Program," 61 *Federal Register* 120, June 20, 1996.
[68] An infant mortality rate that is higher than the average national infant mortality rate or higher than the average infant mortality rate within a state is considered to be a *high infant mortality rate*. Section 502(b)(2)(A) of the Social Security Act (42 U.S.C. §702(b)(2)(A)).

section of this report). The appropriations were not allocated in this manner because under the Consolidated Appropriations Act, 2016 (P.L. 114-113), Congress mandated that no more than $77.1 million (rounded) would be made available to SPRANS, "notwithstanding sections 502(a)(1) and 502(b)(1) of the SSA."[69] As a result of the FY2016 appropriation and as shown in HRSA's FY2018 congressional budget justification report, $77.1 million (12.08%; the SSA calls for 15%) was for SPRANS, $10.3 million (1.61%) was for CISS, and $550.8 million (86.31%) was for block grants to states.[70] Table 1 shows the FY2016 appropriation of $638.2 million if funding allocation followed what is stated in the SSA.

Table 1. Differences between the FY2016 Appropriation and SSA Formula ($ in millions)

MCH Programs	SSA Formula	FY2016 Appropriation	FY2016 Appropriation by SSA Formula	Difference
SPRANS	• 15% of the appropriation that does not exceed $600 million; and	$77.1	$95.0[a]	-$17.9
	• 15% of funds remaining above $600 million after CISS funds are set aside			
CISS	• 12.75% of the appropriation that is above $600 million	$10.3	$4.9[b]	$5.4
Block grants to states	• The remainder of the total appropriation	$550.8	$538.3[c]	$12.5

Source: Table prepared by CRS using data from Health Resources and Services Administration, *FY2018 Justification of Estimates for Appropriations Committees*, 2017, p. 151 https://www.hrsa.gov/sites/default/files/hrsa/about/budget/budget-justification-2018.pdf; 42 U.S.C. §702(a)(1); 42 U.S.C. §702(b)(1); and 42 U.S.C. §702(c).

$95 million is the sum of 15% of $600 million plus 15% of $33.3 million. $33.3 million is what remains after CISS funds are set aside. $4.9 million is 12.75% of $38.2 million. $538.3 million is the remainder after subtracting $95.0 million and $4.9 million from the $638.2 million total appropriation.

---

[69] 129 Stat. 2601.
[70] Health Resources and Services Administration, *FY2018 Justification of Estimates for Appropriations Committees*, 2017, p. 151, https://www.hrsa.gov/sites/default/files/hrsa/about/budget/budget-justification-2018.pdf.

MANDATORY REPORTING AT THE STATE AND NATIONAL LEVELS

At the state and national levels, Section 505 of the SSA[71] requires three reporting mechanisms:

1. A needs assessment, which must be performed every five years (as discussed in the "Requirements to Receive Funds" section of this report).
2. An annual report, including program participation data, state maternal and child health measures, and state pediatric and family workforce measures.
3. An independent audit, which must be performed every two years.

State Reporting Requirements[72]

Each state must prepare and submit an annual report to the Secretary of HHS on all Title V activities.[73] The reports must be presented in a standardized format. States must provide a list of activities and recipients of Title V funding, along with a description of progress toward meeting national and state health objectives, and their consistency with the state's needs assessment. Specifically, these reports must include information on program participation, standardized measures of maternal and child health, and data on maternal and child health systems, including measures of the pediatric and family practice workforce. While the measures are designed to standardize reporting across the states, states vary in terms of their capacity for collecting and reporting data.

For example, states must provide the number of individuals served, either in person or by phone, by the Title V block grant. The numbers

---

[71] 42 U.S.C. §705.
[72] Health Resources and Services Administration, *State Application/Annual Report*, https://mchb.tvisdata.hrsa.gov/ Home/StateApplicationOrAnnualReport.
[73] 42 U.S.C. §706.

provided by states may be estimates if the actual numbers are not available. States are also required to report expenditures by the four broad categories of service (direct health care services, enabling services, population-based services, and infrastructure-building services).

States are required to annually report pediatric and family practice workforce data to HRSA, including information on the number of obstetricians, family practitioners, certified family nurse practitioners, certified nurse midwives, pediatricians, and certified pediatric nurse practitioners who were licensed in the state in that year. States are also required to report data on whether individuals who are eligible for programs such as Medicaid[74] and Supplemental Security Income (SSI)[75] are receiving services, or whether pregnant women have access to adequate prenatal care. For example, states report the number of Medicaid-eligible individuals who received a service paid for by the Medicaid program.

In addition to the above-mentioned annually reported indicators, states select and report 7 to 10 priority needs in their five-year strategic plans; states may annually adjust the strategic plans as their priorities change. Priority needs that were frequently identified in states' FY2017 MCH Services Block Grant applications include family support services, oral health services, childhood obesity prevention and treatment, mental and behavioral health systems, and access to services for children with disabilities.

National Reporting Requirement

HRSA must annually compile the information reported by states and present the data to the House Committee on Energy and Commerce and the Senate Committee on Finance in a report to Congress.[76] This report must include a summary of the information reported to the Secretary of HHS by

---

[74] To learn more about Medicaid, see CRS Report R43357, *Medicaid: An Overview*, coordinated by Alison Mitchell.
[75] To learn about the Supplemental Security Income (SSI), see CRS In Focus IF10482, *Supplemental Security Income (SSI)*, by William R. Morton.
[76] 42 U.S.C. §706.

the states (described in the previous section) and a compilation of specified maternal and child health indicators, nationally and by state. States can access their vital statistics and health data from the National Center for Health Statistics (NCHS) of CDC. The NCHS does not collect vital statistics or health data for American Samoa, Commonwealth of the Northern Mariana Islands, Federated States of Micronesia, Guam, Marshall Islands, Palau, Puerto Rico, or U.S. Virgin Islands.[77] Therefore, these jurisdictions must report their own data. The Secretary must also provide a report on funded SPRANS and CISS projects to those committees.

APPENDIX A. SOURCE OF FUNDING FOR TITLE V BLOCK GRANTS TO STATES, THE DISTRICT OF COLUMBIA, AND OTHER JURISDICTIONS, BY STATE, FY2015

Table A-1. Source of Funding for Title V Block Grants to States, FY2015 ($ in millions)

State	Federal Allocation	Total State Funds (Match And Overmatch)[a]	Other Funds (including local MCH funds)	Program Income (Reimbursements)[b]	Total
Alabama	11.3	30.6	1.6	54.1	97.7
Alaska	1.0	14.1	0	0.1	15.2
Arizona	7.2	7.8	5.9	0	21.0
Arkansas	6.3	6.5	0.6	17.4	30.8
California	35.1	1,553.3	155.6	1,705.4	3,449.4
Colorado	7.5	5.6	0	0	13.1
Connecticut	4.6	6.8	0	0	11.4
Delaware	1.6	9.4	0	1.3	12.3
District of Columbia	6.8	12.7	0	0	19.5
Florida	19.0	169.5	0	0	188.5
Georgia	16.6	91.8	141.4	9.1	259.0
Hawaii	1.4	22.4	0	11.3	35.1

---

[77] Health Resources and Services Administration, *Title V Maternal and Child Health Services Block Grant to States Program*, OMB NO: 0915-0172, p. 12, https://mchb.tvisdata. hrsa.gov/uploadedfiles/Documents/ blockgrantguidance.pdf.

Table A-1. (Continued)

State	Federal Allocation	Total State Funds (Match And Overmatch)[a]	Other Funds (including local MCH funds)	Program Income (Reimbursements)[b]	Total
Idaho	3.5	2.6	0	0	6.2
Illinois	21.1	24.8	4.9	0	50.9
Indiana	12.2	12.5	1.06	1.1	27.0
Iowa	6.3	5.9	6.4	0.5	19.1
Kansas	3.4	3.8	4.0	0	11.2
Kentucky	10.5	17.5	16.9	0	54.9
Louisiana	10.6	9.4	3.4	4.1	27.5
Maine	3.3	3.9	0	0	7.2
Maryland	11.6	8.7	0	0	20.3
Massachusetts	11.0	45.8	0	0	56.8
Michigan	18.0	44.1	0	64.0	126.6
Minnesota	9.1	6.8	12.1	0	28.1
Mississippi	8.1	9.1	0	4.2	21.4
Missouri	11.9	10.5	0	0	22.4
Montana	2.2	2.5	5.2	1.6	11.6
Nebraska	4.0	3.1	0.8	0	7.9
Nevada	2.0	1.6	0	0	3.6
New Hampshire	2.0	5.6	0.7	0	8.4
New Jersey	12.1	112.3	0	0	124.4
New Mexico	3.8	6.7	0	6.5	17.0
New York	38.9	58.9	317.8	274.7	690.3
North Carolina	16.6	33.1	59.0	64.4	173.1
North Dakota	1.2	2.2	0.02	0	3.4
Ohio	22.1	30.5	43.1	0	95.8
Oklahoma	6.9	7.5	0.6	0	15.1
Oregon	6.2	8.5	13.6	0	28.2
Pennsylvania	23.5	44.9	0	0	68.4
Rhode Island	1.6	1.6	0	22.9	26.2
South Carolina	12.3	11.5	33.5	17.0	74.2
South Dakota	2.5	1.8	0.5	0.8	5.6
Tennessee	12.9	30.0	0	4.4	47.2
Texas	34.1	40.2	0	0	74.3
Utah	5.9	14.0	16.7	5.6	42.2
Vermont	1.6	1.4	0	3.8	6.8
Virginia	10.6	8.0	1.2	0	19.8
Washington	16.4	7.6	0	0	16.4
West Virginia	5.9	9.1	0	17.4	32.6
Wisconsin	10.8	9.3	0	5.0	25.1

Maternal and Child Health Services Block Grant 269

State	Federal Allocation	Total State Funds (Match And Overmatch)[a]	Other Funds (including local MCH funds)	Program Income (Reimbursements)[b]	Total
Wyoming	1.1	2.0	0.5	0	3.6
Other Jurisdictions					
American Samoa	0.5	0.5	0.5	0	1.4
Federated States of Micronesia	0.5	0.4	0	0	0.9
Guam	0.8	0.7	0	0	1.4
Marshall Islands	0.1	0.1	0	0	0.4
Northern Mariana Islands	0.5	0.4	0.08	0	1.0
Palau	0.2	.05	0	0	0.2
Puerto Rico	13.3	12.0	0	0.3	25.6
Virgin Islands	1.4	0	1.2	0	2.6
Total	$526.0	$2,614.1	$832.7	$2,314.1	$6,286.9

Source: Table prepared by CRS based on data from HRSA, Title V Information System, Federal-State Title V Block Grant Partnership Budget FY2015, https://mchb.tvisdata.hrsa.gov/.

Notes: Some totals are imprecise because of rounding. Not every state submitted data to HRSA on their other funds and program income. These data is shown as $0 in the table.

[a]States are allowed to exceed the matching requirement of at least $3 for every $4 of federal funds awarded. This amount is an "overmatch."

[b]Program income includes funding from private entities and income collected from insurance payments and Medicaid. For purposes of meeting the state match requirement, states are allowed to use nonfederal program income toward their match.

APPENDIX B. APPROPRIATION HISTORY OF THE FAMILY-TO-FAMILY HEALTH INFORMATION CENTERS

The Family-to-Family Health Information Centers (F2F HICs) program was authorized under the following legislation:

- The Deficit Reduction Act of 2005 (P.L. 109-171) received a direct appropriation of $3 million for FY2007, $4 million for FY2008, and $5 million for FY2009.

270   *Victoria L. Elliott*

- The Patent Protection and Affordable Care Act (ACA; P.L. 111-148)[78] replaced the $5 million to be appropriated in FY2009 and provided $5 million for each of FY2009-FY2012 for the program.
- The American Taxpayer Relief Act of 2012 (P.L. 112-240) funded the program at $5 million for FY2013.
- The Bipartisan Budget Act of 2013 (P.L. 113-67) provided a half year of funding ($2.5 million), which expired April 1, 2014.
- Protecting Access to Medicare Act of 2014 (PAMA; P.L. 113-93) provided $2.5 million for the remainder of FY2014 (from April 1, 2014, to September 30, 2014), and it provided $2.5 million for the first half of FY2015 (October 1, 2014, through March 31, 2015).
- The Medicare Access and CHIP Reauthorization Act of 2015 (MACRA; P.L. 114-10)[79] struck the partial funding provided and provided full-year funding of $5 million for FY2015. It also provided $5 million for each of FY2016 and FY2017.

APPENDIX C. MCH SERVICES BLOCK GRANT FUNDING HISTORY FOR THE PAST 10 YEARS

Table C-1. MCH Services Block Grant Funding History, FY2006-FY2016 ($ in millions)

Fiscal Year	Amount of Grants to States	Amount of Grants for SPRANS	Amount of Grants for CISS	Total Appropriations
2006	566.1	115.9	10.6	692.5
2007	561.7	115.9	10.6	693.0
2008	551.2	99.2a	10.4	666.2
2009	553.8	92.6b	10.4	662.1
2010	558.0	92.4	10.4	660.7

---

[78] To view CRS resources for frequently asked questions about the Affordable Care Act, see CRS Report R43215, *Patient Protection and Affordable Care Act (ACA): Resources for Frequently Asked Questions*, by Angela Napili.
[79] To learn more about MACRA, see CRS Report R43962, *The Medicare Access and CHIP Reauthorization Act of 2015 (MACRA; P.L. 114-10)*, coordinated by Jim Hahn.

Maternal and Child Health Services Block Grant

Fiscal Year	Amount of Grants to States	Amount of Grants for SPRANS	Amount of Grants for CISS	Total Appropriations
2011	555.7	90.2	10.4	656.3
2012	549.7	78.6	10.3	638.6
2013	520.7	74.5	9.7	604.9
2014	545.3	76.9	10.3	632.4
2015c	549.6	77.1	10.3	637.0
2016	550.8	77.1d	10.3	638.2

Source: Table prepared by CRS using annual Department of Health and Human Services, Health Resources and Services Administration budget justifications and appropriations legislation for the relevant years. Funding levels are not adjusted for inflation.

[a] In FY2008, $20 million was transferred from SPRANS to the Autism program line.

[b] In FY2009, $6.9 million was transferred from SPRANS to the Heritable Disorders line. The Autism program and the Heritable Disorder program also are administered by HRSA's Maternal and Child Health Bureau.

[c] The FY2015 appropriation of $637 million is different from HRSA's source of funding, which is shown as $6.29 billion in Table A-1 in Appendix A.

[d] In FY2016, Congress provided $20 million in supplemental funding to the SPRANS program to help territories respond to the Zika virus. In FY2016, HRSA awarded $17 million to American Samoa, U.S. Virgin Islands, and Puerto Rico under the SPRANS program, to help the territories address the Zika virus.

APPENDIX D. ABBREVIATIONS USED IN THIS REPORT

ACA	Affordable Care Act
ACS	American Community Survey
CC	Crippled Children's Program
CDC	Centers for Disease Control and Prevention
CHIP	State Children's Health Insurance Program
CISS	Community-Integrated Services System Program
COBRA	Consolidated Omnibus Budget Reconciliation Act
CSHCNs	children and youth with special health care needs
EMSC	Emergency Medical Services for Children Program
EPSDT	Early Periodic Screening, Diagnosis, and Treatment Program

F2F HICs	Family-to-Family Health Information Centers
FPL	federal poverty level
FY	fiscal year
HHS	Department of Health and Human Services
HMO	health maintenance organization
HRSA	Health Resources and Services Administration
TVIS	Title V Information System
MACRA	Medicare Access and CHIP Reauthorization Act of 2015
MCH Services Block Grant	Maternal and Child Health Services Block Grant
MCHB	Maternal and Child Health Bureau
MIECHV	Maternal, Infant, and Early Childhood Home Visiting Program
OMB	Office of Management and Budget
NHIS	National Health Interview Survey
PAMA	Protecting Access to Medicare Act of 2013
PHSA	Public Health Services Act
SPRANS	Special Projects of Regional and National Significance Program
SSA	Social Security Act
WIC	Special Supplemental Nutrition Program for Women, Infants, and Children

INDEX

A

academic progress, 77, 78
access, vii, 1, 3, 7, 12, 16, 17, 18, 19, 22, 25, 28, 31, 32, 35, 36, 38, 51, 55, 64, 89, 199, 249, 253, 266, 267
accountability, 210, 224, 245
adequate housing, xiii, 189, 195
Administration for Children and Families, 194, 198, 214, 217, 220
age, xv, 77, 82, 123, 131, 137, 181, 182, 204, 242, 246, 247, 248, 255, 256
agencies, xi, xii, xv, 16, 22, 28, 48, 62, 64, 101, 105, 121, 122, 123, 149, 189, 192, 195, 196, 197, 202, 203, 207, 208, 210, 212, 217, 222, 223, 227, 228, 229, 236, 237, 239, 242, 251, 255, 260
agricultural producers, 64
Agriculture Improvement Act, viii, 2, 11, 53, 55
Alaska, 35, 126, 213, 267
American Recovery and Reinvestment Act, 48, 69, 102, 107, 119, 195, 216, 217
American Recovery and Reinvestment Act of 2009, 48
antipoverty efforts, xiii, 189

Appropriations Act, 17, 23, 25, 28, 34, 97, 98, 100, 102, 103, 114, 115, 116, 119, 141, 178, 205, 217, 220, 262
assessment, 16, 22, 31, 48, 50, 61, 167, 170, 171, 197, 217, 222, 224, 245, 254, 265
Attorney General, 226, 227, 228, 230, 235, 236, 237
authority, 6, 10, 18, 23, 26, 27, 30, 31, 32, 46, 56, 58, 65, 101, 104, 105, 107, 159, 200, 233

B

background information, 192
barriers, 22, 29, 62, 138, 191, 204
basic education opportunity grants, ix, 71
basic grants, xi, 121, 122, 123, 125, 126, 128
benchmarks, 210
beneficiaries, 246
benefits, 11, 17, 42, 46, 82, 83, 125, 131, 154, 155, 176, 195, 236, 246, 258
board members, 196
bonuses, 158
borrowers, 10, 14, 20, 21, 26, 37, 38, 42

broadband, vii, viii, 1, 2, 3, 4, 5, 6, 7, 8, 9, 10, 11, 12, 13, 15, 16, 17, 18, 19, 20, 21, 22, 23, 24, 25, 26, 27, 28, 29, 30, 31, 32, 33, 34, 35, 36, 37, 38, 39, 40, 41, 42, 43, 44, 45, 46, 47, 48, 49, 50, 51, 52, 53, 54, 55, 56, 57, 58, 59, 60, 61, 62, 63, 64, 65, 66
broadband access, vii, 1, 3, 10, 22, 31, 32, 36, 51, 55, 64
broadband deployment, vii, 1, 2, 3, 4, 5, 6, 7, 9, 16, 32, 33, 36, 39, 43, 48, 56, 58, 62
broadband loan program, viii, 2, 9, 11, 20, 23, 24, 25, 28, 29, 33, 34, 39, 41, 43, 44, 47, 48, 59, 64, 65
broadband loans, viii, 2, 6, 20, 24, 31, 35, 36, 39, 41, 53, 54, 55, 56, 65, 66
Bureau of Indian Education, 124, 128
Bureau of Justice Assistance, 230

C

cable television, 3
capacity building, 176, 253
cash, 33, 34, 40, 184, 186, 198, 254
Catalog of Federal Domestic Assistance, 235
Census, 5, 90, 124, 128, 172, 182, 196, 258
certificate, ix, 72, 76, 78, 204
challenges, 25, 28, 31, 34, 48, 105
Chicago, 38, 131
Child Health Bureau (MCHB), xv, 242, 271, 272
children, xiv, xv, 123, 124, 131, 137, 138, 139, 143, 158, 160, 161, 162, 165, 182, 184, 204, 229, 241, 242, 243, 244, 245, 246, 247, 248, 249, 253, 254, 255, 256, 257, 258, 259, 262, 263, 266, 271
cities, 35, 38, 41, 131, 144, 145, 146, 149, 151, 164, 191
classroom, 76
clients, 153, 165, 197, 223

cognitive function, 78
cognitive impairment, 78
College Cost Reduction and Access Act, 98, 119
college students, 182
commercial, 3, 49, 95
Commonwealth of the Northern Mariana Islands, 145, 194, 267
Community Connect Grant Program, viii, 2, 13, 23, 58, 66, 69
Community Development Block Grant (CDBG), xii, 130, 144, 145, 146, 158, 163, 164, 173, 179, 180, 181, 182
Community Economic Development (CED), xiii, 189, 190, 194, 197, 198, 199, 205, 206, 207, 208, 209, 212, 218, 219, 220
Community Integrated Service Systems (CISS), xv, 241, 242, 243, 249, 257, 258, 262, 263, 264, 267, 270, 271
Community Services Block Grants (CSBG), v, xii, 189, 190, 191, 192, 193, 194, 195, 196, 197, 198, 201, 202, 203, 204, 205, 206, 207, 209, 210, 211, 212, 213, 215, 216, 217, 218, 219, 220, 221, 223, 224
community-based activities, xiii, 189
competition, 5, 37, 42, 141, 163, 164, 165, 166, 167, 168, 169, 170, 179
competitive grant program, 243, 257
competitive process, xii, 130, 164, 166, 169
compliance, 185, 210, 221, 223, 231, 233
concentration grants, xi, 121, 122, 123, 126, 128
Conference Report, 55, 141, 220
congressional budget, 24, 216, 219, 264
Congressional Budget Act of 1974, 233
Congressional Budget Office, 102, 105, 109, 119, 225, 233, 234
Consolidated Appropriations Act, viii, xiii, 2, 8, 11, 15, 16, 22, 26, 27, 29, 31, 41, 86, 87, 97, 98, 100, 102, 103, 108, 110,

Index

112, 114, 115, 119, 122, 178, 190, 207, 217, 220, 254, 262, 264
construction, 6, 7, 9, 12, 13, 21, 24, 32, 34, 148, 154, 162, 176, 184
Continuum of Care (CoC), xii, 130, 133, 134, 139, 141, 147, 149, 150, 151, 152, 153, 154, 155, 156, 157, 158, 159, 160, 161, 162, 163, 164, 165, 166, 167, 169, 170, 171, 172, 173, 174, 175, 176, 177, 178, 179, 181, 182, 183, 185
coordination, viii, 2, 16, 22, 47, 48, 165, 195, 253, 255
cost, viii, x, 2, 5, 14, 19, 20, 21, 25, 29, 37, 43, 46, 54, 56, 57, 58, 73, 76, 83, 85, 86, 87, 88, 93, 94, 95, 101, 105, 108, 109, 118, 179, 180, 225, 234
Cost of Attendance (COA), ix, 72, 81, 83, 84, 85, 86, 87, 93, 94, 95, 112, 120
counseling, 77, 142, 184, 186, 197, 200, 249, 253, 256
criminal activity, 229, 237
criticism, 33, 37
customers, viii, 2, 5, 12, 36, 49

D

data center, 55
data collection, 174, 176, 178, 208
data rates, 43
database, 50, 59
Department of Agriculture, 9, 10, 11, 12, 13, 25, 34, 35, 52, 208
Department of Commerce, 22, 217
Department of Defense, 100, 114, 115, 178, 217, 220
Department of Education, xi, 73, 74, 80, 82, 86, 87, 89, 111, 113, 118, 120, 121, 122, 128, 137, 252
Department of Education (ED), xi, xiii, 73, 74, 76, 80, 82, 84, 85, 86, 87, 88, 89, 100, 101, 111, 112, 113, 118, 120, 121, 122, 123, 128, 137, 180, 189, 194, 198, 220, 252, 255
Department of Health and Human Services (HHS), xiii, xv, 190, 191, 192, 193, 194, 195, 197, 198, 199, 200, 201, 202, 205, 207, 208, 214, 216, 217, 220, 221, 222, 223, 224, 242, 244, 250, 251, 253, 254, 258, 259, 262, 265, 266, 271, 272
Department of Housing and Urban Development (HUD), v, xi, 129, 130, 132, 133, 134, 135, 136, 137, 138, 139, 140, 141, 142, 144, 145, 146, 147, 149, 150, 151, 152, 154, 155, 156, 158, 160, 163, 165, 166, 167, 168, 169, 170, 171, 172, 173, 174, 175, 176, 177, 178, 179, 180, 181, 182, 183, 184, 185, 186, 187, 203
Department of Justice, 226, 228, 229, 230, 231, 234, 237, 239
Department of the Treasury, 46
Departments of Agriculture, 199
disability, 78, 83, 138, 140, 148, 153, 160, 168, 185, 247, 255
distance learning, viii, 2, 3, 15
Distance Learning and Telemedicine (DLT) grants, viii, 2, 15, 24, 26, 27, 28, 29, 30
District of Columbia, 126, 145, 194, 201, 213, 243, 250, 263, 267
domestic violence, 138, 139, 197

E

economic development, vii, 1, 3, 17, 22, 39, 194, 208, 224
economic growth, 11
education, ix, x, xiii, 11, 15, 18, 71, 75, 78, 90, 94, 121, 132, 142, 153, 176, 189, 191, 195, 197, 202, 228, 238, 253, 255, 263
Education Finance Incentive Grants (EFIG), xi, 121, 122, 123, 125, 126, 128

educational institutions, 51
educational services, 244
El Salvador, 229
Elementary and Secondary Education Act (ESEA), v, x, 121, 122
eligibility criteria, 54, 88, 100, 105
emergency, xi, xii, 26, 130, 135, 136, 140, 141, 142, 144, 149, 174, 195, 197, 202
Emergency Assistance, xi, 130, 133, 135, 140, 142, 150, 151, 172
Emergency Shelter Grants (ESG), xi, 129, 130, 132, 133, 134, 141, 142, 143, 144, 145, 146, 147, 160, 164, 174, 175, 176, 177, 178, 180
Emergency Solutions Grants, xi, 130, 133, 134, 141, 142
employment, xiii, 3, 78, 138, 142, 153, 174, 184, 189, 195, 198, 199, 202, 203, 204, 212
enforcement, 227, 229, 239
enrollment, 76, 77, 78, 80, 83, 84, 86, 87, 88, 90, 91, 101, 107, 109
Environmental Protection Agency, 199, 208
equipment, viii, 2, 7, 8, 9, 15, 24, 26, 43, 51, 156, 253, 254
Every Student Succeeds Act (ESSA), x, 121, 122, 124
expected family contribution (EFC), ix, 71, 72, 75, 76, 79, 81, 82, 83, 84, 85, 86, 87, 90, 92, 94, 95, 104, 106, 108, 112, 120
expenditures, 28, 29, 32, 101, 102, 103, 118, 123, 233, 251, 266

F

families, xi, xii, xiii, xiv, xv, 75, 90, 121, 122, 123, 130, 136, 137, 138, 139, 140, 141, 143, 147, 148, 152, 153, 154, 157, 158, 159, 160, 161, 162, 165, 167, 168, 174, 183, 186, 189, 191, 195, 199, 204, 206, 241, 242, 263

family income, ix, 72, 90, 94, 259
family members, 131
family planning, 249, 255
Farm Bill, 20, 21, 40, 48, 52
federal agency, viii, 2, 62, 243
federal aid, x, 79, 121, 122
Federal Communications Commission, 20, 31, 47, 48
federal funds, xii, 105, 189, 192, 197, 203, 205, 210, 217, 245, 259, 269
federal government, vii, 42, 64, 104, 235, 246, 260
Federal Register, 6, 7, 10, 12, 13, 18, 35, 48, 52, 135, 138, 139, 140, 142, 143, 145, 147, 149, 150, 151, 153, 154, 155, 156, 157, 158, 159, 164, 172, 173, 174, 175, 176, 179, 183, 244, 263
federal student aid, ix, 71, 75, 76, 77, 81, 82, 86, 88, 94, 120
fetal alcohol syndrome, 262
fiber, viii, 2, 3, 5, 29, 31, 32, 43
financial, ix, 34, 40, 41, 42, 51, 57, 59, 71, 75, 79, 81, 82, 83, 92, 95, 106, 108, 200, 202, 221, 222
financial information, ix, 72
fiscal year, x, 8, 9, 13, 44, 47, 49, 55, 58, 60, 63, 65, 73, 96, 97, 99, 100, 101, 116, 124, 146, 164, 178, 216, 217, 220, 227, 228, 237, 238, 252, 259, 272
flexibility, xii, 14, 27, 130, 157, 209, 229, 245, 259
Food and Drug Administration, 17, 23, 28
Food, Conservation, and Energy Act of 2008, 9, 44
formula, xii, xiv, 81, 83, 90, 104, 122, 123, 124, 125, 130, 145, 151, 158, 163, 164, 179, 180, 181, 182, 183, 211, 217, 241, 249, 258, 259
Free Application for Federal Student Aid (FAFSA), ix, 72, 75, 82, 83, 88, 120

G

gang crimes, 227, 228, 236
grant programs, vii, xi, 2, 6, 27, 36, 69, 129, 132, 146, 147, 176, 178
grants, vii, viii, x, xi, xii, xiv, xv, 2, 7, 9, 11, 12, 13, 15, 18, 20, 24, 26, 27, 28, 29, 30, 31, 35, 39, 49, 52, 53, 54, 55, 56, 58, 60, 63, 65, 66, 69, 72, 74, 75, 83, 95, 105, 121, 122, 123, 124, 128, 129, 130, 132, 133, 134, 144, 147, 148, 149, 150, 154, 156, 158, 159, 163, 164, 166, 167, 172, 173, 174, 176, 177, 178, 179, 180, 184, 185, 186, 193, 194, 198, 199, 200, 201, 211, 217, 220, 222, 227, 228, 229, 234, 241, 242, 244, 245, 246, 249, 253, 256, 257, 258, 259, 263, 264
guidance, 38, 112, 139, 181, 222, 223, 229, 243, 249, 250, 255
guidance counselors, 229
guidelines, 13, 35, 204, 244, 259

H

health, xiv, xv, 11, 15, 18, 26, 51, 132, 139, 142, 143, 153, 173, 184, 186, 203, 204, 241, 242, 243, 244, 245, 246, 247, 248, 249, 250, 251, 253, 254, 255, 256, 257, 258, 259, 260, 262, 263, 265, 266, 267, 271, 272
Health and Human Services, xiii, 104, 114, 115, 190, 205, 220, 251, 258, 259, 262
health care, xv, 11, 15, 18, 51, 132, 142, 184, 186, 242, 244, 246, 247, 248, 251, 253, 254, 256, 257, 262, 263, 266, 271
health care system, 253
health expenditure, xv, 242
health insurance, 204
health services, xv, 153, 203, 242, 243, 244, 249, 253, 254
Helping Families Save Their Homes Act, xi, 130, 133
high school, 76, 78, 106, 138, 204, 229
high school degree, 138
high school diploma, 76, 78, 106, 204
higher education, v, ix, 71, 72, 73, 74, 75, 76, 89, 94, 104, 109, 120
history, vii, 11, 77, 80, 81, 89, 98, 101, 102, 138, 192, 194, 244, 262
Homeless Assistance Grants, v, xi, 129, 130, 132, 133, 134, 139, 141, 144, 147, 149, 175, 176, 177, 178, 179, 180, 181, 182, 185
Homeless Emergency Assistance and Rapid Transition to Housing (HEARTH) Act, v, xi, 129, 130, 133, 134, 135, 136, 137, 140, 141, 142, 144, 145, 147, 149, 150, 151, 154, 155, 157, 158, 159, 160, 162, 163, 165, 172, 180, 181, 183
homeless persons, xi, 129, 131, 132, 141, 147, 149, 160, 163, 180, 184
homelessness, xi, xii, 130, 131, 132, 133, 134, 135, 139, 140, 141, 142, 143, 149, 152, 153, 157, 158, 159, 162, 163, 165, 166, 167, 168, 171, 172, 174, 175, 178, 180, 182, 183, 197
House of Representatives, xiv, 225, 231, 233, 236, 262
household income, 90
housing, xi, xii, 44, 83, 130, 131, 132, 134, 135, 136, 137, 138, 139, 141, 142, 143, 146, 147, 148, 149, 152, 153, 154, 155, 156, 157, 158, 159, 160, 161, 162, 165, 166, 167, 168, 169, 170, 173, 174, 175, 176, 178, 179, 180, 181, 182, 183, 184, 185, 186, 194, 199, 202
Housing and Urban Development, xi, 129, 132, 135, 140, 141, 142, 145, 149, 150, 151, 166, 169, 170, 171, 172, 179, 181, 182, 183, 185, 186, 203, 239
human, 134, 135, 136, 141, 228
hybrid, 43, 183

I

immunization, xv, 242, 250
improvements, 22, 51
in transition, 135, 138, 168
income, ix, xi, xiii, xiv, xv, 35, 41, 54, 56, 72, 82, 90, 92, 95, 106, 121, 122, 143, 146, 154, 174, 175, 181, 183, 189, 191, 193, 194, 195, 196, 197, 198, 199, 200, 203, 204, 206, 208, 211, 217, 241, 242, 243, 244, 245, 246, 249, 253, 258, 259, 260, 269
income threshold, ix, 72, 90, 106
Independence, 200, 201, 220
Individual Development Accounts (IDAs), xiii, 189, 190, 194, 195, 198, 200, 201, 205, 206, 207, 209, 213, 218, 219, 220
individuals, vii, xiii, xv, 3, 89, 131, 132, 134, 136, 137, 139, 141, 143, 147, 148, 149, 152, 153, 154, 159, 160, 161, 162, 167, 168, 180, 181, 183, 184, 185, 186, 189, 194, 195, 197, 204, 206, 208, 242, 246, 248, 265, 266
industry, 3, 26
infant mortality, 256, 263
infants, 247, 248, 254, 257
infrastructure, vii, viii, xv, 2, 7, 9, 13, 15, 16, 20, 22, 24, 28, 29, 32, 54, 58, 60, 242, 251, 266
institutions, 3, 55, 75, 76, 78, 83, 88, 89, 90, 91, 92, 94, 109, 118, 256, 257
intellectual disabilities, 78
interest rates, 14, 26, 46, 58
interim regulations, 141, 145, 151, 153, 154, 163, 181
intervention, 227, 228, 237, 238, 239
investment, 7, 14, 21, 22, 25, 29, 34, 39, 62, 200

J

job creation, 208
job training, 153, 186, 197
jurisdiction, 173, 183, 238, 243
justification, 23, 264
juvenile justice, 227

K

K-12 education, x, 121

L

labor market, 90
land grants, vii
law enforcement, 227, 229, 237, 238, 239
legislation, xiv, 17, 38, 63, 96, 99, 103, 105, 107, 116, 179, 181, 182, 190, 192, 193, 210, 212, 229, 230, 233, 269, 271
limited liability, 10, 18
living arrangements, 131
Loan Guarantee Program, viii, 2, 8, 9, 10, 13, 14, 21, 23, 38, 48, 52, 55, 69
loan guarantees, viii, 2, 13, 20, 23, 49, 52, 53, 54, 55, 56, 58, 60, 63, 64
loans, viii, 2, 6, 9, 10, 11, 13, 14, 15, 17, 18, 20, 21, 23, 24, 26, 27, 28, 29, 30, 31, 32, 33, 34, 35, 36, 37, 38, 39, 41, 42, 43, 46, 47, 49, 52, 53, 54, 55, 56, 57, 58, 60, 61, 63, 64, 65, 66, 69, 94, 95, 200
local community, 193, 196, 197, 198, 211
local educational agencies (LEAs), xi, 121, 122, 123, 125
local government, vii, 10, 11, 15, 18, 42, 146, 147, 148, 149, 151, 155, 173, 184, 186, 202, 212, 216, 234, 238
low-income families, xi, xiv, 121, 122, 191, 195, 199, 200, 241, 242

Index

M

Maternal and Child Health (MCH) Services Block Grant, xv, 242, 243, 244, 245, 246, 247, 248, 249, 250, 251, 253, 254, 255, 256, 257, 258, 259, 261, 263, 266, 267, 270, 272
McKinney-Vento Homeless Assistance Act, xi, 129, 132, 162, 219
Medicaid, xiv, 203, 241, 243, 246, 252, 255, 257, 260, 266, 269
medical, 8, 26, 29, 32, 246, 253, 254
medical assistance, 246
Medicare, 203, 270, 272
mental health, 138, 143, 148, 153, 155, 184, 186
metropolitan areas, xii, 130

N

nonprofit organizations, 146, 147, 148, 151, 155, 173, 184, 185, 196, 199, 200, 220, 263
nonprofits, vii, 11, 15, 161
nutrition, 53, 137, 143, 197, 203, 253

O

Office of Management and Budget, 244, 259, 272
operating costs, 156, 176
opportunities, 18, 22, 32, 62, 191, 198, 199
outreach, 47, 140, 157, 227, 229, 253
outreach programs, 253

P

Pell Grant program, v, ix, 71, 73, 74, 75, 76, 77, 79, 88, 89, 92, 96, 97, 98, 99, 100, 102, 103, 104, 105, 106, 107, 108, 109, 112, 117, 118
Pell Grants, ix, 71, 72, 73, 74, 75, 83, 85, 86, 87, 89, 91, 92, 94, 95, 104, 106, 108, 110
per capita income, 35
permanent housing, xi, 130, 132, 136, 138, 141, 147, 148, 149, 152, 153, 155, 156, 157, 158, 159, 160, 161, 166, 167, 168, 169, 174, 179, 180, 183, 185
personal responsibility, 244
persons with disabilities, 160, 184
policy, 22, 47, 63, 89, 101, 107, 112, 192
policy initiative, 47
policymakers, 41, 104
population, vii, xv, 1, 4, 5, 6, 8, 13, 35, 41, 44, 56, 63, 90, 107, 124, 131, 139, 145, 160, 162, 172, 173, 181, 183, 242, 247, 251, 257, 259, 266
population density, vii, 1, 5, 173
post traumatic stress disorder, 140
postsecondary education students, ix, 71
poverty, xiii, 90, 124, 181, 182, 183, 189, 191, 192, 195, 198, 204, 205, 211, 223, 244, 258, 259, 272
President, viii, 2, 11, 22, 37, 48, 55, 62, 99, 100, 116, 118, 182, 191, 193, 206, 209, 215, 216, 217
prevention, xi, xii, 130, 141, 142, 149, 174, 227, 228, 229, 232, 236, 237, 238, 239, 244, 245, 253
private investment, 6, 25, 28, 31, 37
private sector, 7, 191
profit, 11, 15, 18, 88, 91, 120, 146, 254, 261
project, 16, 17, 18, 19, 34, 38, 44, 48, 50, 51, 54, 56, 57, 58, 59, 60, 61, 66, 142, 148, 155, 156, 157, 158, 165, 166, 167, 168, 169, 170, 179, 180, 185, 186, 230
proposed regulations, xii, 130, 133, 140, 172, 173, 174, 175
public health, xv, 242, 249
public housing, 146, 147, 151, 184

public policy, vii, 37
public safety, 3, 11, 51, 238, 239
public-private partnerships, 56
Puerto Rico, 124, 128, 145, 171, 179, 194, 201, 211, 214, 243, 250, 262, 267, 269, 271

R

recommendations, iv, 39, 48, 63, 222, 223, 233
regulations, 11, 34, 38, 39, 46, 48, 62, 133, 135, 137, 139, 143, 145, 151, 152, 153, 156, 159, 172, 210, 235, 237
rehabilitation, 77, 142, 148, 162, 176, 184, 185, 246
rehabilitation program, 77
rent, 142, 148, 154, 155, 174, 183, 186
rent subsidies, 148, 186
requirement, ix, 33, 40, 41, 50, 56, 71, 135, 148, 159, 160, 162, 186, 222, 223, 245, 254, 269
resources, xiv, 16, 23, 28, 34, 136, 139, 143, 150, 151, 166, 167, 169, 181, 191, 217, 221, 224, 229, 237, 253, 255, 270
risk, 37, 39, 45, 82, 143, 158, 165, 174, 175, 221, 222, 229, 246, 247, 254
roots, xiii, 190, 191
rules, ix, 11, 39, 48, 62, 72, 74, 75, 78, 79, 86, 87, 88, 90, 98, 106, 108, 109, 155, 227, 235, 237, 245
rural America, vii, 1, 2, 3, 6, 7, 22, 24, 30, 48, 52
rural areas, vii, viii, 1, 2, 3, 4, 5, 6, 7, 8, 9, 10, 11, 13, 14, 15, 29, 35, 37, 41, 42, 43, 45, 49, 52, 55, 58, 59, 61, 62, 205, 257
rural communities, vii, xii, 1, 4, 7, 8, 9, 16, 24, 26, 33, 35, 36, 41, 42, 49, 55, 56, 130, 133, 172, 173, 199, 206, 208

Rural Community Facilities (RCF), xiii, 189, 190, 194, 197, 199, 205, 206, 207, 208, 209, 212, 218, 219
rural development, 47
Rural Utilities Service (RUS), v, viii, 1, 2, 6, 7, 9, 10, 11, 12, 13, 15, 16, 17, 18, 20, 21, 22, 23, 24, 25, 27, 28, 29, 30, 32, 33, 34, 35, 36, 37, 38, 39, 40, 41, 42, 43, 44, 48, 49, 50, 51, 52, 54, 55, 59, 60, 61, 63, 64, 65, 66, 69

S

school, 3, 7, 76, 77, 78, 83, 88, 123
secondary education, 122, 123
secondary schools, x, 121, 122
Secretary of Agriculture, 16, 17, 31, 39, 43, 45
Section 8 Moderate Rehabilitation for Single Room Occupancy Dwellings (SRO), xi, 129, 130, 132, 133, 148, 150, 156, 159, 160, 161, 162, 176, 177, 185
Senate, xiii, 17, 24, 25, 26, 29, 32, 33, 34, 37, 48, 49, 53, 54, 55, 180, 181, 190, 193, 206, 207, 208, 209, 210, 220, 266
sensitivity, 116
September 11, 83
service provider, 8, 10, 45, 50, 51, 53, 57, 139, 149, 153, 155, 157
shelter, xi, xii, 130, 132, 134, 135, 136, 138, 140, 141, 144, 149
Shelter Plus Care (S+C) program, 133, 148, 155, 160, 178, 183, 186
shortfall, x, 73, 74, 96, 97, 101, 103, 104, 105, 106, 107, 118
Social Security, xv, 193, 242, 243, 244, 245, 256, 259, 260, 261, 263, 272
South Dakota, 125, 128, 214, 268
Special Projects of Regional and National Significance (SPRANS), xv, 241, 242,

Index

243, 249, 256, 258, 261, 262, 264, 267, 270, 271, 272
spending, 50, 59, 100, 103, 125, 202, 207, 208, 234, 235, 259, 260
stakeholders, 56, 62, 103, 151, 208
State Children's Health Insurance Program (CHIP), xiv, 241, 243, 252, 255, 270, 271, 272
state-of-the-art telecommunications, vii, 1, 4
statistics, 89, 259, 267
statutes, 137, 139, 143, 158
statutory authority, 74, 104
statutory provisions, 81, 107, 112, 208, 209
substance abuse, 153, 186, 205
Supplemental Nutrition Assistance Program, 137, 143
Supplemental Nutrition Assistance Program (SNAP), 137, 143
Supportive Housing Program (SHP), xi, 129, 130, 133, 147, 148, 150, 152, 154, 155, 156, 159, 160, 161, 162, 176, 177, 178, 179, 183, 184, 186

T

targeted grants, xi, 121, 122, 123, 125, 126, 128
technical assistance, viii, 2, 15, 16, 57, 176, 178, 194, 195, 199, 211, 221, 222, 223, 224, 253, 263
technologies, viii, 2, 3, 5, 17, 31, 35, 43, 45, 58
telecommunications, vii, viii, 1, 2, 3, 4, 6, 8, 9, 13, 14, 15, 18, 20, 28, 29, 44, 54, 60, 61, 63, 64, 66
Telecommunications Infrastructure Loan, viii, 2, 7, 13, 14, 20, 23, 26, 27, 30, 31, 32, 63, 69
telecommunications services, 3, 6
telemedicine, viii, 2, 3, 6, 7, 8, 9, 11, 15, 23, 30, 31, 32, 41, 69

telephone, 3, 8, 13, 21, 61
Telephone Loan Program, viii, 2
Title I, v, ix, x, xi, 6, 71, 72, 73, 74, 75, 76, 77, 79, 81, 82, 88, 94, 96, 106, 108, 120, 121, 122, 123, 124, 125, 126, 128, 162, 172, 200, 220, 262
Title II, 6, 96, 120, 262
Title IV, ix, 71, 72, 73, 74, 75, 76, 77, 79, 81, 82, 88, 94, 106, 108, 162, 172, 200, 220
Title V, xv, 9, 52, 193, 219, 242, 243, 244, 245, 246, 248, 249, 250, 251, 254, 255, 256, 257, 259, 260, 265, 267, 269, 272
training, viii, 2, 57, 78, 156, 176, 194, 195, 203, 211, 221, 222, 223, 224, 243, 253, 254, 256
training programs, 203, 256
transmission, 6, 11, 17, 29, 32, 43, 45
transparency, 49
transport, 55
transportation, 18, 26, 83, 94, 153, 197, 253
traumatic brain injury, 140
Treasury, 14, 19, 26, 27, 28, 29, 30, 31, 32, 199
treatment, 15, 62, 153, 199, 244, 245, 246, 249, 255, 266
tuition, 83, 88, 92, 94, 95, 116

U

U.S. Department of Agriculture (USDA), v, viii, 1, 2, 6, 7, 14, 15, 18, 22, 23, 25, 26, 27, 28, 29, 30, 31, 32, 33, 34, 35, 36, 37, 38, 39, 43, 47, 48, 51, 52, 54, 61, 62, 63, 65, 66, 69, 199, 200
U.S. Department of Commerce, 5
U.S. Department of the Treasury, 119
U.S. economy, 3
United States, 3, 22, 33, 36, 43, 44, 63, 77, 90, 126, 191, 226, 227, 228, 229, 236, 256

urban, vii, 1, 3, 4, 5, 17, 38, 42, 131, 144, 145, 164, 195, 199
urban areas, vii, 1, 4, 5, 17, 38, 42
Urban Institute, 195
USDA, v, 1, 6, 7, 14, 15, 22, 23, 25, 26, 27, 28, 29, 30, 31, 32, 33, 34, 35, 37, 39, 43, 47, 51, 52, 54, 61, 62, 63, 65, 66, 69, 199, 200

V

validation, 60
variables, 90
vehicles, 26
Vice President, 37
violence, 139, 198, 227, 228, 230, 237, 238
violent crime, 227, 229, 234, 237, 238
vision, 250
vocational education, 197
vocational rehabilitation, 244
vote, 230, 231, 232, 239
vouchers, 148, 155, 186

W

waiver, 211
war, 191
War of 1812, vii
War on Poverty, xiii, 190, 191, 192
Washington, 90, 128, 191, 201, 214, 233, 268
waste, 199
waste water, 199
water, 194, 199
welfare, 134, 154, 195, 244
welfare reform, 195
WIC, 203, 252, 255, 260, 272
Wisconsin, 128, 214, 268
Women, Infants, and Children, 137, 143, 252, 255, 272
work-study, 95

Y

young people, 238
Youth program, 137, 138, 143

Related Nova Publications

Welfare Programs and Policies: An Overview and Issues for Congress

Author: Gail Harper

Series: Government Procedures and Operations

Book Description: The Supplemental Nutrition Assistance Program (SNAP) provides benefits to low-income, eligible households on an electronic benefit transfer (EBT) card; benefits can then be exchanged for foods at authorized retailers.

Softcover ISBN: 978-1-53614-109-2
Retail Price: $95

Federal Benefits and Services for People with Low Income: Spending Trends and Program Fact Sheets

Editor: Barry Hammond

Series: Government Procedures and Operations

Book Description: Federal programs intended to help poor and low-income people are of ongoing interest to Congress. The federal government spends billions of dollars annually on a wide range of low-income benefits and services and lawmakers routinely conduct oversight and consider legislation related to these programs.

Hardcover ISBN: 978-1-53610-454-7
Retail Price: $125

To see a complete list of Nova publications, please visit our website at www.novapublishers.com

Related Nova Publications

FEDERAL GRANTS: BACKGROUND, ISSUES, AND MANAGEMENT

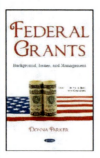

EDITOR: Donna Parker

SERIES: Government Procedures and Operations

BOOK DESCRIPTION: Chapter 1 is intended for Congressional members and staff assisting grant seekers in districts and states and covers writing proposals for both government and private foundation grants.

HARDCOVER ISBN: 978-1-53615-521-1
RETAIL PRICE: $230

SOCIAL SECURITY: BENEFITS, CHANGES AND PROPOSALS

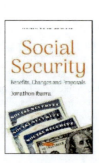

EDITOR: Jonathon Ibarra

SERIES: Government Procedures and Operations

BOOK DESCRIPTION: The CRS reports included in this book provide an overview of Social Security financing and benefits under current law. It also covers how the Social Security program is financed and how the Social Security trust funds work

SOFTCOVER ISBN: 978-1-53614-153-5
RETAIL PRICE: $82

To see a complete list of Nova publications, please visit our website at www.novapublishers.com